Fierce Females on Television

The Cultural History of Television

Fierce Females on Television

A Cultural History

NICOLE EVELINA

ROWMAN & LITTLEFIELD
Lanham • Boulder • New York • London

Published by Rowman & Littlefield
An imprint of The Rowman & Littlefield Publishing Group, Inc.
4501 Forbes Boulevard, Suite 200, Lanham, Maryland 20706
www.rowman.com

86-90 Paul Street, London EC2A 4NE, United Kingdom

British Library Cataloguing in Publication Information Available

Library of Congress Cataloging-in-Publication Data

Names: Evelina, Nicole, author.
Title: Fierce females on television : a cultural history / Nicole Evelina.
Description: Lanham, MD : Rowman & Littlefield, [2023] | Series: The cultural history of television | Includes bibliographical references and index. | Summary: "Fierce Females on Television provides a fascinating deep-dive into how shows such as Buffy the Vampire Slayer, Charmed, Homeland, Orphan Black, and The Equalizer have changed the way women are portrayed on television and paved the way for the strong female characters we know and love today"—Provided by publisher.
Identifiers: LCCN 2023008601 (print) | LCCN 2023008602 (ebook) | ISBN 9781538165652 (cloth) | ISBN 9781538165669 (epub) Subjects: LCSH: Women on television. | Feminism on television. | Television programs—United States—History.
Classification: LCC PN1992.8.W65 E94 2023 (print) | LCC PN1992.8.W65 (ebook) | DDC 791.45/6522—dc23/eng/20230313
LC record available at https://lccn.loc.gov/2023008601
LC ebook record available at https://lccn.loc.gov/2023008602

To Shauna Granger, Lyra Selene, Liv Raincourt, and Kristen McFarland, my fellow Spellbound Scribes and four of the strongest women I know

Contents

Introduction

The American women of late Gen X and beyond are lucky. Why? Because we were never limited in our life goals based on what we saw on television. Xennials—those of us on the cusp of Gen X (1964–1979) and Millennials (1980–1994), usually defined as those born between 1977 and 1983[1]—and Millennials came of age during a time when our TV role models were shifting from career-and-family-focused second-wave feminists to third-wave "girl-powered" feminists who literally kicked ass. Buffy Summers, the Halliwell sisters, Sydney Bristow, and Nikita Mears showed our high school- and college-aged selves that we could be anything, kick the patriarchy to the curb, and look good doing it. While most of us weren't spies or didn't have magical powers, they showed us that it was possible to balance the competing priorities in our lives, fight for what we knew was right, and come out a little wiser on the other side.

Similarly, our younger sisters in Gen Z (1995–2012) and Gen Alpha (2013–2025) have grown up with even stronger role models, thanks to the boundaries not only pushed but broken by those before them. These young women looked up to a new generation of superheroes in Agent Carter and Jessica Jones, watched Carrie Mathison protect the United States while Claire Underwood governed it as the first female president, and explored the future of "crazy science" with the Clone Club; the only Equalizer they know is played by Queen Latifah. Not only do they have women of color to emulate, but also women in science, technology, engineering, and math (STEM) and levels of government not yet seen in real life in the United States.

Housewives to Heroines: The History of Fierce Females on Television

It wasn't always this way. When television really caught on in the United States after World War II, its women mirrored those who had been featured in popular radio shows of decades prior. In fact, many of the most popular radio shows migrated over to television,[2] taking their damsels in distress with them. (*Agent Carter* does a beautiful job recreating these ladies, but more on that later.)

Even though many of these shows starred powerhouses like Lucille Ball, Eve Arden, and Gracie Allen, who also were very influential in shaping their shows,[3] their characters had less agency than the actresses who played them. Reflecting the prevailing values of the time, female characters were almost always white and usually were portrayed as middle-class housewives and mothers who catered to their husbands' every whim and indulged their sons while teaching their daughters to grow up just like them. These ladies vacuumed in their pearls and high heels and always had dinner on the table and a drink in hand for their husbands when they arrived home from work. (Think June Cleaver.)

Female characters who did have jobs were limited to the traditional roles of nurses, teachers, and secretaries.[4] But having a job didn't stop them from focusing on marriage as the be-all-and-end-all of their lives. Take, for example, the popular teacher Connie Brooks (played by Eve Arden) in *Our Miss Brooks*. She spent more time during the show's four-season run trying to get a husband[5] to save her from her underpaid life than she did in the classroom.

Even in westerns, which were ubiquitous in the 1950s, women were seldom seen in roles outside of saloon owners, prostitutes/temptresses, and wives/girlfriends of the cowboy hero. (Calamity Jane and Annie Oakley were rare exceptions.)[6]

When the threat of the Cold War began to dominate America's fears, spy shows rose in popularity.[7] The first woman to lead such a series was Ilona Massey who played Resistance singer Nikki Angell in the short-lived ABC show *Rendezvous* (1952).[8] Then came Gena Rowlands as Agent Powell in the syndicated show *Top Secret* (1954).[9] It wasn't until 1961 that the genre got its first meaty female role—and it was a British, not American, show—that of Emma Peel in *The Avengers*. Sociologist Thomas Andrae called her "television's first feminist," writing that she "offered an image of a liberated woman well before the emergence of an organized feminist movement . . . [and] emblematized changing morals overseas."[10]

But in the United States, women were pretty much stuck in the same roles—although a few characters who were actresses did appear on shows like

Gilligan's Island,[11] and American viewers got their first supervillain in Julie New-mar's Catwoman.[12]

In 1966, the groundbreaking television show *That Girl* debuted on ABC. Starring Marlo Thomas as Ann Marie, it follows the life and work of a young actress who just moved to New York and is trying to get her big break. Thomas, who was in her twenties at the time,[13] had the idea for the show after reading Betty Friedan's second-wave-feminist classic *The Feminine Mystique.* She recalled, "I remember saying to the network, 'I don't want to be the wife of somebody, I don't want to be the daughter of somebody, I don't want to be the secretary of somebody, I WANT TO BE THE SOMEBODY!'"[14]

Herbie J. Pilato, writing for the Television Academy, says,

> Her role influenced millions of women to take charge of their own lives, this at a time when the country was feeling the first jolts of the new feminist movement. Indeed, Ann Marie became one of the medium's first "emotionally intelligent" characters, female or otherwise, bursting with a unique blend of vivaciousness, innocence and smarts, and seizing control whenever she faced adversity.[15]

Despite network reservations that "there wasn't a great deal of enthusiasm for a television series about an independent woman; [*sic*] viewing audiences weren't fond of show business stories, and they didn't like female characters without families," the show became an instant hit.[16]

And female viewers took notice. They wrote to Thomas by the thousands, disclosing their unwanted pregnancies and spousal abuse and confiding their dreams.[17] Thomas recalled to the Comedy Hall of Fame:

> It wasn't until the mail started coming in [and we realized] we were talking to a whole bunch of young girls and women and grandmothers . . . who saw in this young girl, their dream that they hoped for, the dream that they didn't realize, the dream they wanted their daughters to have, their granddaughters to have, and that's when it started to feel not just important, but responsible, to the story and that's why I would say such a thing as "I will not let her get married in the end" [of the series]. I can't do that to them.[18]

Thomas kept her promise. Instead of ending with Ann Marie getting married to longtime love interest and fiancé Donald Hollinger, they walk out of the elevator they had been trapped in, hand in hand, on their way to a women's lib meeting.[19] This ending showed women that, despite what they had been taught from girlhood and saw all over television, marriage was not their only choice in life.

This was a theme that would be carried on in a similar show that began airing in 1970, the same year that *That Girl* ended, *The Mary Tyler Moore Show*. *The Mary Tyler Moore Show* was focused on "a single woman in her thirties . . . [who] was not widowed or divorced or seeking a man to support her."[20] Instead, she found a "workplace family" on which to depend and with whom to have relationships.

As popular as the show was, it was still an outlier for female characters. By mid-decade TV also featured attorneys Beth Davenport (played by Gretchen Corbett), who worked for Jim Rockford on *The Rockford Files*, and Kate Mc-Shane (played by Anne Meara), the titular character in the first television series with a female lawyer as its main character.[21]

But for the most part, in the 1970s, if young women wanted a role model—especially one who had a career and was physically strong—she would have to watch shows focused on superheroes and fighting crime.[22] Wonder Woman—who was considered to be the first female superhero[23]—gave girls throughout the country someone to cheer for while their male counterparts emulated Batman and Superman. Even today, Wonder Woman is still credited as "one of the toughest female superheroes alive."[24]

At about the same time, *The Bionic Woman*, a spin-off from *The Six Million Dollar Man*—there is irony there, as well as shades of Adam and Eve—aired and became a cultural phenomenon throughout the world.[25] The decade also gave us such female TV superheroes as Isis, Electra Woman and Dyna Girl, The Girl from U.N.C.L.E, Microwoman, Web Woman, and Spider-Woman.[26]

In the 1980s, the TV woman was generally a working mother. The most iconic is undoubtably Clair Huxtable (played by Phylicia Rashad) on *The Cosby Show*. Clair was the first black female TV main character who was a lawyer. On top of that, she was also a mother of five children. This was important because balancing the needs of family and career wasn't something generally shown on television at the time,[27] but this would change as the '80s progressed. Other working mothers included Carol Brady (real estate) in *The Brady Bunch* spin-off *The Brady Brides*; Elyse Keaton (architect) in *Family Ties*; Angela Bower (advertising) in *Who's the Boss*; and perhaps most famously, Murphy Brown (newscaster)[28] in the show of the same name. In 1992, during the show's fourth season, Murphy became a single mother at the age of 42 and was subsequently attacked by Vice President Dan Quayle for "mocking the importance of fathers, by bearing a child alone, and calling it just another 'lifestyle choice.'"[29] His words, despite being aimed at a fictional character, spoke volumes about just how far American culture had to go on women's equality.

The Scope of This Book

This book covers television heroines from 1994 to 2022, which was a formative and progressive time for female characters in television. Thanks to the effects of third-wave feminism (discussed at length in chapter 3), a new generation of stronger, more independent women appeared on-screen to guide the daughters of the Cosby generation into their own era of power.

Although they lived in times as varied as post–World War II to an alternative version of the present, women on television in the last three decades knew how to kick ass, literally and figuratively. They have battled vampires, demons, corrupt government officials, and secret scientific programs while dealing with the same issues their (mostly female) audience faced, including the meaning of female identity; issues of sex, gender, and sexuality; and how to fight back against a patriarchal society.

Though by no means the majority of shows on TV, the ten shows covered in this book—*Buffy the Vampire Slayer, Charmed, Alias, Nikita, Agent Carter, Jessica Jones, Homeland, House of Cards, Orphan Black,* and *The Equalizer*—changed the way women were portrayed in science fiction, fantasy, spy, and political shows. Previously, television's "strong women" were all superheroes like Wonder Woman or Catwoman. Other "tough" women, like Charlie's Angels, weren't exactly the feminist ideal.

In the '90s, for the first time, television heroines were ordinary women like Buffy Summers and the Halliwell sisters who just happened to develop extraordinary abilities but, otherwise, led mundane lives—they were relatable. The "woman warrior" dramas they helmed all featured "highly physically adept, linguistically 'sassy' white, middle-class heroines [who] undert[ook] supernatural quests.... Mixing melodrama, martial-arts, and highly feminized self-presentation . . . [to] explore complex questions of gender in a format that often shed the shackles of reality."[30] Even when they were set in the past or a present with advanced cloning technology, they represented modern women's desires (to be taken seriously and experience equality in *Agent Carter*) and fears (loss of agency and being forced to conform to patriarchal society in *Orphan Black*). As a result, these shows developed rabid cult followings that changed the cultural landscape for women.

While much has been written about the cultural impact of *Buffy*, to date the show has not been examined in context with others like it, and some of the shows in this book, like *Nikita* and *Alias*, have received little, if any, cultural analysis. With the '90s now thirty years in our rearview mirror and coming back into style as the daughters of the original viewers come of age, the time is ripe for an analysis of these shows and how they paved the way for the strong female characters we know and love today.

As of the end of 2022, we've come close to achieving gender parity for main characters on TV for the first time in history, with 48 percent of characters being female.[31] (Nonbinary and trans roles are growing as well; according to a report by GLAAD, in the 2021–2022 television season, forty-two characters were trans and eight were nonbinary, although they made up about only 0.1 percent of characters.[32]) While that is something to be celebrated, we still have a long way to go. As this book will show, we're still fighting many of the same battles in 2022 that Buffy Summers attempted to stake through the heart in 1994. The good news is, there are more of us with each passing day who are willing to do so, thanks in no small part to the fierce females we grew up or came of age with on television.

A Few Disclaimers

This should go without saying, but be warned, this book is full of spoilers, so read at your own risk. Throughout the text you'll see the words "women" or "all women" used a number of times. By that I mean female-presenting people who are of a feminist mindset. That, of course, doesn't include *all* women; we have as many philosophies and ways of seeing the world as there are people. This language is simply an easy way to group those of like mind.

Similarly, when I refer to "men," I mean the patriarchy—those who enable and participate in the systematic oppression of women. Many male-presenting people are our allies in the fight for equal rights, and it is important to acknowledge that. Again, this terminology is used for ease of writing and reading.

Part I

THE SHOWS AND THEIR LEADING LADIES

CHAPTER 1

Women in Fantasy and Science Fiction Programs

She saved the world. A lot.

These are the words engraved on Buffy Summers's tombstone when she dies for a short period of time in season 5, but they could apply to all the women discussed in this book. The women of science fiction and fantasy shows from the '90s to the '10s varied from vampire hunters and witches to superheroes and clones. But they all shared a thoroughly modern viewpoint in which their independence and personal agency motivated them to help others, and as a result, they ended up saving not only themselves and their friends/family but also the whole of humanity from whatever evil they faced.

How these forms of evil translated into larger societal issues will be explored in part II of this book. For now, let's get to know *Buffy the Vampire Slayer*, *Charmed*, *Jessica Jones*, and *Orphan Black* and the female characters who shaped the culture in which we live.

Buffy the Vampire Slayer: Turning the Tables

Buffy the Vampire Slayer is the story of Buffy Summers, a normal teenage girl living in Sunnydale, California, who finds out she is The Slayer, the girl chosen from her generation to save the world from vampires and other preternatural creatures—all while going through the normal trials of high school and the drama that goes along with it. The series was loosely based on a 1992 movie of the same name that was also written by Joss Whedon.

Buffy the Vampire Slayer premiered March 10, 1997, on the CW network. From the opening scene of the pilot (season 1, episode 1, "Welcome to the Hellmouth")—in which the audience is led to believe a girl was going to be harmed by her boyfriend during an after-dark visit to their school, but it turns out that

3

the girl is the vampire and the boy her victim—it was clear this show was going to be different from anything audiences had ever seen before. Within the first five minutes, the show turned traditional gender roles on their heads and didn't let up for seven seasons.

It carried viewers on a journey not only through the hell that is high school but also through the characters' self-discovery, which is precipitated by the vampires, demons, and other "Big Bads" they face each week. In turn, these antagonists represent larger problems in society.

SEASON 1

The Master led Buffy to a reluctant acceptance of her role as Slayer. She tried all season to fight it and be a normal teenager, but finally The Master grew too powerful to ignore and she had to face up to what he represented—responsibility.

SEASON 2

Buffy faced off against Angelus, the soulless version of her vampire boyfriend, Angel. While millions of viewers rooted for their romance, it was actually a toxic relationship symbolized by the evil Angelus who is everything Buffy shouldn't want, but does.

SEASON 3

Here we are introduced to Mayor Richard Wilkins, who was willing to do any-thing—even transform into a giant snake—to achieve ascension, which is the ultimate source of power. He represents the truth of the aphorism "Power cor-rupts; absolute power corrupts absolutely." He is symbolic of all the politicians who promise one thing on the campaign trail but do the opposite once they are in office.

SEASON 4

Adam, a bionic man who is also part demon and part vampire, is created in an attempt by the military to learn how to control, and ultimately defeat, these creatures. Like Frankenstein's monster, he kills his creator and then is left to learn how to handle human emotion. Through the vampire Spike, he turns the

Scooby Gang against each other until they realize they have to work together to kill him. Thus, Adam represents forces that try to divide people and countries when they should really be working together for the common good.

SEASON 5

Glory is a banished goddess of hell bent on going home and unleashing any evil necessary to get her way. She was cursed into a parasitic relationship (seen by some as a symbol of pregnancy) with Ben, whose body she shares until she grows powerful enough to possess it. Dawn, the unwitting key to Glory's portal home, causes Buffy similar irritations as she learns to parent her new sister amid the sudden death of her mother. In this way, both Glory and Dawn represent motherhood and the responsibilities of adulthood.

SEASON 6

This season can be said to have two Big Bads. The first is the group of incel teenage boys, led by Warren, who are blatant symbols of misogyny and the patriarchy. They go so far in their hatred of women as to kill Tara. Her death triggers Willow to invoke dark magic to get revenge. When killing the trio isn't enough, she becomes a threat to all of Sunnydale. Both Willow and the boys had been bullied earlier in life and let their feelings of being alone and outcast fuel a search for power, which ultimately turned them into bullies themselves.

SEASON 7

The First Evil is the villain of this season. As it is unable to take on a human body, it must use Buffy and her friends— the Scooby Gang—against one another to weaken them. Like Adam in season 5, The First represents forces of disunity.[1]

Journalist Katharine Schwab writes in *The Atlantic* that this metaphor goes beyond the Big Bad to include all sorts of monsters:

> Vampires symbolize sexual predators, werewolves represent bodily forces out of control, and witches tap into tropes about how female power and sexuality is seen as threatening. . . . The monsters everyone faces—oppressive authority figures, meaningless rules, confining social norms, sexual awakening, loneliness, redemption—[are really] the terrors of growing up and finding one's way in the world.[2]

Another way of looking at the show is that Buffy, in her outsider and demon-slaying status represents the very teenagers who were so attracted to the show. They watched her adventures to get a better handle on their own lives, which evolved as they grew, just as each season reflected a new season in life for Buffy. As F. R. Kesby wrote for Women's Republic,

> In season 1, she was 16 and trying to navigate making new friends and finding her place. . . . Season 2, she's in love for the first time and it goes horribly wrong, what could be more accurate for 17-year-olds? Season 3, she's on that line between childhood and adulthood and the baddies are bigger, more powerful and represent the control she doesn't yet have. Season 4, she's just starting college, she's lost and unsure of who she is and a government agency comes in to do her job for her. . . . Season 5, she's an adult, alone, independent, and the biggest bad she's ever had to face comes to kick her arse. Adulting is hard, guys. Season 6, often hated, is a perfect representation of the disappointment of growing up. You go through all that work to find yourself being undermined by men. And season 7? Hello, motherhood.[3]

As these examples show, *Buffy* is very much a modern-day allegory that blends myth, legend, literature, philosophy, and real-life issues to provide entertainment while commenting on modern life. It is that unique combination that drew both young people and academics to the show in a shared quest to understand their lives and the meaning behind them. The result was thousands of blog posts, pop culture articles, and creative fan-fiction written by viewers, as well as a plethora of academic articles and books, including this one.[4]

The Man behind the Myth

Normally a book like this wouldn't address the creator of a show, but Joss Whedon was so influential in '90s and '00s feminism and now is so problematic it would be irresponsible to leave the issue unexplored.

From the very beginning, Whedon was different for his open espousal of feminism and willingness to talk about it, especially for a male in Hollywood. He often recalled in interviews that he came up with the idea for Buffy when he was watching a horror flick and wondered what would happen if someone let "that blonde girl who's always getting herself killed" fight back; he wanted her to be "the thing the monsters were afraid of, not the other way around."[5] Not long after, Buffy was created, patterned after the stereotypical airhead cheerleader so common in the genre, but with an unexpected twist: "she was practically unrivaled in both physical strength and steel-willed emotional fortitude but also a far cry from the few and often grim female action heroines who had preceded her. . . . She was funny, smart, frustrated, and flawed."[6]

Not only that, she wasn't just some jock's girlfriend or the heroine's friend; she was the main character. "Buffy was the ringleader; she called the shots," Emily St. James and Caroline Framke wrote for *Vox*.[7] Two years before *Scream* allowed Sidney Prescott to helm a horror film and (spoiler) live to tell about it for five movies and counting, Buffy broke the well-established mold of the "big-breasted girl who can't act who is always running up the stairs when she should be running out the front door."[8]

Fans and the media responded by christening Whedon "an icon of Hollywood feminism"[9] a moniker he would go to great pains to protect in the press, ensuring "fans thought of him as a feminist ally, an impression bolstered by his fund-raising efforts for progressive causes"[10] and by his own words in hundreds of interviews. "A sort of cult of personality formed around Whedon,"[11] wrote Lila Shapiro for Vulture. Even TV powerhouse Shonda Rhimes admitted to binge-watching all seven seasons of *Buffy* and being influenced by the show to write her own strong female characters.[12] In 2006, Whedon was honored by Equality Now at an event for "men on the front lines" of feminism.[13]

The adulation leaked into academia on preposterous levels as well, with David Lavery, a professor of English at Middle Tennessee State University, hailing Whedon as "the 'avatar' of a new religion, the 'founder of a new faith . . .' [who had] taken a stand against a panoply of oppressive 'social forces,' most obviously the 'forces of gender stereotyping.'"[14] In 2009, Lavery and fellow American scholars Rhonda V. Wilcox (professor of English at Gordon State College in Barnesville, Georgia) and Tanya R. Cochran (professor of English and communication at Union College in Lincoln, Nebraska) formed the Whedon Studies Association,[15] an official "non-profit organization devoted to the study of the works of Joss Whedon and his associates." (In the wake of Whedon's dethronement, the organization is now called the Association for the Study of Buffy+, and its mission has been refined "to promote the scholarship of Buffy+ Studies, focusing on inclusivity, intersectionality, and excellence.")[16] To this day, the association holds an annual conference/party to bring together *Buffy* scholars from around the world at universities in the United States, Canada, and the United Kingdom.[17]

However, Whedon's girl power attitude turned out to be all for show and commercial value. While the cast of his shows must have known, or at least suspected, the duplicity for years, it wasn't until 2017 that the veneer of Whedon's feminist mask began to tarnish. The inciting incident was an open letter Whedon's ex-wife, Kai Cole, published on *The Wrap*, a popular movie blog. She branded him a "hypocrite preaching feminist ideals" and listed the sexual and "inappropriate emotional [affairs] that he had with his actresses [on *Buffy*], co-workers, fans and friends," which he had confessed to her. She continued, "I believed, everyone believed, that he was one of the good guys, committed to fighting for women's rights, committed to our marriage, and to the women he worked with. But I now see how he used his relationship with me as a shield, both during and after our marriage, so no one would question his relationships with other women or scrutinize his writing as anything other than feminist."[18]

Just when it looked like that scandal would blow over with minor repercussions, in summer 2020 Ray Fisher and Gal Gadot, stars of Whedon's *Justice League* movie, claimed he'd mistreated them. Gadot said he "threatened [her] career,"[19] and Fisher described his behavior as "gross, abusive, unprofessional, and completely unacceptable."[20] This prompted Charisma Carpenter, who played Cordelia on *Buffy* and *Angel*, to write a long Twitter post accusing Whedon of being a "glorified abuser" and having a "history of being casually cruel," including terrorizing her while pregnant by asking if she was going to keep her baby, calling her fat, "mock[ing] her religious beliefs, accus[ing] her of sabotaging the show, and fir[ing] her a season later, once she had given birth."[21] Fellow *Buffy* actors Sarah Michelle Gellar (Buffy) and Alyson Hannigan (Willow) flocked to her side to show support, and Michelle Tratchenberg (Dawn) released her own statement regarding a rule that she couldn't be alone with Whedon on set because she was a minor.[22] Writers and costume designers told stories of outrageous and offensive behavior.[23]

Fans, meanwhile, felt devastated and betrayed by the hero who had created the strong woman they had grown up with and admired. Liz Shannon Miller, a reporter for Collider, posits that the situation hit fans so hard because Buffy "inspired them to believe in their own power and use it to change the world . . . [and] Whedon was supposed to be different. Better."[24] Shapiro told NPR that though most people didn't see them at the time, the warning signs of Whedon's imperfection were there all along.

> When he was sort of cast by us as this feminist hero, we were thinking that like, oh, he brought Buffy to life. He gave us Buffy, you know. And not necessarily thinking, well, he also showed us that the world is full of monsters. And most of those monsters are men. And most of those monsters want to destroy Buffy, kill her, try to rape her, endlessly brutalize her. I mean, that's in his brain, too, you know.[25]

Whedon's response to these accusations was to deny the specifics but admit he had some anger issues and that sometimes he "was not mannerly," which he blamed on being young and not yet "civilized."[26] While this was certainly not the apology victims and fans were looking for, many urged fans not to give into the urge to cancel Whedon completely but, rather, to separate the man from the work and remember the good that his shows and characters did for society.[27]

Indeed, the legacy of the show—if not its creator—is a lasting one still being felt and debated by fans and scholars alike. Sarah Dobbs, writing for the website Den of Geek, notes that

> Buffy wasn't pop culture's first female superhero, not by a long shot. But she was the first to anchor her own TV series, and her success paved the way for others like her. Post-*Buffy*, we've seen a lot of other superheroines take center stage in supernatural stories of their own. Without Buffy, we'd never have had *Alias*, or *Lost Girl*, or *Underworld*, or *Orphan Black*, or *Wolfblood*, or the *Resident Evil* movies, or *Jessica Jones*.[28]

And without *Buffy*, we wouldn't have had many of the other shows included in this book. In that way, *Buffy* could be said to be the feministic foremother to an entire movement that urged women to speak up and kick ass—and changed the television landscape forever.

A Trio of Strong Women

According to Whedon, *Buffy*'s mission statement was "the joy of female power,"[29] which can be seen reflected in many of its main characters. While there were dozens of strong female characters on the show—apologies to Cordelia, Tara, Glory, Dawn, Kendra, Anya, Drusilla, Harmony, and others—for the sake of brevity, this book will focus on the main three: Buffy, Faith, and Willow.

BUFFY SUMMERS

Buffy Summers earned the top spot in *Entertainment Weekly*'s 2020 ranking of TV's "Top 20 Badass Female Characters,"[30] which covered shows from roughly the same span of time as this book. And it's not hard to see why. Though she has special powers, Buffy is very much an every woman, which made it easy for an entire generation (or two) to relate and look up to her.

Like her movie counterpart, Buffy is a former Valley Girl and cheerleader who sees herself as just another teenage girl with typical teenage problems. Having caused a bit of a scandal at her previous school (an allusion to the events of the movie), she relocated to Sunnydale, California, to try to live a normal life. That hope is dashed when she finds out she is still her generation's Slayer, a line of supernaturally strong women chosen to protect the world from vampires and other forces of darkness.[31] At first Buffy fights against this idea—she never asked for this and doesn't want it; all she wants is to survive high school, make some new friends, and maybe have a boyfriend or two—but eventually she sees the harm that would come to innocent people if she shirked her responsibility and accepts her calling,[32] inspiring young women to embrace that which makes them different because it is that very thing that will allow them to leave a unique mark on the world.

FAITH LEHANE

Faith's place in the Buffy-verse is as complicated as Faith is dangerous. When Buffy was temporarily killed by The Master in season 1, a new Slayer named Kendra was called. The two Slayers fought side-by-side for a year before Kendra was killed by the unstable vampire Drusilla, triggering Faith to be named Slayer in her place.

Faith is Buffy's polar opposite in everything. She prefers black and red with lots of leather to Buffy's pastel wardrobe of dresses, skirts, and jeans. Faith's upbringing wasn't exactly good; her mother was an alcoholic, and her absentee father owed money to the mob so she was left to fend for herself on the streets

Buffy (Sarah Michelle Gellar, center) is surrounded by her friends, including Willow (Alyson Hannigan, left) and Spike (James Marsters, behind Buffy) and fellow Slayers, including the potentials and Faith (Eliza Dushku). *UPN/20th Century Fox/Photofest*

of Boston. Yet Buffy's mother, while flighty, genuinely loved and cared for her daughter and provided a stable home life. Most telling, perhaps, are their attitudes toward life; Faith's "want, take, have" philosophy and open, casual regard for her sexuality is in stark contrast to Buffy's ethical approach to her life and embracing of love and monogamy.

In many ways, this "dark Slayer" is a fantasy fulfillment for fans of all genders. To men, she is the bad girl of their sexual dreams, and to women, she is the unrestrained version of themselves that they would be if not constrained by the rules of society, religion, and decorum. She provides a clever foil for Buffy as an antihero who is eventually transformed after a long journey (more on that in chapter 9), serving as a messenger that no one is beyond redemption, regardless of what they have done.

WILLOW ROSENBERG

Willow began the series as a sidekick, one of several members of the Scooby Gang who were Buffy's friends and allies. Smart and sweet, she is the nerdy girl who takes school very seriously, loves computers, and can be trusted to come to the rescue when no one else could solve a problem.

But over the seasons, Willow evolved into a main character in her own right. She discovered her powers as a witch when going through her murdered teacher Jenny Calendar's things and trying a few spells. She later found the text of the ritual that would restore Angel's soul to him if Buffy couldn't kill Angelus. Her successful completion of that spell led Willow to study magic for the next several seasons and grow in power, which she sometimes struggled to control.

Willow's first foray with the dark side came after her boyfriend, Oz, cheated on her with a werewolf named Veruca. Willow attempted to curse them both, but chickened out, doing a ritual to have her "will be done," instead, which inadvertently attracted demons to her friends before she reversed it. A while later, she met fellow witch Tara at a college campus Wiccan group, and the two fell in love. Willow's power increased quickly, scaring Tara, who was worried Willow was using too much magic. Willow continued to work increasingly complex and dangerous magic, culminating in bringing Buffy back from the dead when she died at the end of season 5.

Willow then became addicted to magic, using it to remove people's memories, even Tara's when it suited her, causing the lovers to fight and eventually break up. Without Tara there to guide her, Willow succumbed to dark magic until she and Tara reunited. But then Tara was accidently killed by a stray bullet Warren intended for Buffy. Enraged and grief stricken, Willow surrendered completely to her darker side, becoming Dark Willow, a woman bent on revenge at any cost. After brutally killing Warren and his two friends, Willow fought Buffy, absorbing her Slayer power as well as that of the witches who attempted to stop her. Super sensitive now, she could feel all the pain in the world, which nearly drove her mad, and she attempted to bring on the end of the world. Giles and Xander were finally able to get through to her, and Giles took her to England to recover and face what she had done.

Weakened and vulnerable to demons, Willow falls victim to several before once again being called on to restore Angel's soul. As the inevitable battle with The First drew near, Buffy tasked Willow with empowering all the potential Slayers in the world, those like Kendra and Faith who would be called in the event of the current Slayer's death. Willow did so using a combination of her computer skills and magic, before being deified as a goddess by her lover, Kennedy. The couple fled Sunnydale before Buffy's final battle with The First.

Willow's descent into dark magic was in some ways foreshadowed by the character of Vampire Willow who appeared in seasons 3 and 5. Vampire Willow was created when Cordelia made a wish to vengeance demon Anya that Buffy had never moved to Sunnydale. In the alternate reality this created, Willow had been turned into a vampire and was a leader of the vampires running Sunnydale. She crossed over into reality when a spell the real Willow and Anya attempted went awry. Bored of wandering the streets in a world that allowed humans to roam freely instead of "keeping them in chains" like they did in her world, she allied with a group of vampire assassins hired by the evil mayor and attempted to take over the world. Eventually, Willow, Anya, and Giles succeeded in banishing Vampire Willow back to her own realm, where she was quickly killed by Oz and Xander. (Fun fact: Dark Willow utters Vampire Willow's favorite phrase, "Bored now," just before killing Warren and getting her revenge for Tara's murder.)

Like Buffy, Willow can be seen as an everywoman, but for outcasts rather than cool, popular people. Fans derided as nerds, geeks, or other forms of "uncool" related to her early character, taking pride in a show that valued her beyond the butt of jokes and used her skills to help the hero. As Willow grew into her magic, many fans found they had their own power inside them and used their newfound confidence to step out of the shadows and claim their place in the world. For them, Willow's embrace of the darkness was a warning not to forget from whence they came, lest they become the abusers they used to so despise. And like Faith was for the cool kids, Vampire Willow was wish fulfillment for those who never fit in, as she used her situation to her advantage, gaining power and sex appeal in the process.

Charmed: The Power of Three

When *Charmed* debuted on October 7, 1998, on the WB (the same station on which *Buffy* aired), it appeared to some as a rip-off attempting to capitalize on the Slayer's success and the popularity of the supernatural among high school and college students. In fact, *Charmed* was conceived at the request of the network for a "*Buffy the Vampire Slayer* companion piece,"[33] leading some to refer to it as "Buffy's less sophisticated younger sibling."[34] And it's easy to see where the comparison comes from—after all, both feature beautiful heroines battling the forces of evil with their supernatural powers, but as Caroline Preece from Den of Geek points out, "whereas *Buffy* was about growing up, *Charmed* was concerned with what happens once you have."[35]

From left: Phoebe (Alyssa Milano), Prue (Shannen Doherty), and Piper (Holly Marie Combs) were the original Charmed Ones, the most powerful witches in history. *WB/Photofest*

The show soon proved itself to be a force to be reckoned with in its own right. The pilot, "Something Wicca This Way Comes," had more than 7.7 million viewers, becoming the WB's highest-rated debut episode.[36] "Charmed existed in a sort of mid-90s golden-age of the super-powered female lead on television," writes Sophie Moss for literary journal *Luna Luna*. "There was Buffy. There was Sabrina. There were the Charmed Ones. What remains so unique about the latter, for me, is the show's postfeminist values and the way it challenged traditional notions of what it meant to be a 'strong woman.'. . . The sisters were multifaceted, powerful women with a 'girl-power' rhetoric, though never entirely paradoxical to second-wave feminist ideals."[37]

Charmed is the story of the Halliwell sisters—Prudence or "Prue," Piper, and Phoebe—three ordinary San Francisco women who are well into their twenties before they discover that they have mystical powers after the death of their beloved grandmother, whom they call Grams, and are the latest in a long line of Wiccan witches in their family. They are, in fact, the Charmed Ones, the most powerful good witches in history, and have the responsibility to protect "innocents," aka ordinary people, from all sorts of evil, including demons, warlocks, and other mythical creatures.

The show can be seen as having two very different halves. The first half, encompassing the first three seasons, helmed by executive producer Constance M. Burge, took its story lines and its witchcraft very seriously, striving to portray the Wiccan religion accurately and show respect for those who practiced it. (For the record, Wicca is a distinct religion within the overall umbrella of witchcraft, and not all witches are Wiccan.) From their Book of Shadows—a spell book most witches keep, especially when witchcraft is passed down between generations—and their familiar, a lilac-point Siamese cat named Kit, to their spells, potions, and tools, the show is careful to be at least semi-accurate in its depiction of the faith. The sisters also followed a prohibition that stated they could not use their powers for personal gain, a rule followed by many real-life Wiccans.

This makes sense, considering Burge herself studied Wicca and aimed to "portray the Halliwells as decent women who looked and acted like actual people with differing magical abilities."[38] Not coincidentally, Burge left her role at the end of the second season, but she agreed to stay on as an executive consultant until the end of season 3.[39] That was when the dedication to the religion was pushed to the back burner in favor of increasingly ridiculous story lines, which drew the viewer out of the emotional relationship of the sisters and forced them to focus on the bad-guy-of-the-week. "When the show's writers began to trade drama for campy comedy, [it] made for either amazing television or cover-your-eyes disaster," writes Jenny Crusie in the introduction to the book *Totally Charmed.*[40]

Season 3 also saw the departure of Shannen Doherty—for reasons still unknown except to insiders—and the heart-wrenching death of Prue, the sister she portrayed, in the season finale.

With this major change and the end of Burge's oversight, season 4 began the second half of *Charmed*. It began by introducing Paige Matthews (played by Rose McGowan), the conveniently forgotten-then-discovered fourth "Charmed One," who was the product of their mother's affair with her white-lighter. With Burge no longer at the helm, the show developed a new tone. "Suddenly *Charmed* was a whole lot sillier, with mermaids, fairytale creatures and leprechauns becoming weekly occurrences, and any groundedness it could have boasted before was thrown out of the window," writes Preece.[41] That wasn't the last of the show's troubles. In the final season, Leo, Piper's white-lighter and husband, was written out for half the season due to budget issues, and Paige's protégée, Billie, was "universally hated [and] . . . often cited as the beginning of the end for a show already on its last legs."[42]

Yet despite these problems, *Charmed* endured for eight seasons. What made the show such a long-running success was that it "focused as much on the ordinary lives of Prue, Piper, and Phoebe as it did on their extracurricular magical activities, living by the mantra of 'not witches who happen to be sisters, but sisters who happen to be witches.'"[43] The show sits comfortably on the line between fantasy and reality, able to move back and forth with ease. One moment we see the Charmed Ones at work or out shopping,[44] and the next they are fending off demons with their powers or by using a spell. Like *Buffy*, by grounding the views in lives that look like their own, *Charmed* "encourages the viewers to apply information learned about the fictional *Charmed* universe to the events and occurrences taking place in their own lives."[45]

The Charmed Ones

Even with the skimpy outfits worn to draw in male viewers, *Charmed* is an essentially female show written for a female audience. Not only do each of the sisters face "challenges that are all too familiar to any woman,"[46] they are very much mortal and get themselves out of situations using their intellect, rather than the "mindless rage" of stereotypical male superheroes such as Superman and Wolverine.[47]

PRUDENCE "PRUE" HALLIWELL

As the eldest sister, Prue has spent her life feeling responsible for her younger siblings, but especially after the deaths of their mother and grandmother.[48] In the first season, she works as an antiques specialist at an auction house but later leaves that job to pursue her dream of being a photographer.[49] As a typical firstborn child, Prue is driven, strong, and a rule follower, to the point that her sisters mistake her caution and concern for them as being overbearing and uptight.

In an interview with *In Touch Weekly*, Burge explained that each sister's power came from their unique psychology. "Prue, who is very in her mind, very smart, is someone who it seemed to make sense would have the powers that would be mind-related, hence the power of telekinesis."[50] Her gift soon grows to the point where she can move objects as fast as her temper requires. Later on, she finds she has the ability to astral project, or be in two places or on two planes at once. "Her character is, therefore, a presentation of her inner battle with her emotions, self-control and the balance she learns to find in between," writes Abdullah Idrees of Ryerson University in Toronto. "The writers clearly kept this representation of a concerned, yet powerful woman in an oppressive world alive, making sure to put her character through a temporary empath transformation in Season 3's 'Primrose Empath' to comment on the good and bad that comes with empowerment."[51] Prue was so powerful, in fact, that she was viewed as the strongest of the four Halliwell sisters and given nicknames like "Super Witch" and "Wicca Wonder."[52]

PIPER HALLIWELL

High-strung, anxiety-ridden middle sister Piper is the mother-like nurturer and peacemaker of the sisters, often mediating in disputes between authority figure Prue and free-spirited youngest sister Phoebe.

Piper initially works at a restaurant called Quake as its manager and is in training to become a chef but, like Prue, leaves that job to fulfill her dream of opening her own club, P3, whose name is a nod to her sisters and the "power of three." More than her sisters, Piper's deep desire is to be normal, to have "a career and a life outside magic" rather than in the "family business" of magic, and is constantly torn between the two.[53]

Piper's power is the ability to freeze time. "The middle sister always has trouble with time because she's people-pleasing simply by her nature. It felt like that would be a good power for her, the ability to freeze time," Burge said. Piper is the most reluctant of all the sisters to accept her power as a witch. She fears that her gifts may not come from a good source and so she initially rejects them. But they would not be denied, and her reluctance results in a lack of control of her powers, especially when she panics.

As the most emotional of the sisters, Piper takes Prue's death particularly hard, especially since she inherits the mantle of most powerful of the Charmed Ones. Nearly crazed with rage and grief, she forgets the rules of interacting with demons and ends up turned into a Fury.

Piper is best known for her romance with her white-lighter, Leo. Though their relationship is forbidden by The Elders, Piper and Leo eventually marry and have two sons named Wyatt and Chris. She splits her time between her club and being a mother to the boys. "Her power metaphorically represents her ability to manage both lifestyles, with the writers adding molecular combustion to her powers as her inner frustration in a world that expects her to choose a lifestyle when she shouldn't have to," writes Idrees. "For the audience, this reinforces the idea of a visual culture that represents the sacrifices one individual must experience to ease the lives of those in future, and hopefully, more open-minded generations."[54]

PHOEBE HALLIWELL

As the baby of the family and a free spirit, Phoebe was restless and less dedicated to the traditional life path of college, job, and marriage. Because Phoebe dropped out of college and returned home without a job or any money, Prue wrote her off as reckless and irresponsible. But she was just really trying to find her way. After accepting her powers as a witch, Phoebe goes back to school, graduates with a degree in psychology, and becomes a popular advice columnist. This job leads to her later penning a book.

Phoebe initially possesses the power of premonition, which enables her to see into the future and the past. "Because [she] was viewed as having no vision of the future, because she lived in the moment, I thought it would be nice to give the power of premonition to her, because there's something so ironic in the ability to see everyone else's future but her own," Burge said.[55] Because her power is passive, rather than active like her sisters, she trains in martial arts so she can defend herself and her sisters in battle. Later, she develops the powers of levitation and empathy.

Phoebe is known as the sister who is most dedicated to the craft—she was the one who found the family Book of Shadows, after all, and accidently performed the spell that gave the sisters their powers. She is also seen as the most feminist of the sisters because she "juggle[s] work, school, relationships, and the daily responsibilities of domestic life on top of saving humankind" and is a self-made success even amid very unusual circumstances.[56]

PAIGE MATTHEWS

Paige Matthews is the half sister of Piper and Phoebe, born from their mother's extramarital liaison with her white-lighter, Sam. The sisters knew about the affair, but not that their mother was pregnant because of it. Not long after the birth, Paige's parents left her at a church, hoping to protect her from The Elders if they found out she was part white-lighter, as affairs between them and witches were forbidden. She was briefly in the care of Sister Agnes—who mistook her parents for angels—before being adopted by Mr. and Mrs. Matthews. (Their first names are never mentioned.) They raised Paige as their own until she was 17 years old, and they died in a car crash. She only survived because she was able to "orb" (or teleport) out of the car. That was the only time her power manifested before she met her half sisters.

Before meeting Piper and Phoebe, she regularly attends P3, feeling drawn there for reasons she can't explain. She meets Phoebe at Prue's funeral where the former has a vision of Paige being killed by a demon. Phoebe and Cole later rescue her from that very attack. They bring her home to Halliwell Manor where the sisters summon their mother and Grams who explain Paige's backstory. Paige struggles for some time with guilt over her parents' deaths and the anxiety of living in Prue's shadow.

Paige works as a social worker. When she later quits that job to become a full-time witch, she begins working at the School of Magic created by The Elders to help new witches learn to use and control their powers.

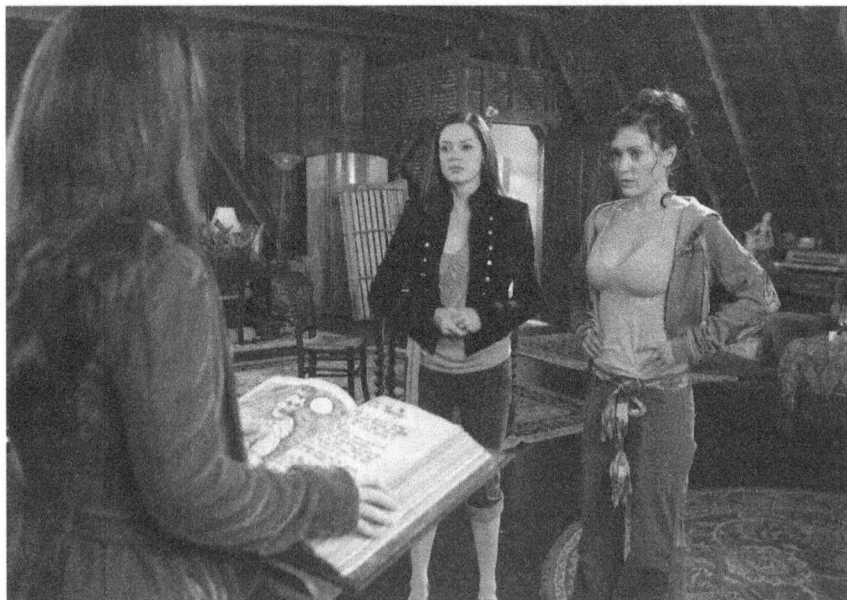

From left: Piper (Holly Marie Combs), Paige (Rose McGowan), and Phoebe (Alyssa Milano) were the second group of Charmed Ones on *Charmed*. *Warner Bros. Television/Photofest*

Paige has both the powers of a witch and a white-lighter because of her parentage. She has telekinesis like Prue, but it manifests differently. She inherited the ability to "orb" anywhere in the world from her white-lighter father, but it is also similar to Prue's ability to astral project. This gift allows Paige to travel to distant lands to relay "the message of the Charmed Ones: to battle injustice, spread peace, enforce empowerment in the helpless, give hope to the hopeless, and promote a world where the concept of patriarchy is frivolous and equality reigns."[57] Over time, she discovers that she can also heal and create an "orb shield," a type of forcefield that protects from danger.

Orphan Black: "Crazy Science"

Orphan Black may be one of the strangest and most intense sci-fi shows in recent years. It is difficult for fans who have seen the show multiple times to try to explain the plot to those who haven't yet experienced *Orphan Black*'s particular form of twisty storytelling in which no one is who or what they seem and the explanations are always far crazier than one could ever imagine. This intricacy led *A.V. Club* to call the show "one of television's most confidently complex sci-fi dramas."[58]

Premiering on March 30, 2013, on BBC America, this thriller follows the five women who try to understand their lives after finding out they are clones. In the process, they meet other clones and end up fighting against several corrupt government and private organizations that are determined to use the science behind human cloning for their own nefarious purposes—Dyad, Neolution, Topside, the Proletheans, and another shadowy organization that isn't named.

Over time the clones come to find out they are the offspring of Project LEDA, an illegal experiment from the 1980s by Susan and Ethan Duncan. The clones, no more than fertilized eggs, were carried to term by surrogate mothers and grew up unaware of their status as clones, though they were secretly monitored by employees of Dyad who posed as people who would logically be part of their lives (parents, boyfriends, husbands, etc.).

When the series begins, Sarah, a rough-living English grifter, witnesses a woman who looks just like her, Beth Childs, step off a subway platform in front of an oncoming train. Astonished but always wily, Sarah takes Beth's purse and shoes from the platform and assumes her identity, while faking her own death with the help of her best friend and adoptive brother, Felix. She is also trying to regain custody of her daughter, Kira, from Mrs. S, the woman who raised her and Felix.

Over time, she comes to find out her identity as a clone and meets dozens more clones, including four others who are desperately searching for answers and have banded together into what they call the "Clone Club" to pool their resources and knowledge toward their common goal. Beth had been part of the club, which also included founding members Alison, an uptight suburban soccer mom, and Cosima, a pot-smoking lesbian scientist who is trying to find a cure for a disease that is killing clones all over the world and from which she suffers. Later on, Helena, an Eastern European killer-turned-defender of the clones, would join them, along with Rachel, a clone raised self-aware by Neolution who is sometimes friend, but usually foe.

Subsequent seasons would add in additional complexity, including male clones created through Project Castor, which was similar to LEDA; an unexpected biological relationship between two of the clones that explains why only they can reproduce naturally; a truly mind-blowing origin story for the cloning experiments; and another generation of clones.

Tired yet?

Adding to the truly unique nature of this show is the fact that Tatiana Maslany, who won an Emmy for her work on *Orphan Black* in 2016, played all of the clones, of which there were nearly twenty[59] throughout the show's five-season run. What's more, with the aid of a stunt double and some truly spectacular technology, she often played more than one clone in the same scene.

The sheer number of female characters in the show—forty-four including the clones—was highly unusual as well. "There are a lot of women," Jill Lepore observes for the *New Yorker*. "The show's lush with them. It's shocking."[60] In addition to the clones, female main characters included Delphine, Cosima's lover; Mrs. S (Siobhan), who raised Sarah and is now helping to raise Sarah's daughter Kira; Susan Duncan, the scientist who is responsible for the experiments that led to the clones; and Charlotte, a next-generation clone who views Rachel as a mother figure.

For feminists, seeing so many strong female characters is not only unprecedented but also a sign of hope. While most of Hollywood still writes off female characters as second-class supporting roles whose character and concerns don't matter, *Orphan Black* has placed them center stage. Communication scholar Jessie Commerce notes in a paper on *Orphan Black* that not only does the show pass the Bechdel test with flying colors, it takes it a step further. Created in 1986, the Bechdel test "judges gender bias by asking if a work of fiction features at least two women who talk to each other about something other than a man."[61] *Orphan Black* goes on to posit that "not only should women be able to talk about something other than a man, they should have plot lines, thoughts, and even conflicting characteristics, because that would show a world in film that is more like real life."[62]

Well-rounded characters like this are one of the many reasons audiences flocked to give *Orphan Black* a home in their living rooms. Through its heart-pounding story line, the show is able to explore a number of female-centric issues including "notions of womanhood, identity, the politics of science, and the prickly notions of autonomy for women, all wrapped in an immensely engaging science-fiction tale about clones."[63]

Five Clones and a Lover

The beating heart of *Orphan Black* is undoubtedly the five main clones. Their relationship and the adventures they take the audience on as they seek to unravel the mystery of their existence is what kept audiences tuning in week after week, even amid some very bizarre story lines. Like the Scooby Gang of *Buffy* and the Halliwell sisters on *Charmed*, every viewer related to and cheered for at least one clone, praying with each episode their favorite would live to see another day—on this show nothing was guaranteed.

SARAH MANNING

Orphan Black's main character is Sarah Manning, a "feral" clone who was considered lost by Dyad. As such she grew up without a monitor or any oversight by Dyad. She was rescued from Project LEDA as a baby and raised by Mrs. S along with a human boy named Felix. Somewhere along the line Sarah fell in with a rough crowd, and she started drinking, doing drugs, and committing petty crimes. She eventually got pregnant and gave birth to a daughter named Kira, whom Mrs. S took custody of until Sarah could prove she was clean and mature enough to be a mother.

Getting Kira back is Sarah's main concern at the beginning of the series, but as she finds out more and more about the program that created the clones, she also realizes she needs to keep Kira away from Dyad. The clones were created to be sterile, but yet Sarah had Kira, which means Dyad would want to study her to find out how this happened.

With her maternal hackles up, Sarah "faces tough choices that transform her from a rebel on the run to a devoted mother, sister, and friend. She experiences [more] development in twenty episodes than some female characters receive in six seasons,"[64] writes Commerce. "Sarah was a selfish, destructive, wrecking ball of a woman," agrees Angelica Jade Bastién, "but there's something triumphant and admirable in tracking her evolution toward regaining her own autonomy, which finally happens when she takes an oxygen tank to the head of P.T. Westmoreland, the final Big Bad whose own ego and quest for immortality is behind the sprawling Neolution mythology."[65]

While she can accept that she is a clone and shares a face with hundreds of others—273 to be exact[66]—Sarah is determined to maintain her individuality. When she tells Felix she is a clone and he questions her, she responds, "They're not me. They're not. They're completely different people" (season 1, episode 3, "Variation under Nature").

But perhaps Sarah's most defining characteristic is her tenacity, a trait she likely developed on the streets with Felix, same as her cunning and adaptability. Once she finds out about the clone conspiracy, she's all in and determined to see the fight to the end, no matter the cost. "Sarah's way of reclaiming her power comes from forcing her way in and going after the outcome she wants, whether it's by assuming another identity, meeting face-to-face with the very people who want to strip away her freedom, or taking a loaded gun to potential threats," writes Caroline Framke for the *A.V. Club*.[67] Nothing and no one is going to stop her from getting to the bottom of the mystery, not a crazed clone (Helena and Rachel), a government institution (Dyad, Neolution, etc.) and especially not a man (scientist Aldous Leekie).

Sarah is relatable to mothers, of course, but also to women who are just trying to do the right thing but have somehow lost their way. (And haven't we all at some point?) She wants to be a better person, but at the same time, she's living the only life she's ever known.

COSIMA NIEHAUS

Cosima Niehaus is a PhD student at the University of Minnesota who is studying experimental evolutionary development biology. She has a particular interest in this field because she is dying from a genetic defect that causes a lung disease that is slowly killing all of the clones of her generation. Incredibly smart, Cosima is also free-spirited and fun, and is the most loving, happy, and innocent of the clones. She wears her hair in dreadlocks and smokes pot, as befits her age and West Coast roots. "She could have had a brighter future than most people in this world had she not been born of a science experiment with damaged DNA," writes Tanya Ghahremani for Complex.[68]

Cosima is the only clone that is known to be a lesbian. She falls in love with Delphine Cormier, whom she later finds out is her monitor (or handler) from Dyad. The two break up because Cosima feels she can no longer trust Delphine, but they eventually get back together. As Delphine is also a scientist, the two work together—aided by the other clones as much as they can help—to conduct "crazy science," their term of endearment for their research into the disease that may take Cosima's life. "Cosima goes after the 'why' [behind their existence] more aggressively than her co-clones," Framke points out. "She treats their genetic material like a map to their independence, because more than anything, Cosima believes that knowledge is power."[69]

Cosima is also the only clone to have a real-life counterpart and namesake. Dr. Cosima Herter is *Orphan Black*'s science consultant and one of the unofficial cocreators of the show due to her significant influence on its story line. Herter's job is to use her knowledge in her specialty of the history and philosophy of science, technology, and medicine to ensure episodes as correct as possible in their science and medicine so they are more believable.[70]

The real Cosima also influenced the character's look, especially her tattoos, which are modeled on Herter's. Tatiana Maslany also copied the scientists' hand gestures to give her more authenticity.[71]

Like the real Cosima, the fictional clone is a much-needed example of women in STEM on television. While she may not have any supernatural powers, Cosima's brilliant mind easily puts her in the category of a superhero. She makes science exciting for the viewer, hopefully inspiring generations of girls to emulate her. Through her work, she shows how women in science and related fields can contribute to health care, save lives, and perhaps even save the world.

ALISON HENDRIX

On the surface, Alison Hendrix is a stereotypical suburban soccer mom, right down to the doting husband (Donnie), minivan, house in an upper-middle-class neighborhood, two adopted children (a boy and a girl), and an immaculately organized craft room. Anxious, uptight, and more than a little repressed, she is the textbook definition of a Type A personality and a perfectionist, an image she is even more desperate to maintain after finding out that she is a clone. "She deeply resents being a clone," writes Framke.[72] When she tells Sarah they are clones, she follows it up with "We're *someone's experiment* and they're killing us off" (season 1, episode 3, "Variation under Nature"). All Alison wants is to live a normal life and make her own choices—two things she fears she will never be able to do again after finding out about being a clone.

But dig deeper and you'll find this PTA paragon has a wild side. She's also an alcoholic who carries a gun, has an affair, deals drugs to pay the bills, ends up in rehab, accidently kills a woman she believes is threatening her children, and buries another body beneath her garage floor with her husband's help. After finding out that Donnie is also her monitor, Alison freaks out and holds him captive but eventually comes to realize he really does love her. He truly believes the cover story he was given: that his role has to do with a study on families. Alison tells him about the clones, and the two join forces in some truly outrageous schemes, which serve as comic relief in an otherwise tense and serious show.[73]

Alison is the result of what happens when the idea of perfection and the adherence to societal expectations is taken too far. So tightly wound she makes everyone around her miserable, Alison is clearly hurting as well. The inner confidence she finds lacking she makes up for with outer perfection. And when she finally explodes, she does so with wild abandon, recklessly breaking the law and any sense of ethics she previously held. She can be seen as a cautionary tale for women of what takes place when one follows the rules too closely to the detriment of fun and freedom.

HELENA (MANNING?)

Helena is the only clone whose last name isn't given in the show. Raised in a strict Eastern European convent, she was terrorized by the nuns; her blonde hair and red-rimmed eyes are said to have come from one of the nuns dunking Helena's head into a bucket of chemicals. Rescued from them at age twelve, she went from the frying pan into the fire, as her saviors ended up being extremists who trained Helena to kill the other clones, brainwashing her to believe she was the original and the others are evil copies.

Rendered insane because of this upbringing, she kills several other clones before meeting Sarah and attempting to kill her as well. Helena is severely wounded by Sarah in the battle and survives only because she performed bloody surgery on herself before carving angel wings into her back with a knife as punishment for failing in her quest.

Helena instinctively recognizes something unique that she and Sarah share, calling her "sestra," which means "sister" in several languages, including Ukrainian. Not long after they find out they are twin sisters separated at birth to protect them. Helena kills their birth mother in revenge for leaving her to be raised in such horrible conditions. Helena and Sarah fight once again, and Sarah shoots Helena, believing she is dead. It is not until toward the end of season 2 that the two meet again and reconcile after Helena saves Sarah's life.

When Helena becomes pregnant (she and her twin, Sarah, are the only fertile clones) as a result of an in vitro procedure forced on her by the Proletheans, a cult that believes synthetic biology is God's will, Helena's humanity really comes to the fore. Her maternal instincts win out over her insanity and complement her killer instinct as she defends her unborn twins at all costs. "Others may have doubted Helena's ability to raise her children, and on another show there may have been a protracted debate about whether Helena should keep her babies," writes Delia Harrington for Den of Geek. "But the perspective of the show was clear: regardless of the violent means by which she became pregnant, what to do next was Helena's choice. Those babies were hers and hers alone, and she and her sestras were going to handle it just fine."[74] During her pregnancy, Helena is taken care of by Alison, whose steady presence helps tame her feral nature. Slowly, Helena relearns how to live and love, becoming for the rest of the series as fierce a defender of her sister-clones as she was once a killer of them.

Helena clearly stands for what happens when extremism—especially in religion—is taken too far. It is the zealots—both the Catholic nuns and the two Proletheans who rescue Helena—that turn her into what she is. As Framke points out, "the show often paints Helena in a feral light, a stray made wild by abuse,"[75] but Maslany sees her as more of a fallen angel-type, "a girl-monster who'd lost her way from a fairytale," as one critic put it.[76] As such, Helena is also a symbol of redemption, proving that any woman, no matter how far gone, can find her way back to good with enough time and love.

RACHEL DUNCAN

Rachel Duncan is the only clone to be raised completely self-aware. Her adoptive parents, Susan and Ethan Duncan, the scientists responsible for project LEDA, raised her as if she was their own, and she is seen in flashbacks having a happy, close relationship with them.

What happened to make Rachel into the "corporate ice queen . . . in a Wintour-worthy bob"[77] is unclear. In the first season, her primary objective is to get Kira into Dyad custody so they can study her and perhaps learn why, out of more than two hundred clones, only Sarah (and Helena, but they don't know that yet) can get pregnant. Over the next two seasons, she ruthlessly pursues this objective, playing Dyad and the clones against one another and proving herself to be a cold-hearted master manipulator. Rachel later proves that she will do anything in "her desperate search for power and freedom"[78] by removing her own bionic eye that was implanted when Sarah stabbed out her real one.

Like Jeri in *Jessica Jones*, Rachel illustrates what can happen when a woman pursues power for its own sake with single-minded focus. Alicia Lutes, writing for Nerdist, observes, "For all its science, *Orphan Black* is also about power: who has it, who controls it, how do you get it, and what does it look like in the hands of a woman."[79] One of the things that is so fascinating about the show is that the answer is different for every female character. For Rachel, it is unfeeling and self-directed, a force wielded without pity and to be used to her greatest advantage.

DELPHINE CORMIER

So much attention is given to the clones (and with good reason) that it is easy to overlook Delphine. While not a clone, she is undoubtedly one of the most important characters on *Orphan Black*; one critic went so far as to call her the "unsung hero of the show."[80]

We first meet her on the campus of Cosima's school, when Cosima mistakes her for a student like her, a natural assumption that Delphine does not correct. Later, we find out that Delphine actually works for Dyad and is in some sort of intimate, if not sexual, relationship with Dr. Aldous Leekie. Despite this, she and Cosima date and become lovers. They break up briefly after Cosima finds out Delphine is her monitor, a revelation that breaks their trust, but in time their love wins out. "Delphine's relationship with Cosima has produced both incredible happiness and devastating heartbreak," writes Framke. "Her love for Cosima and the LEDA clones contrasted sharply with her slow and steady embrace of harsher techniques as she got more and more entrenched in Dyad's 'whatever it takes' mentality. She . . . [is] a woman on an incredibly personal mission."[81]

Delphine's love for Cosima is so deep that finding a cure for the clone's disease becomes the driving force in her double life as a dedicated worker for Dyad and Neolution who is secretly helping the clones. "I think she's very strong because she's fighting for a love that you only find once in a lifetime,"[82] says Evelyne Brochu, who played Delphine. "[Neolution] science affects the love of her life, so she can't just walk away from it. . . . She's fascinated by and curious about the idea that we could live forever and cure everything, but the big issue for her is Cosima's life."

Delphine is a woman driven by her dedication to her work, which she wholeheartedly believes can do good, but she also loves intensely, making her like an interesting combination of Rachel without the hard edges (or maybe with them softened by her love) and Cosima, but without the wide-eyed optimism of a sheltered life; through her work with Dyad, Delphine has seen and experienced things whose effects can't be undone. But at the same time, she has made a promise to Cosima that she will protect and love all of the clones equally,[83] and she is nothing if not a woman of her word.

Delphine represents women who are good at heart but find themselves trapped in an untenable situation. Like those who stay in abusive relationships for the sake of their children or who remain in toxic or soul-crushing work environments to provide for their families, she puts the greater good above her own happiness, doing what she must in the present to achieve her endgame and protect those she loves.

Jessica Jones: Not Your Average Superhero

Jessica Jones is the bridge between the supernatural and the spies covered in this book. She's a superhero with minor powers in comparison to others. She is very strong and can sort of fly, which is really more the ability to jump high and land gracefully. But she also works as a private investigator, which makes her a spy of sorts.

She is a relatively new addition to the Marvel universe, having been created in 2001 as the heroine of a graphic novel called *Alias* as part of the launch of Marvel's "Max" line for adults. The graphic novel was not related to the TV show of the same name, though it came out within a few weeks of the show.[84]

Jessica's backstory is that "she existed in the background of the Marvel adventures that had been published in the preceding thirty years—she went to high school with Peter Parker, she was best friends with Ms. Marvel, and she knew Luke Cage from adventures they had shared during her brief time as a superhero."[85]

Jessica Jones was successful on many levels; it was a hit with female viewers because it was made by women for women. The production team was mostly female.[86] A year before #MeToo brought the sins of powerful men to light, the show's creators were already planning to have every episode of the second season directed by women; they succeeded, and nine of thirteen episodes also were written or cowritten by women.

The show captured not only viewers but also critical acclaim. It won the prestigious American Peabody Award for "storytelling that expands our horizons"[87] for season 1's focus on Kilgrave's abuse of Jessica and what it said about real-life abuse, power, and consent, subjects few shows—much less those about superheroes—dare to touch. "Showrunner Melissa Rosenberg took a subplot from the original comic series about Kilgrave, a character who uses his mental abilities to bend others to his will, and turn[ed] it into a season-long exploration of how a powerful woman can reclaim her life and stand up against her abuser," the jurors said.[88] By being willing to have a heroine who suffers posttraumatic stress, treats it by abusing alcohol, and does not flinch away from the causes and effects of abuse, *Jessica Jones* proved it was as far away from camp and fluff as its titular heroine was from perky and sweet.

Three Viewpoints on Power

Little kids may idolize perfect superheroes who always fight for justice and live on the side of right, but jaded adults need more three-dimensional characters to cheer for; if they are flawed and real, the audience takes notice. And *Jessica Jones* "always treated its female characters with care. They're fully fleshed-out, realistic, flawed, sympathetic, powerful, and above all, wildly interesting."[89]

JESSICA JONES

Jessica Jones (played by Krysten Ritter) is not your mother's superhero; she's closer to your father's hard-boiled PI. She is about as far from Wonder Woman's bright smile and optimism as a total eclipse is from the summer solstice. From her first moment on-screen, it was clear she was a hard-drinking, foul-mouthed, depressed, and bitter woman who scared away nearly everyone who tried to help her; but yet it was clear that a keen mind, kind heart, and sharp sense of humor lay hidden underneath her protective shell.[90] "What makes Jessica such a riveting character is that she wears her damage on her sleeve, something that many 'strong' female characters, aren't allowed to do,"[91] writes Jenna Scherer for *Rolling Stone*.

Though she was recovering from terrible abuse, Jessica "wasn't a one-note vengeance machine in a revenge saga. She was a walking wound, too busy numbing herself with alcohol and casual sex to actually face her past, until her past came back to life and she couldn't ignore it any longer,[92] notes Chelsea Steiner. Jessica's quest to confront and heal from that past—even if it wasn't her idea and meant facing it head on—is what attracted audiences. Who doesn't have something in their past they are running from or trying to forget ever happened? Seeing Jessica's struggle—with herself, her guilt, and her abuser—gave viewers hope that they, too, could face down their demons and win—even if it hurt and even if it took every ounce of their strength to do it.

TRISH WALKER

At the beginning of the series, Jessica's best friend/foster sister, Trish, appears to be no more than a beautiful journalist who is rich because she was a child star. There are hints that she suffered from drug addiction and had a Britney-esque public meltdown and subsequently fell from grace, but the extent of the damage caused by her fame isn't revealed until season 2.

That is when we learn that not only could her mother, Dorothy, give Joan Crawford a run for her money, but also Trish was sexually abused by a director when she was young, and mentally by her fiancé, who was more concerned with his own needs than hers. Couple this insecurity with her past addiction issues and jealousy over Jessica's superpowers, and it's no wonder why when Trish broke again, it was in a spectacular fashion.

Trish's downfall begins when she takes a drag off of an inhaler left behind by her former boyfriend, Simpson, who became hyper-focused after using it. What she doesn't realize is that it contains "a potentially fatal cocktail of chemicals."[93] Addicted to the power it gives her, she decides to take justice into her own hands, subverting the legal system and meting out whatever punishment she sees fit, including death. "This aligns her with the attitude of a vigilante who has given up on a hopelessly corrupt system," writes scholar J. M. Tyree in the *Michigan Quarterly Review*.[94] In making this transformation into a vigilante, she becomes her alter ego, Hellcat. "Trish became a monster just as Jessica—learning more about her past and discovering that her mother was still alive—became more human," notes Sophie Gilbert in *The Atlantic*.[95]

Trish's plight shows that even good women can be corrupted when their vulnerabilities are continually exploited. Had her mother's stage managing stopped after her teenage meltdown, Trish may have had the chance to grow into a strong woman in her own right, but by constantly living under Dorothy's thumb, Trish was never able to find out who she really was, only who everyone (her mother, the press, her boyfriend, etc.) wanted her to be. As a result, when she took her identity into her own hands, becoming Hellcat, she did so to an extreme. She wasn't going to let anyone—especially not Jessica, for whom she long harbored jealousy—stop her.

JERI HOGARTH

Played by Carrie-Anne Moss, Jeri Hogarth is a high-powered lawyer and the queen of boss-bitches—entitled, unfeeling, and proud of it. She works and lives like a stereotypical man, doing what she wants when she wants. This "Prada-wearing python" doesn't apologize for anything, including trading in her long-time wife for her secretary, ordering Jessica around like a slave, or breaking any and all ethical codes (and occasionally the law) if the ends justify the means. As she tells Jessica, "The real world is not about happy endings. It's about taking the life you have, and fighting like hell to keep it" (season 1, episode 9, "AKA Sin Bin"). Marykate Jasper of the *Mary Sue* describes Jeri's attitude as a perverse form of entitlement:

> She feels entitled to Jessica's time whenever and however she requires it, because she pays well and Jessica needs the money. She feels entitled to use Kilgrave's powers in her divorce case. She even feels entitled to Pam saving her life: "*You* chose to pick up that thing and crush her skull. *You* did that." Jeri has fought hard for her wealth, rather than inherited it, but that almost makes her delight *more* in the power that comes with it. She fought for that wealth because of

what she wants it to mean: that she can control whoever she wants and get whatever she wants.[96]

This mindset was no doubt created out of the struggle Jeri faced to rise from poverty to greatness. "I grew up in a trailer the size of this dining room with four siblings . . . school [was] as much a living hell as home. Everything I have, I built from nothing," she tells Inez Green in season 2, episode 8, "AKA Ain't We Got Fun."

After flaunting her power in the first season, Jeri is faced with the harsh reality that she really is human in season 2 when she is diagnosed with amyotrophic lateral sclerosis (ALS), for which there is no cure and which leads to a particularly painful and humiliating death. As she says in season 2, episode 3, "AKA Sole Survivor," "It's ironic, isn't it? I've spent my whole life amassing this power and control, thinking somehow it would protect me. If I believed in God, I'd say her sense of humor is for shit."

Faced with having at most eight years to live, many characters would try to reform their lives, but not Jeri. When her law firm partners try to force her out, she asks Jessica to find dirt on them so she can blackmail them. She even buys potentially dangerous medication from overseas to try to curb her mortality. When she is robbed by a supposed "healer," Inez Green, Jeri even goes so far as to arrange a situation in which Inez would be forced to shoot her boyfriend and then called the police to report the shooting, ensuring she got her revenge.

Unlike Trish, Jeri knew that vulnerabilities in women were often seen as weaknesses rather than a natural part of human nature, so she created for herself a persona that was seemingly impenetrable. In her mind, she was untouchable. She was so used to getting what she wanted that she forgot she was a mere mortal until her body betrayed her. Jeri is a symbol of what can happen when the fight for gender equality is taken too far and corrupted to serve the needs of the individual rather than the whole. In trying to prove—over and over again throughout her life—that she was just as good as her male counterparts, Jeri became the worst of what she was fighting against until she no longer cared.

CHAPTER 2

Smart Spies and Political Paragons

In a male-dominated world, women make great spies because no one ever suspects them of being capable of duplicity, sweet obedient things that they are. Women can walk among men unnoticed because, to them, women aren't worth the attention—until they are. The very novelty of their existence makes them assets in the world of espionage. The danger inherent in this work necessitates that any woman participating in it must be able to defend herself, and as such, that was one of the first ways in which fierce females could be shown on television. By the 1990s, though, female spies had come a long way from the days of Emma Peel and, by the 2020s, when *Homeland* ended, would be running entire divisions, thanks to the ground she broke.

In their own way, politicians are a lot like spies, constantly watching for the next opportunity for advancement or way to take down a rival. They traffic in secrets and lies and live double lives, promising their constituents one thing while doing another. Politicians live and work in a constant state of hypervigilance, never knowing who to trust or what to believe. They've even been known to resort to murder and cover-ups when circumstances warrant. That is why Claire Underwood is included in this section. The women of the FBI and CIA could learn a thing or two from this master manipulator.

Alias: I Can Be Whoever I Want to Be

"The greatest thing would be if Felicity was recruited by the CIA."

That statement from *Alias* creator J. J. Abrams was the genesis of a hit, the first germ of the idea that would become *Alias*.[1] Premiering only ten days after the world-changing September 11, 2001, terrorist attacks on the World Trade

Center in New York City, it was "one of several series to sympathetically portray American intelligence services after the fall of the Twin Towers."[2] Lucky for all involved, despite America's real-life troubles being focused on the Middle East, the show's Big Bad was a throwback to Cold War Russia; otherwise it may have hit too close to home and tanked. But it was a hit with viewers, though strange story lines over the course of its run alienated some, causing one critic to call *Alias* "the greatest spy drama of 2002 . . . [and] the worst spy drama of 2005."[3]

Sydney's (Jennifer Garner) wild wigs became a famous part of her disguises on *Alias* and helped distinguish her from the mild-mannered student she portrayed by day.
ABC/Touchstone Television/Photofest

The premise? The main character gives it to us in a nutshell in a voiceover at the beginning of the pilot:

> My name is Sydney Bristow. Seven years ago I was recruited by a secret branch of the CIA called SD-6. I was sworn to secrecy, but I couldn't keep it from my fiancé. And when the head of SD-6 found out, he had him killed. That's when I learned the truth: SD-6 is not part of the CIA. I've been working for the very people I thought I was fighting against.
>
> So, I went to the only place that could help me take them down. Now I'm a double agent for the CIA, where my handler is a man named Michael Vaughn. Only one other person knows the truth about what I do—another double agent inside SD-6. Someone I hardly know, my father.

Sydney Bristow was, then, an all-American good girl who just happened to become a spy. She was in many ways, according to critic Charles Taylor, the spiritual daughter of Mary Richards of *The Mary Tyler Moore Show*. Just as Mary was "a path-breaking representation of the female professional on the small screen," thanks to her efforts, characters like Sydney could boast "'I can be whoever I want to be' . . . at the frontier of endless and available life choices."[4]

Indeed, the fact that Sydney was a spy was groundbreaking in and of itself. "Historically, the spy oeuvre has manifested resistance if not antipathy towards women," writes Sarah Whitney.[5] Outside of Emma Peel, it is hard to name many female agents before Sydney who weren't playing the role of seductive Bond girl or Mata Hari. "I ultimately realized that elegant Emma was merely another taste of eye candy," wrote film historian Mark Cotta Vaz, who wrote the official companion book to the series, *Alias*. "Sydney Bristow, however, is not only beautiful, but exceptionally brainy and very two fisted—I think series creator J. J. Abrams broke the mold with this female secret agent."[6]

Because *Alias* was so different from anything TV audiences had ever seen, the industry coined a new subgenre to describe it: "spy-fi, a mash-up derivation of both the espionage and science-fiction genres," perfect for a show that "felt like it was looking to the past in order to create the future; it had a pulpy, 1960's [*sic*] adventure vibe updated for modern audiences."[7]

Alias goes deeper than your average spy caper. Taken as a whole, it is about the quest for identity. Like any spy, Sydney has to juggle two lives and two personas, but there is so much more to question and uncover. She learns through the violent death of her fiancé that the company she works for isn't what it seems, then that her estranged father has been protecting her all along, and that her mother, long presumed dead, was really alive but had been hiding her identity as a Russian operative.[8] In the face of such revelations, what even is truth? That is the question Sydney spends five seasons trying to answer amid increasingly outrageous assignments.

SYDNEY BRISTOW

Unassuming English graduate student Sydney Bristow might seem the least likely of any heroine in this book to be ranked number 5 in *Entertainment Weekly*'s 2020 ranking of TV's "Top 20 Badass Female Characters" (in shows from approximately 1990 to 2020).[9] That is, until you realize she is also "a globe-trotting American undercover agent by night."[10]

"Sydney brings a sweetness to the spy genre that it has never had,"[11] Charles Taylor wrote in 2005. That disarming nature comes from the way she was written; she's just the girl-next-door who happens to save the world for a living. She's no superhero; she accomplishes her missions with only "her ability to think on her feet and fight in a series of increasingly outlandish disguises."[12]

That very ordinary-ness is what makes Sydney so easy to relate to. Like every other working person, she has her job, and her personal life is separate. "She gets in, she kicks ass, she gets out again. Except, when she gets captured, in which case the ass-kicking is slightly delayed,"[13] writes Karl Hodge.

With her dysfunctional family, no-nonsense attitude, and genuine heart, Sydney represents what every woman could be if she chose a different path in life. "Sydney had a loneliness and desperation about her, and this desire to be normal," Jennifer Garner, who played Sydney, said. "That's what makes [her] believable to me."[14] Normality is what every person dreams of, right? Being accepted, not standing out, not feeling "other." There is irony in that a character so many people idolize *because* of her exotic lifestyle would want exactly what those people have: a plain ol' boring life.

Nikita: Rogue Assassins on the Run

The 2010 TV remake of *Nikita* is the third version of her story since she first appeared on film in the 1990s French movie *La femme Nikita*. Next came the 1997 TV series of the same name starring Peta Wilson. While there are some changes between versions, the basic plot is the same. Nikita, a directionless teenage drug addict, is arrested for murder and sentenced to life in prison. But instead of that fate, she is chosen to take part in a secret government program that turns her into a killing machine adept at martial arts, gunplay, seduction, and technology. The organization faked Nikita's death when she was recruited, so when she decides to leave the organization, she can easily disappear into the wind.

This is where the 2010 series picks up. Nikita has been off the grid for three years and returns looking for revenge. Her backstory is a little different—she fell in love with a civilian during her time at Division (the government program that made her an assassin), and when he was murdered, she realized Division betrayed her and then she escaped. She is the only one to ever do so—all other recruits who run or are deemed unsatisfactory are killed via a tracking chip in their heads—so Division is anxious to clean up their mess.

Nikita is training Alex, the daughter of a man Nikita assassinated years ago—though Alex is not aware of the true nature of their relationship—to be a mole inside Division. Using intelligence Alex gains for her, Nikita manages to convert several people inside the organization to her side, including Nikita's former handler, Michael, and foil the director's attempt to take over the CIA. Alex leaves Nikita when she learns Nikita was responsible for her father's death and is identified as the mole inside Division. Amanda, the new head of the organization, sees a lot of her younger self in Alex and so offers her a deal: if Alex helps Division stop Nikita, Division will help Alex her kill the man who ordered Nikita to kill her father. Alex agrees.

While Nikita and Michael are on the run and systematically killing people involved in Oversight, an organization closely linked to Division, Alex is on the hunt for Sergei Semak, her father's trusted confidant, who had him killed to take over the organization. Over the next two and a half seasons, Alex regains control of her father's organization and reconciles with Nikita. Together, Nikita, Alex, and Michael expose Amanda as a traitor in league with the Russians, stop a plutonium bomb from destroying the nation's capital, kill the leaders of Division, and install people from their side instead. When that backfires, Nikita and crew go after Amanda, who is on the run with the clones, or "Doubles," she created of top government officials. She is eventually captured, but instead of killing her, Nikita locks her away somewhere no one will ever find her.

Den of Geek called this iteration of *Nikita* closer to "*Alias'* spiritual younger cousin"[15] than a remake of the original story. And in many ways that is true; the two shows have remarkably similar premises. By starting this *Nikita* where the original left off, it is more of a sequel than a retelling. The show also turned the prevailing image of a female spy as an over-sexualized, deadly vamp—a femme fatale, if you will—on its head by focusing on the intertwined stories of two "damaged and co-dependent female protagonists," who had depth, emotion, and story line beyond their Bond-like skills.[16] That's not to say Alex and Nikita were not drop-dead gorgeous when they needed to be, nor were they above seduction when required or desired, and they most certainly could kill, but they had much, much more going on in their lives and in their minds than their historical counterparts.

Three Very Deadly Women

Trained by Division, Nikita and Alex are serious threats to the organization because they know its ins and outs, its strengths and weaknesses. Amanda is equally dangerous because she has access to all of the resources and intelligence of Division to use against them. In pitting them against one another, the show creates a feminist form of spycraft perfect for the twenty-first century.

NIKITA MEARS

In this version of the story, Nikita escapes death row rather than life in prison, increasing the stakes for her to join Division, and her skills have been amped up to the point "she's practically a superhero; albeit a very deadly one."[17]

Nikita is serious, constantly thinking and plotting, which can make her seem cold and distant, but it is really just a result of her training. She can be charming, funny, and witty when the occasion (or assignment) requires, but she prefers to keep to herself. She holds grudges very easily and is quick to anger.

Under her warrior armor, Nikita is a caring woman who harbors much guilt over what she did while a part of Division. While she knows she didn't really have a choice, she still regrets some of her actions, especially not being able to

Nikita (Maggie Q) and Alex (Lyndsy Fonseca) are both strong female characters but have a maternal-/sororal-like bond. *The CW/Photofest*

save Alex from being sold into human trafficking. Nikita is also protective of those she lets into her heart, especially Alex, Michael, and Seymour Birkhoff, a Division hacker whom the group befriends. Though motivated by revenge, Nikita is actually a rather selfless person who is willing to sacrifice for the greater good and wants what is best for everyone.

Nikita can be seen as an allegory for women who fall outside of the confines of ordinary life in America. Many don't survive or go unnoticed, but Nikita makes her own success, using everything she has to get back on her feet. Though her methods are often suspect, her intentions are noble, and many of her actions can be forgiven as they were forced by circumstance.

ALEX UDINOV

Alexandra Udinov is the wealthy daughter of a Russian kingpin whom Nikita is sent by Division to assassinate. At only thirteen years old, she is present when this takes place, though she doesn't see who killed him. Fearing for her, Nikita sends a man to protect her, but he betrays her by selling Alex into human trafficking. During her time as a sex slave in the United States, Alex gets hooked on drugs, which Nikita helps her kick when the two reunite.

Bent on revenge, Alex is willing to do anything necessary to bring down Division and those who killed her family. She suffers from PTSD and flashbacks that she cannot control, but she cannot take any medication for them lest she become addicted again.

Alex had to grow up fast, so she is mature beyond her years and often serious like Nikita, but occasionally the child within shines through. Given her past, Alex is naturally distrustful. In season 1, episode 15, "Alexandra," Amanda remarks that Alex is "like one of those Russian dolls; you open one version of her, only to find there's another hidden inside her." Nikita is the only one who manages to break through her walls and gain her trust over time, which makes it all the more painful when Alex finds out the secret Nikita has been keeping from her.

Alex can be seen to represent those who are caught in the middle of unfortunate situations and aren't at liberty to extract themselves from them. She can also be seen as those who do manage to get out and help change the situation that they were subject to.

HELEN "AMANDA" COLLINS

Amanda Collins is Division's psychologist and unofficial head of torture. She is a trained manipulator who is tasked with interrogating enemies (sometimes by force) and breaking new recruits so that they give Division cult-like loyalty. Only two people have been able to resist her attempts—Nikita and Alex—and as a result, Amanda is fixated on them.

As befits her job, Amanda has the personality of a shapeshifter, able to take on any role that will benefit her. She can be kind and friendly, even motherly, to gain trust or manipulate people using their mistakes and greatest fears against them. Her skills are so great that most people aren't even aware she is influencing their every thought, word, and deed.

Amanda has an obsessive personality that, on one hand, drives her to succeed and, on the other, causes her to fixate on people (like Nikita) and concepts (like power). She enjoys finding new and inventive ways to torture people physically and mentally and doesn't hide her pleasure. She can be particularly violent, bordering on psychotic, when she thinks people are keeping information from her.

Like Jeri in *Jessica Jones*, Amanda can serve as a warning to women that, while pursuing power and success is encouraged, everyone should be careful to watch over their ambition and not let it run away with them. She also embodies the dangers of overconfidence in one's own abilities and putting one's own needs first all the time.

Agent Carter: Marvel's Best-Kept Secret

In 2023, we have Black Widow, Harley Quinn, and a host of other female main characters based on graphic novels, but at the time *Agent Carter* premiered in 2015, the last female character adapted from a graphic novel was *Elektra* in 2005.[18]

Agent Carter follows Peggy Carter, a woman who has returned to her job as the first female agent at the Strategic Scientific Reserve (SSR) after the end of World War II. Having made a name for herself overseas, Carter is annoyed to find that back on the home front she is treated with the same chauvinism as before the war. As she says to Chief Dooley, "I conducted my own investigation because no one listens to me. I got away with it because no one looks at me. Because unless I have your reports, your coffee, or your lunch, I am invisible" (season 1, episode 7, "SNAFU").

But she gets a new lease on life when Howard Stark, who is wanted by the SSR, asks her to track down some of his dangerous inventions that have gone missing and might be being sold to enemies of the state on the black market. Working with Edwin Jarvis, Stark's butler, Peggy recovers Stark's stolen weapons but also uncovers an organization called Leviathan that wants to use them for evil.

Agent Carter (Hayley Atwell) is a take-no-prisoners female spy holding her own in the male-dominated world of 1940s New York City. *ABC/Photofest*

Agent Carter happened to premiere right as the fourth wave of feminism was about to begin and women in America were about to endure five years of blatant misogyny and the gradual peeling back of their rights. Like a superhero swooping in to save the day, "Carter was the 'I can take care of myself thank you very much' hero we needed."[19] What's more, the show was the "first major project set within the Marvel Cinematic Universe to be headlined by a woman."[20]

PEGGY CARTER

Dr. Margaret Elizabeth "Peggy" Carter, PhD, may be best known as Captain America's girlfriend, but she is far more than simply someone's love interest, and she'd be the first to tell you. She is also a brilliant, loyal agent—most of the time she's the smartest person in the room[21]—and takes her job seriously. But she can also be by turns charming, outspoken, and witty. She believes that her gender shouldn't stop her from doing anything, especially when she is more capable than the men around her.

Peggy takes slights stoically, but she isn't above tossing back a witty bon mot when the situation calls for one. She can be sarcastic and flippant in her takedowns, but also loving to her small group of trusted friends. She has a strong sense of right and wrong and is usually on the side of right, even if she has to lie to protect her cover.

Peggy is clearly the feminist in every woman. She has a keen eye for injustice and the will to fight against it, whether that means pinning a rude customer's hand to a diner table when he takes liberties with the waitress or foiling a plot to blow up Los Angeles with Zero Matter. Equality is her mantra, and she will do everything she can to get closer to that goal.

Homeland: Pushing the Envelope on Acceptability

On October 2, 2011, 2.8 million people tuned in to the first episode of a new Showtime series, making it the network's most watched premiere in nearly a decade and the most talked-about show in America.[22] President Obama said he was "obsessed" with *Homeland*, calling it his favorite show of 2012.[23]

Based on *Prisoners of War*, an Israeli drama,[24] *Homeland* follows the exploits of bipolar CIA agent Carrie Mathison, who becomes obsessed with newly released al-Qaeda prisoner of war Marine sergeant Nicholas Brody, whom she believes to be a turned man secretly working for terrorists. For three seasons, she travels the Middle East in relation to this theory, eventually falling in love with Brody and having his child. Season 4 finds her as a drone operation lead in Afghanistan and then Pakistan. All the while she repeatedly defies authority, breaks the law, and ignores potential consequences. Removed from her position several times, she is always saved by her mentor, Saul Berenson, until he can no longer help her and she leaves the CIA to go into private security before working for the first female president of the United States, whom she later believes to have ties to the Russians.

The first two seasons earned near universal acclaim from critics,[25] winning two Golden Globes for best drama series, and a total of eight Emmys—four for outstanding drama, one for writing, one for best lead actor (Damian Lewis, who played Brody), and twice for best lead actress (Claire Danes, who played Carrie).[26] Danes, in fact, became only the second actress to ever win all five main TV acting awards for her performance in the lead actress categories.[27] The series also garnered Emmy nominations for four of its supporting cast members.[28]

CARRIE MATHISON

CIA operative Carrie Mathison is fiercely patriotic, dedicated to the CIA and her country. She is incredible at her job, but she lives by her own rules, doing whatever is necessary—including not taking her medication for bipolar disorder—if she believes it will help her mission. Like Amanda in *Nikita*, she has an obsessive personality, but in her it manifests as single-minded fixation on solving whatever riddle is before her, which some might even say makes her a danger to the agency. Her heart is in the right place, but she is often misguided in her methods. Danes herself says Carrie "is a mess. . . . The challenge is finding a way to play the truth of her being chemically unstable and also a really proficient, highly capable CIA agent."[29]

When Carrie loves someone—be it her family, Brody, or even Saul—she does so deeply and with great loyalty. The one exception is that she is a terrible mother, pawning her daughter off onto her sister while she focuses on her work and later losing her to Child Protective Services.

"Mathison is multi-faceted, flawed and real. She is intense, secretive, and promiscuous. . . . I dislike her at times; her actions and mannerisms often frustrating me. However I also respect her, empathise with her and relate to her," writes Mary Hartnett for *TN2 Magazine*. Carrie's complexity, juxtaposed with her unquestionable competency, makes her just as interesting as her male counterparts.[30] It is no wonder, then, that *Vox* called her "the most influential TV character of the 2010s"[31] and she ranked number 15 in *Entertainment Weekly*'s 2020 ranking of TV's "Top 20 Badass Female Characters"[32] (from approximately 1990 to 2020).

Carrie can be seen as the unstable genius potential in all of us. It is difficult to tell if her mental illness feeds her genius or if her genius feeds her mental illness, but she definitely uses both in her quest for justice. She is a powerful example of how those with mental illness can do great work even with their struggles.

The Equalizer: Black Women Finally Have Their Time

Like *Nikita*, the 2021 version of *The Equalizer* is the fourth rendition of the story, but the first to feature a woman—and a woman of color at that—as the main character. The original 1985 television show took place in the grimy, dangerous streets of a New York that is unrecognizable by today's standards, save for the corruption that persists.[33] The next adaptations were movies starring Denzel Washington that came out in 2014 and 2018.[34]

The 2021 reboot follows the same basic premise as the original show. Former military and CIA agent Robyn McCall may claim to have just quit her job at a charity to spend more time with her family, but what she really does is mete out justice for those who don't have any way to help themselves, prompting the *New York Times* to style her "a gun-toting Robin Hood."[35]

In a society where Black people, especially Black men, have negative experiences with the police on a daily basis and Black women too frequently mourn the lives of boyfriends, husbands, and sons taken too soon in police-related shootings, having a Black woman be "the face of justice" is a bold move.[36] The show not only makes a Black woman a key part of fighting back against corruption that affects her own community, it asserts that Black women are just as capable of kicking ass and solving crimes as their white counterparts have done for decades. Candice Frederick for *TV Guide* writes:

> *The Equalizer* steadies its narrative on restoring justice for people who we don't often see blockbuster action films portray in the same light. . . . Amid its cool action sequences with [McCall] strongarming everyone from extremists to gang members, *The Equalizer*'s mission to expand beyond the homogenous landscape of victims and villains is apparent and necessary.[37]

The show has been well received by viewers, regularly topping the scripted-series charts for the network with an average of 9.46 million viewers and 1.2 billion potential social media impressions.[38]

LOSING A MAIN CHARACTER

As with Joss Whedon and *Buffy*, the elephant in the room on the set of *The Equalizer* must be addressed. Actor Chris Noth, who played William Bishop, Robyn's former CIA director and friend, for one and a half seasons, was fired from the show in December 2021. This action came after several women publicly accused him of sexual assault and misconduct. While Noth denies the claims, calling them "categorically false," his character was quickly written out of the show, being killed in a plane crash caused by an electromagnetic pulse fired by Robyn's nemesis, Mason Quinn.[39]

ROBYN MCCALL

Robyn McCall's past is a bit of a mystery. All that has been revealed so far is that, as a teenager, she got in trouble with the law and was given the opportunity to choose whether she went to jail or joined the military. She chose the latter, which led her to the CIA, both of which made her uniquely qualified for her role as The Equalizer.

Years after she put all of that behind her, Robyn is a divorced single mother who tries to balance her responsibilities to her family with her promise to the people of New York that she will be there when they need her. This sounds like the setup for a superhero series, but showrunners Andrew Marlowe and Terri Miller are adamant that Robyn is very much human. "She hurts when she's hit, she has a family, she cares deeply and has tremendous empathy about the people that she encounters in the world," Miller says, "and as a former CIA operative, she has the skills necessary to help those people."[40]

Robyn is both a "bad-bitch" and "a soothing, maternal figure";[41] she turns both sides of her personality on the bad guys and just as often on her daughter, Delilah. Even though she "isn't always home to say goodnight to her child," family is Robyn's top priority, and she is always there when Delilah really needs her for a pep talk,[42] a life lesson, or some tough love. She is close to her aunt, Viola, and often relies on her to take care of Delilah when she can't.

Robyn is very much the "everywoman" of the 2020s. She is intelligent, confident, and witty, and she is unashamed to claim her talents and successes. As a woman of color, she is an empowering role model for women of all races and helps welcome BIPOC (Black, Indigenous, and People of Color) women into fourth-wave feminism. She faces the same problems as the average woman: how to balance work, home life, and some semblance of a personal life, as well as how to deal with a teenage daughter who is rapidly coming into her rebellion and sass—she just happens to fight crime in her spare time. In her championing of the downtrodden, Robyn represents the social justice of today, especially in the #BlackLivesMatter movement.

House of Cards: The Dark Underbelly of Politics

None of the characters on *House of Cards* are officially spies, but they spend so much time embroiled in the backstabbing and constantly shifting alliances of Washington, DC, politics that they may as well be.

House of Cards, an American adaptation of a British show of the same name, premiered in February 2013. The series follows Democratic Majority Whip Frank Underwood's elaborate plan of blackmail, promises, deceit—and occasionally murder—to gain increasingly high political standing for himself and his equally ruthless wife, Claire. By season 4, the couple are running for the White House, with Frank as the presidential candidate and Claire as his running mate.

Frank may have ascended to the presidency, but at the same time, the actor who played him, Hollywood icon Kevin Spacey, wasn't so fortunate. Like Joss Whedon before him and Chris Noth after, Spacey was fired after being accused of sexual misconduct by actor Anthony Rapp (further allegations would follow). While he never admitted to doing the things he was accused of, Spacey apologized to Rapp and entered treatment.[43]

While some shows would crumble under the loss of their main character, the *House of Cards* team found a clever way around the problem that also served to highlight the current political mess for women in the U.S. government. When Frank dies suddenly of an accidental medication overdose, Claire finds herself in the top office in the nation. "The reign of the middle-aged white man is over," she declares in the trailer for the show's final season.

While that sounds like an uplifting feminist message, in Claire's hands it is anything but. She manipulates the press, the public, and her fellow politicians into seeing her as both a victim of circumstance—which gives her sympathy and time to plot—and a capable ruler determined to advance the cause of women in the United States, which she does but only to her own ends. Claire eventually realizes that Frank was murdered, and Doug, the man who did it, comes to her begging for a plea deal. When she rejects him, he tries to kill her as well. Claire defends herself and kills Doug with a letter opener. This ending angered and confused many viewers, causing Mashable to accuse the show of being "limited in its capacity to imagine the potential of a woman-led country or even TV show."[44]

House of Cards was the first TV series to have been produced by a studio for Netflix and is the first original online-only streaming television series to receive major Emmy nominations—a total of thirty-three.[45] The show also earned eight Golden Globe Award nominations, with its two leads, Kevin Spacey and Robin Wright, winning best actor and actress in a drama, respectively.[46]

CLAIRE UNDERWOOD

Does a female character need to be moral or likable to be a model of female strength? Claire Underwood and Jessica Jones certainly say no, and as we get further into the twenty-first century, more antiheroines are emerging to agree with them. "Men like Walter White and Frank Underwood get to play bad guy protagonists without the burden of representing something larger about their entire gender,"[47] notes Jess Joho. If they can, Claire asks, why can't women?

"If *House of Cards* is like chess, then Claire Underwood is the queen—the most powerful piece in the game."[48] With that statement, Amanda Marcotte nails Claire's character. She's ambitious, cunning, and cold. "In a perfect world, we should be free to delight in Claire's masterful play of letting men make the fatal mistake of underestimating her. But unfortunately, we live in this world . . . [where] even fictional women are judged more harshly than their male counterparts. On-screen narratives can and do impact public opinion."[49]

While Claire is willing to play second fiddle to Frank for most of the series, she is doing it with an endgame in mind. After all, she is a powerhouse in her own right as founder of a multimillion-dollar nongovernmental organization (NGO). She has often been compared to Hillary Clinton, who put her own political desires on the back burner in favor of her husband's.[50]

Like Hillary, Claire is an extremely intelligent woman, having attended Radcliffe and Harvard, and is well versed in the ways of Washington politics. She is a well-known advocate for women's reproductive rights, having had several abortions herself, and after a failed assassination attempt on Frank, she becomes a gun control advocate. She is not afraid to speak out on either issue, or anything else she cares about.

Despite being willing to betray him, Claire really does love Frank (their relationship will be detailed in a later chapter). Their special bond is symbolized in the fact that she is the only one who is allowed to call him Francis and in the way they work together to plot their next move. She keeps her heart hardened and closed most of the time, but every so often she allows a glimpse of her love to slip through, such as when she interacts with Frank's friend's children.

As with Jeri and Amanda, Claire is a symbol of power that has gotten out of hand and the results that can come from using unethical practices to gain it. Though she rises to the most powerful office in the country—possibly the world—she loses everything in the process. She has repeatedly pushed away her friends, her colleagues know they can't trust her, and her husband dies. They say that it is lonely at the top, and by the end of the series, Claire's ruthless brand of feminism has left her to deal with the fallout on her own.

ZOE BARNES

Though she is only part of the show for a short period, journalist Zoe Barnes is a fierce female who deserves a brief examination. Young, attractive, ambitious, and ethically pliable, she has no compunction about using sex to get information that will advance her career. After failing with other Washington, DC, elite, she strikes a bargain with Frank Underwood to place his messages in the media in exchange for the advancement such scoops will bring her.

At first their relationship is purely a business arrangement, but after a short period, it becomes a sexual affair. "I can play the whore. Now pay me," she demands (season 1, episode 9, "Chapter 9"). Just like a prostitute with a client, their sex is transactional, pleasure for information, no feelings involved.

Zoe quickly gets in over her head when she and a colleague start investigating the death of Frank's friend, Peter Russo. She uncovers details that point to Frank's involvement, but she is hesitant to believe it. Even though she swears off additional digging into what happened, Frank comes to realize she knows too much and pushes her in front of an oncoming subway train.

Reporter Zoe Barnes (Kate Mara) made the mistake of learning too much about Frank Underwood's personal affairs in *House of Cards*. A-Pix Entertainment/Photofest

House of Cards was "criticized as sexist for featuring the ugly stereotype of the female journalist who sleeps with sources,"[51] but it is a reality of the industry. More important, it demonstrates the lengths Zoe is willing to go to get ahead. In many ways, it's no surprise that Frank was willing to have an affair with Zoe since she isn't that much different from Claire. For viewers, she is an example of a headstrong young woman who allows her ambition to cloud her judgment and, in the end, pays a heavy price for it.

Part II

THE ISSUES

CHAPTER 3

The Influence of Third- and Fourth-Wave Feminism

Television shows of the 1990s and 2000s owe a great deal to the wider feminist movements taking place in the culture in which they were written. Coming into their own in the early 1990s, the daughters of second-wave feminists created their own brand of feminism that focused more on intersectionality and sexuality than on the laws and workplace that occupied their predecessors' concerns.

The so-called third wave of feminism—the first being the suffrage movement (1843–1920) and the second encompassing the press for equality under the law and in the workplace (ca. 1960–1989)—began in 1992 with the courageous testimony of Anita Hill against her former boss, lawyer Clarence Thomas, who was in the process of being confirmed as a U.S. Supreme Court justice. Hill testified that Thomas had sexually harassed her, and her courage enflamed a new generation of women who decided they wouldn't wait until they were older to fight against the patriarchy and its practices. The *New York Times* wrote that Hill was "personally responsible for revitalizing feminism."[1]

Having suffered a sound defeat after nearly fifteen years of fighting to pass the Equal Rights Amendment (ERA)—which remains unratified even in 2023—and worn out from trying to balance the demands of being working mothers, many second-wave feminists had all but given up. But then came Anita Hill, with her courage, insistence on justice, and steely unwillingness to back down, even in the face of the nation's most powerful men. "What she's done is to make sexual harassment the great connector among women," said Irene Natividad, chairwoman of the National Commission of Working Women. "This is one of those awakenings. It's like before, and we feel powerful again, and she did this."[2] When, despite Hill's testimony, Thomas was confirmed as a Supreme Court justice, one of the first and most prominent names of the third wave, Rebecca Walker, wrote in *Ms.* magazine:

> I write this as a plea to all women, especially women of my genera-
> tion: Let Thomas' confirmation serve to remind you, as it did me,
> that the fight is far from over. Let this dismissal of a woman's experi-
> ence move you to anger. Turn that outrage into political power. Do
> not vote for them unless they work for us. Do not have sex with
> them, do not break bread with them, do not nurture them if they
> don't prioritize our freedom to control our bodies and our lives.[3]

With this rallying cry, a new generation rose up to tell their own personal stories[4] of harassment, abuse, and being treated as second class or inferior, simultaneously assuring others they weren't alone and creating the personalized structure that some thought brought the third wave into conflict with those before. Whereas their mothers and grandmothers rallied together in protests and parades, the women of the third wave used new technology of e-zines and the internet to protest from a distance yet reach more people than ever before. It wasn't that these feminists shunned the collective, they just formed it in a figurative way, rather than a literal one; they were still working together for the same causes, just from the comfort of their own homes, which hadn't been an option in the past.

Having been raised with feminism as the norm, this generation of women were confident of their rights and willing to push for greater freedom in areas that were formerly taboo, specifically sexual and reproductive rights, domestic abuse, and race, class, and gender rights. This movement was much more concerned with including women of color who had been actively ignored by previous generations of feminists, as well as those with disabilities and of all sexualities. They continued to pound on the metaphorical glass ceiling, sending women to the pinnacle of all industries and finally seeing them holding board seats at top companies. They also fought for the rights of single and working mothers, insisting that their lifestyles were valid choices even though they didn't fit into the traditional model of the nuclear family.

Suddenly the spotlight of pop culture was on women—young women in particular—who took up the mantle and the charge to change the country for the better for all women. Female rockers like Sarah McLachlan, Tori Amos, Alanis Morissette, and the Spice Girls dominated the airwaves, proclaiming girl power; books on Wicca and female spirituality crammed bookstore shelves, signaling that women would no longer be subject to patriarchal religions; and of course, the shows discussed in this book changed television forever, allowing women to show aspects of their lives and power that were verboten in past years. While some shows, like *Alias* and *Nikita*, did this primarily by making their heroines physically strong (more on that in the next chapter), *Buffy* and *Charmed* were excellent examples of how multifaceted third-wave feminism could be.

Third-Wave Poster Child:
Buffy the Vampire Slayer

For many Americans, *Buffy* was their first encounter with a strong female character who embodied this new movement, a young woman who was determined to make her place in the world on equal terms with men from the get-go. This was a show in which the previous patterns were reversed: Buffy, Willow, Cordelia, Anya, Faith, and other women took center stage while men like Xander, Oz, Giles, and Wesley were relegated to friends and sidekicks and a large portion of the bad guys—including Angel and Spike—were men. The commentary was subtle but unmistakable. "The show lived and breathed the credo that girls are powerful. . . . For a long time, *Buffy* was one of the central examples of what it meant to be a 'feminist TV show' in the '90s. It didn't just define those conversations in pop culture—it helped to jump-start them into the 21st century."[5]

As the first in a line of fierce females on television, Buffy faced significant obstacles and barriers. She forced audiences to rethink the way they approached women in horror and well as what they expected from a female heroine. No longer was it a sign of impending death when Buffy or another member of the Scooby Gang walked alone in a graveyard late at night or went to investigate a strange noise; rather, it was a sign that an ass-kicking of epic proportions was imminent. "Viewers did not yell at their TVs for Buffy to avoid going into the dark dens of monsters, but learned to cheer on her strength and inevitable victory over the evil monsters," writes Chris Jenkins in a roundup of ways *Buffy* changed American culture.[6]

Buffy's relatability "did more to turn a generation onto feminism than the intellectual drudgery of gender studies or . . . [the] Twitter-scolding that now passes for activism," writes Stephen Daisley for *The Spectator*. And as he notes, this was in the days before anyone had ever heard of safe spaces or trigger warnings. The show was unabashed in showing violence—even a controversial rape scene—and dealing with heavy issues, trusting its viewers would deal with the emotions such visuals created. Daisley continued, "Buffy and Willow teamed up to unleash the Slayer power across the world. Instead of 'one girl in all the world' fighting evil alone, women would now struggle together against the bad guys."[7]

While *Buffy*'s feminism was far from perfect, it was progress, nonetheless. Yes, Buffy was beautiful and her outfits often were tight or skimpy, but so was fashion in the '90s. She wore the same things her fans wore to school every day, which not only made her relatable but also grounded her in the here and now, increasing her relevance. "The show avoided explicitly sexualizing Buffy," writes Jenkins. "That is, she saved the day without running around in a metal bikini or star-spangled underwear. In this sense, *Buffy* helped lay considerable groundwork for later feminine heroes, such as Katniss Everdeen, who show viewers that women can kick ass without showing their ass."[8]

Entire books have been written on the numerous instances of feminism in *Buffy*. Most of these moments are quiet and could be missed if one isn't paying close attention, but the entirety of *Buffy*'s final season is a clarion call for the female fans and their allies to work together to carry on the show's message even after it is over. It is also a not-so-subtle reflection on the struggle of third-wave feminism with the opposing forces of individualism and collective action.[9]

The crux of the season is that The First Evil (the patriarchy, thinly veiled) has risen against Buffy and she can't possibly defeat it alone. Because The First can't take on human form, it possesses a misogynistic preacher named Caleb, who kills girls who are considered future potential Slayers, with the goal of ending the entire line of Slayers for good. Buffy and Willow work together to track down these women and activate their powers. This act is representative of the call of feminism to every woman to fight against old expectations of society and take up her own power. Buffy's speech in season 7, episode 8, "The Chosen," is as much directed at the viewers as it is to the potential Slayers she's addressing:

> Here's the part where you make a choice. What if you could have that power now? In every generation one Slayer is born, because a bunch of men who died thousands of years ago made up that rule. They were powerful men. This woman [Willow] is more powerful than all of them combined. So I say we change the rules. I say my power should be our power. Tomorrow, Willow will use the essence of the scythe to change our destiny. From now on, every girl in the world who might be a Slayer will be a Slayer. Every girl who could have the power will have the power. Can stand up? Will stand up. Slayers—every one of us. Make your choice: are you ready to be strong?

In the end it takes everyone—Buffy, Faith, Dawn, Willow, Spike, Anya, Xander, and all of the potential Slayers—to defeat The First, just as it will take collective action for feminists to finally vanquish the patriarchy and gain equality once and for all.

Charmed: Three Witches Reflect a Movement

Third-wave feminism was very much about authenticity and being who you are loudly and proudly. "*Charmed*'s commitment to depicting the lives of women going through their 20s and 30s was never superficial or cynical—from start to finish this was the series' mission statement, and it succeeded," Preece asserts.[10] Some criticized the show for being too stereotypically feminine to be feminist—irony if ever there was any. Assertion of feminine identity was part of the movement, as reflected in its sex-positive nature. So the fact that, like Buffy, the Halliwell sisters cared as much about fashion and romance as they did about their mission to save the world[11] was completely in keeping with the holistic nature of the third wave.

Similarly, this new breed of feminism was often contradictory, holding two polarities in perfect tension, and so were *Charmed*'s witches. Sophie Moss elaborates:

> They are desiring and desirable. They are independent and dependant [*sic*]. They are superhuman and human. They see and are seen. They are imperfect. They sleep with men who are rotten. They save humankind in high-heels. They are both dependent on, and dismissive of, traditional feminist ideals. . . . They kicked demonic ass and raised babies. They held down demanding jobs and threw fireballs at ex-boyfriends. The sisters were multifaceted, powerful women.[12]

Like Buffy and her Scooby Gang, *Charmed* was a story where going it solo wasn't an option. While they each had powers that could be used separately, the Charmed Ones needed "the power of three" to vanquish their demons, both literal and figurative. Contradicting the popular notion that the third wave was individualistic, they "create[d] a whole community of powerful, unique women . . . [who] represented 'the interconnection of empowered individuals and collective action.' Power, style, sin, sisterhood, desire: suddenly, these tough girls with innate supernatural capabilities found themselves understood within the wider context of contemporary feminism,"[13] Moss adds.

SOMETHING WITCHY THIS WAY COMES

One of the few things that is predictable about feminism is, when it is active, there is a corresponding rise in interest in witchcraft,[14] which makes sense if you think about it. Witches, or at least the women accused of witchcraft in the United States and Europe, have always been the resistance. They often lived alone, which in itself was bucking the system because it kept them out of the control of men. They had power in their independence and in the healing arts (herbs, midwifery, etc.) that they provided the community. People feared their magic and spells, regardless of whether or not any were ever cast. "The fact [is] that to be a witch is to be a woman with power in a world where women are often otherwise powerless," writes Anne Theriault for *The Establishment*.[15] In other words, they were the original "nasty" women.

One could argue that the spiritualism trend of the 1800s and early 1900s was the witchcraft of the first wave of feminism. Many early suffragists like Sojourner Truth and Victoria Woodhull were also spiritualists, people who believed they could communicate with the dead.[16] This practice gave them a valid reason to speak in public in a time when women who proclaimed their ideas from the podium were thought to bring shame upon themselves and their families; spiritualists were given a pass because they were not the ones speaking but, rather, the spirits through them. As Ann Braude asserts, "Spiritualism became a major—if not the major—vehicle for the spread of women's rights ideas in mid-nineteenth-century America. . . . While not all feminists were Spiritualists, all Spiritualists advocated woman's rights."[17]

Although not a practitioner, even Susan B. Anthony wished she had the inspiration and freedom given to spiritualist women. She wrote to Elizabeth Cady Stanton in 1855, "Oh, dear, dear! If the spirits would only just make me a trance medium and put the right thing into my mouth. . . . You can't think how earnestly I have prayed to be made a speaking medium for a whole week. If they would only come to me thus, I'd give them a hearty welcome."[18]

Witchcraft again came to the fore in the 1960s, right in time with second-wave feminism, this time through the religion of Wicca, which had been founded in 1954 by Gerald Gardner, who claimed it revealed ancient rituals that had been forced underground for centuries. Throughout the next three decades, as women fought for equality and workplace rights, pop culture carried the idea of the witch into the public consciousness through television shows like *Bewitched*,[19] the music of Stevie Nicks, and books like Marion Zimmer Bradley's best seller *The Mists of Avalon*.

The next witchcraft boom came in the 1990s with the advent of third-wave feminism. This was the time of *The Craft* in theaters and *Buffy* and *Charmed* on TV. Writing for *Teen Vogue*, Kelsea Stahler astutely points out that "realistically speaking, '90s witches (and the new set of witches) likely became a trend because studios and TV networks realized that it was financially beneficial to deliver the witch stories women crave, similar to the vampire craze that hit pop culture around 2009."[20] But the desire for that content had to be there first, and it was fueled by the longing for "gender balance within the divinity system . . . an appealing prospect for teens growing up in a patriarchal society, who are constantly exposed to news stories about abuses of male power."[21]

Indeed, *Charmed* mirrored this exact disdain "for toxic masculinity when its first season focused largely on the Halliwell sisters battling sexual predators and other bad men."[22] A similar clientele of kindhearted but fed up women patronized Treadwell's bookshop in London looking for books on witchcraft. Owner Christina Oakley-Harrington recalled:

> I [kept] seeing that they want to be kind to one another, and all un-
> usual people, and indeed to have understanding for others—and yet
> to destroy a patriarchy which destroys the earth, animals, and them.
> They are aware that it's the patriarchy that has infiltrated their con-
> sciousness and has them self-harming, self-loathing, and struggling
> with eating disorders.[23]

In short, women wanted their power back and were looking to magic to reclaim it, much as the Charmed Ones did. The television "witches took control of their own destinies and helped others do the same—and there's danger whenever a woman decides to do that, whatever the cost, no matter what she calls it. The magic might not be 'real'—but it works anyway," Laurie Penny notes in *The Baffler*.[24]

Twenty-something years later, when the original *Charmed* audience has daughters of their own, "witchcraft is back in vogue, a heady brew of nineties nostalgia, goth revivalism and plain, arcane fun."[25] Instead of relying on e-mails and message boards, these "baby witches" of the fourth wave of feminism use so-cial media to connect and spread their message of resistance. "The fourth wave of feminism we're riding right now is more inclusive and intersectional than its for-bears, uniting women in the wake of #MeToo and a Trump presidency. We are finding a closeness with one another through sharing our stories and taking part in both online and IRL [in-real-life] activism," says Sarah Assenti for *Stylist*.[26]

And '90s favorites are back right along with interest in crystals, herbs, tarot, and the moon. Both *Charmed* and *Sabrina* had much darker reboots to fit with a culture mired in hatred and bigotry and women who have so much more to fight for—with *Roe v. Wade* overturned, our remaining reproductive rights being threatened by the states, and women being taken even less seriously on issues of sexual violence (see the appointment of Justice Brett Kavanaugh to the Supreme Court and high-profile rape cases like Brock Turner for evidence). With women's rights sliding backward and the patriarchy trying to reassert itself, fourth-wave witches could hardly be blamed for being attracted to magic a few shades darker than the white and green of their '90s foremothers. "If past trends have taught us anything," Stahler writes, "when the witches arrive en masse, it's an almost direct reflection of the ills society is leveling against women."[27]

Children of the Fourth Wave

Because some second- and third-wave feminists took a hard line against men and employed radical tactics to get attention, some prominent figures in the media labeled them as misandrists and "femi-Nazis." Their image of a feminist froze as "the masculinized stereotype of women of the second wave . . . 'a hairy-legged, karate-chopping commando with a chip on her shoulder the size of China.'"[28] As a result, "feminism" became a dirty word for a portion of women who no longer wished to be associated with the movement. Scholars who agreed declared that feminism was dead and that society had moved into a period of "post-feminism." Those who ascribed to this mindset claimed feminism had achieved its goals and was no longer needed.

At the same time, third-wavers continued fighting, albeit in a culture that was much less inclined to listen. This was not unusual in the history of feminism. After each period of intense activity (the "waves"), there were years— decades even—when feminism fell out of public consciousness and was considered "dead." But in reality, the fight never stopped; it simply moved underground for a while, employing more subtle tactics until the public was ready for another round of open protest. That is exactly what happened from approximately 2000 to 2016.

The catalyst for this fourth wave lies firmly at the feet of former president Donald Trump. While some feminists were already supporting Hillary Clinton's attempt to become the first female president of the United States, a new generation rose up in the wake of Trump's loudly vulgar, sexist campaign for president. In one of the most overt insults to women, he asserted it was fine to "grab 'em [women] by the pussy" because "when you're a star, they let you do it. You can do anything."[29]

After his surprise win on election night, women could see that dark days were ahead for their rights and did what they had been doing since the Seneca Falls convention in 1843: they gathered in protest. The Women's March on Washington took place on January 21, 2017, in Washington, DC, with 470,000 people in attendance (more than three times the number who had attended the presidential inauguration the day before);[30] another one to three million in other U.S. cities, like Chicago, Seattle, Los Angeles, and St. Louis;[31] and two to three million people at 673 marches worldwide,[32] on all seven continents, including Antarctica.[33]

The protesters took Trump's ugly rhetoric and turned it into a new symbol for a new movement—the Pussy hat, a knit pink cap with cat ears worn as a sign of unity and resistance.[34] Like the third-wave feminists who reclaimed the words "bitch," "queer," and "slut" as their own, giving them positive connotations, these fourth-wavers stole Trump's pejorative for Clinton—"nasty"—and made it a moniker of strength, outspokenness, and feminism.

On October 5, 2017, the *New York Times* bookended the year by breaking a story that Hollywood mogul Harvey Weinstein had been sexually harassing and abusing young actresses for decades.[35] The resulting outcry by women around the world who shared their stories of similar experiences with men in the entertainment industry created a movement called #MeToo because it was used by women on Twitter to join the conversation. (In reality, the hashtag had been co-opted by white women from Black creator Tarana Burke who had used the hashtag as early as 2006 to unite Black and other minority women who had suffered from sexual abuse.)[36] The ramifications would be felt for years, with powerful men in the entertainment, culinary, publishing, and other industries losing their careers in the face of accusations of sexual misconduct—including showrunner Joss Whedon, and actors Chris Noth and Kevin Spacey, whose stories are included in this book because they affected shows discussed.

Women's resistance continued throughout the four years of Trump's presidency as they watched their rights be slowly eroded by his regime. From the first day of his presidency, "his administration used every tool in its arsenal to chip away at women's health, employment, economic security, and rights overall"—including threatening private abortion coverage, weakening birth control access under the Affordable Care Act, negatively impacting women's pay, weakening Title IX sexual harassment and assault protections, lessening Title X health care services, and eroding nondiscrimination protection in health care—all of which are harmful to women.[37]

On June 24, 2022, two years after Trump left office, his long game paid off, when the conservative Supreme Court he engineered overturned *Roe v. Wade*, ending women's right to legal abortion in the United States. Because of trigger laws in many states' constitutions, abortion immediately became illegal in those places. In addition, Supreme Court justice Clarence Thomas issued a statement that the court might reconsider other established rulings, including those concerning the right to contraception access, same-sex relationships, and same-sex marriage.[38]

Naturally, these six years and the devastating changes they wrought concerned many Americans, and those concerns were, in turn, reflected in the art they created. Like the second- and third-wave feminists before them, writers, directors, and producers allowed these modern concerns to populate their TV shows both to educate and motivate their audience. In an age of constant access to streaming media and binge-watching, television proved to be the perfect format to get their message across.

Jessica Jones: The Angry Superhero

Jessica Jones is a bitch, and she is proud of it. But the only reason she can unapologetically show it is thanks to third- and fourth-wave feminism. As chapter 4 details, this progress allows women to show real emotions on-screen and fight back against a patriarchal society that would have us "smile more" and be Stepford happy no matter what life throws at us. When Jessica was held up next to the "fluffy and inconsequential"[39] female superheroes of the past, the country was shocked to see a real, wounded woman staring back at them.

Indeed, it's not just Jessica who is hurting. "All of the women in *Jessica Jones* are in pain, but they refuse to be passive. They cry, they rage, they self-destruct, but they are always active, always moving. No one is coming to save them. They can only save themselves and each other," writes Chelsea Steiner for the *Mary Sue*.[40]

Jessica is struggling with the PTSD brought on by her time as a mind-controlled captive of Kilgrave, who mentally and sexually abused her; Trish is at war with who she wants to be and who her overly controlling mother has shaped her to be; and even before she receives her fatal ALS diagnosis, Jeri is constantly on guard against anyone—especially another woman—who might seek to usurp or surpass the power she has fought so hard to gain. Yet, they all work together at one time or another to help fight a bigger evil, a relationship Eric Deggans of NPR calls "an uneasy alliance of women . . . [that is] an expression of female-centered empowerment . . . rarely seen in a superhero-themed TV show."[41]

None of these female characters live in a black-and-white world; rather, they exist in the "morally gray"[42] area between polarities where right and wrong have different definitions depending on who is interpreting them. This freedom of choice or interpretation is one of the spoils of the third wave's personalization feminism, where each woman can embrace the parts that fit her life rather than being restricted by specific rules and tenets like previous generations.

Each season shows a different character grappling with that gray area as she struggles to overcome her pain. In season 1, the focus is on Jessica's guilt and rage over Kilgrave's abuse. She is dealing with issues of control and consent, of things she did not of her own volition, and how she can live with herself in the aftermath. This is the same situation many victims of rape and/or domestic violence find themselves in. They don't have superpowers to save them, and for Jessica, even the ones she has don't help. She has to struggle through this very human story as best she can.

Season 2 continues Jessica's recovery, but now the spotlight falls on Trish, who is tempted by "ratings, power, and stardom," as Jessica points out. Trish tries to persuade herself that her intentions are good and she is doing what she is "because those things will help [her] help people," but deep down she knows that isn't her true motivation. She wants to be powerful like Jessica, but she ends up becoming more like her mother as her drive increases and her sense of personal ethics slowly disappears.[43] In the face of "a lifetime of resentment and exploitation, Trish's arc . . . was one of self-destruction and harmed many who crossed paths with her."[44]

In both seasons 2 and 3 we see Jeri, who seems to have no ethical qualms whatsoever—in fact, she behaves much "like someone abusing her power in the workplace (if she were a man, she'd be precisely the kind of character the #TimesUp movement is coming for)"[45]—face the consequences of her actions just when she must also face her mortality. When she is given an ultimatum by the partners of her firm, instead of asking for help, she figures a way to trick Jessica into helping her so that she can feel she remains in control.[46] Jeri is a walking contradiction, but that is often the case for women who dare step into male-dominated spheres, like that of corporate power. "We see Jeri's admirable tenacity, intelligence, and confidence in a world that tells her to shrink herself," writes Marykate Jasper. "We also see her loathsome entitlement and exploitation of those with less power, or less talent, than she has. We see her at her cruelest and least compassionate. We see her at her most vulnerable and most human. Jeri is a powerful, successful queer woman in a world that makes it really, really hard to be such a thing and still be decent."[47]

Jessica Jones is at heart a show about what it is like to be a woman in a world where the demands are constantly changing and everyone is somehow traumatized by their past. In other words, it clearly mirrors real life. "Our show has always been about female empowerment and always been about how women use their voices and all of the complications that can sometimes come with that," Rachael Taylor, who played Trish on the show, told *Bustle*. "The fact that we kind of speak to what has been happening right now [with the #MeToo movement] is very timely. . . . If I can be part of a show that adds to the conversation in any way, I think that's awesome."[48]

Agent Carter: Standing Up and Being Counted

On the surface, it's strange to think about how the feminism of the '90s and '00s affected a show set in the '40s, but of course, it influenced the writers and was an expectation of the audience. One of the biggest things the show did was use the historical sexism of the period to put feminism front and center where anyone watching the show couldn't fail to see it. Kaitlin Thomas, writing for Salon, found that emphasis refreshing. "In an age where 'difficult men' populate many television shows and female characters are often disregarded. . . . *Agent Carter* makes feminism its priority."[49]

In the first season, feminism is felt most keenly in Agent Peggy Carter's fight to be taken seriously in the workplace as a full agent of the SSR, on par with the male employees. The woman who was so highly regarded during the war was then in peacetime relegated to a glorified secretary and errand girl. With her caustic wit, she makes the best of the hand she is dealt. When her boss calls an "all hands on deck" meeting and Peggy makes to join the men, he clarifies that for her it means she should "cover the phones." Unfazed, Peggy says to the switchboard operator, "Rose, forward all calls to the briefing room" and joins the men in the meeting (season 1, episode 1, "Now Is Not the End"). Similarly, in the same episode, when her colleague Daniel Sousa stands up for her after another man insinuates Peggy is a tart by saying she "knew a lot of men during the war," Peggy responds, "Thank you, but I wish you hadn't. I'm more than capable of handling what these adolescents throw at me."

This systemic willingness to believe Peggy is somehow "less than" because she is female comes from the fact that the men of the SSR are so steeped in the misogyny of the time that they barely even notice her presence. She points this out to them rather bluntly, "You think you know me, but I've never been more than what each of you has created. To you, I'm a stray kitten left on your door-step to be protected, the secretary turned damsel in distress, the girl on a pedestal transformed into some daft whore" (season 1, episode 7, "SNAFU"). Her point is that to treat her like an agent, they would have to see her as she really is, which they refuse to do.

In the second season, which many have called the show's most feminist season, *Agent Carter* shifts its location from New York to Los Angeles and brings on a whole new set of characters and conundrums, even introducing Peggy to more women in response to criticism that she spent too much time with men in the first season.[50] Peggy becomes close with Jarvis's wife Ana quickly, with none of the envy and cattiness typically portrayed between women on TV, especially between a wife and her husband's female friends.[51] The show is mature enough to trust that viewers will believe that two women secure in their femininity and in their relationships will be able to have a bond without the pesky patriarchal concepts of lust and territorial jealousy getting in their way.

Critics argue that "it seems that the series was devised as a way to dialogue with feminist arguments and, at the same time, remain low profile enough that rabid male audiences wouldn't feel 'threatened' by a strong woman."[52] But to level such accusations is disingenuous to the character and the show. Peggy natu-rally has a lower profile, than, say, Wonder Woman or Black Widow, given her lack of superpowers. She is an ordinary woman even though her wit and cunning might at times make her seem supernaturally smart. Historian Otto L. notes, "She behaves like a real-life woman who is trying to get her job done in an era of indomitable *machismo.*"[53] Actress Hayley Atwell, who played Carter, explained her take on the spy: "I likened her character to that famous Ginger Rogers quote. She can do everything Captain America can do, but backwards and in high heels. . . . She doesn't need to be rescued. That's exciting to me—her strength."[54]

It is that strength that makes Peggy attractive to audiences, especially to women who see their plight today mirrored in hers, for women are still fighting many of the same issues as they were in the 1940s. In a character analysis for Mar-velous Geeks Media, Gissane Sophia writes about Peggy's effect on audiences:

[W]here Peggy Carter is concerned, they've rightfully written a woman for whom agency matters. A woman whose agency is respected. It's no wonder she's so beloved. Peggy is both admirably badass and fiercely feminine, but she's been a constant reminder to audiences that women can be whoever they want as long as they respect their own worth.[55]

One aspect of Peggy's feminism that doesn't get much attention but deserves a mention is the way she eats. Hear me out. Viewers are living in an age when skinny is revered and women are willing to starve themselves to try to achieve an unrealistic body image. Peggy's love of food is refreshing. Ignoring the societal expectation that a woman should eat something light like a salad and do so with utmost decorum, Peggy isn't afraid to eat large amounts of food like she is still at war and doesn't know when or where her next meal may be. "She does not delicately bite into sandwiches; she stuffs them into her mouth as quickly as possible," notes Rebecca Even for the *Cornell Daily Sun*. "In episode [season 1, episode 4], 'Smoke and Mirrors,' she drips mayonnaise on an important document and quickly wipes it off with her finger, licking her finger clean."[56] In this way, she is on equal footing with the men in her office, who eat with abandon and don't think twice about manners.

Peggy Carter's experience of sexism in post–World War II New York should cause audiences to question exactly what we have gained in the fight called feminism over the last eighty years. After all, "women still experience pressure to be all things sexy, brilliant, well-mannered, tough, and blasé enough about her own femaleness so that it does not interfere with the daily goings-on in the business world."[57] Just as Peggy was tolerated in the SSR office, even into our fourth wave of feminism women are allowed to be present in the workplace, but when women "lean in" and demand their rightful place on par with men (or God forbid, equal pay), women are called overly assertive and brash and reminded to be grateful for what they have. Sometimes it feels like women are still taking lunch orders while men do the real work.

Homeland: The Feminism of Representation

Homeland's form of feminism is more subtle than other shows covered in this book. It lies in the acknowledgment that women are just as capable of espionage as men. While this might seem like an obvious or outdated notion, it's a much-needed message. As of 2022, only 28 percent of the FBI's special agents were female,[58] despite women being allowed to serve in the agency for fifty years. Over at the CIA, things are a little better, with its workforce being 39 percent female as of late 2021,[59] but that is nowhere near parity, so showing a woman in the top ranks was still a reach. *Homeland* ran from 2011 to 2020, and it was only in 2019 that women finally held the top three CIA directorates for the first time.[60]

In addition to being female, Carrie (who is based on real-life retired CIA agent Valerie Plame)[61] is not a Mata Hari or femme fatale. She is valued for her intelligence rather than her sex appeal, though that doesn't stop her from using sex to get what she wants. "When it comes to the show's premise, Carrie being a woman isn't intrinsic to what the show is trying to do," writes Inkoo Kang for Yahoo. But as a woman, "she could be underestimated and . . . she occasionally used that to her advantage."[62]

The reality is that the CIA is actively recruiting women and other minority groups. In 2012, the head of their al-Qaeda tracking team, Michael Scheuer, said, "If I could have put out a sign on the door [after 9/11] that said 'No men need apply,' I would have done it."[63] In fact, NBC News reported that "women made up the majority of analysts—at one point all the analysts—in 'Alec Station,' the unit charged with finding [Osama] Bin Laden."[64]

Like Carrie, real-life female agents are lauded for their "distinctly female view of security" that includes "relentless focus," long-term thinking, "intense dedication and incredible attention to detail."[65] And also like Carrie, women are allowed and are, in fact, "especially effective at interrogating terror suspects." While much of what is portrayed on *Homeland* is fiction—including its more brutal interrogation techniques—one former CIA operative suggested that women are a kind of secret weapon in the war on terror because they cause "surprise and shame" in those being held captive. "Jihadis were stunned that women, whom they saw as inferior, had been chosen to question them," the operative said.[66] They may have been surprised, but Carrie Mathison wouldn't be.

Homeland's feminism is also accurate in that not all female agents are likeable and some will do anything they must to get to the top, an attitude that can and often does backfire, just as it does for Carrie. One real-life operative, known only as "Maya," "was denied a promotion and a $16,000 pay raise—perhaps, suggested one former CIA official, because she doesn't 'play well with others. She has very sharp elbows.'"[67] Women who choose to go their own way may end up with great rewards—"Maya" received "a cash bonus and a medal" when Osama bin Laden was killed—but they also risk everything, as Carrie repeatedly learned.

House of Cards: The Weaponization of Feminism

While most adherents to feminism are nothing more than genuine women fighting for equal rights, not all women use it for altruistic purposes. *House of Cards* takes the usual positive assumptions about women and turns them on their head to explore the darker side of feminism. "Claire weaponizes feminism as a political tool . . . [which] feels not only true to her character, but to what women in politics are forced to do in order to even the playing field of a man's game," writes Jess Joho for Mashable.[68]

When her husband becomes vice president, Claire—who was known in Washington circles, but not beyond that—is suddenly thrust into the national spotlight as Second Lady. Forced to conduct an interview with CNN alone when Frank is on lockdown in the Capitol, she uses this unexpected opportunity to her full advantage. The reporter fixates on the fact that, in nearly thirty years together, she and her husband have not had children and keeps asking why and if she's ever been pregnant, questions that would never be posed to a man. To avoid admitting the truth she knows the public couldn't handle—that she and Frank put their careers ahead of having a family and Claire has had three abortions, two in her youth and one while married to Frank—she slyly admits that yes, she had been pregnant, but had chosen to have an abortion.

For a political figure to admit this on national television was shocking and unheard of, especially by one in such a hallowed office as the vice presidency. But Claire knew exactly what she was doing—controlling the narrative around her and telling her own story the way she wanted to before someone else leaked it and it could damage her image.

She knew the reporter would ask the natural follow-up question about what happened to lead her to such a decision, so Claire told a version of the truth. She explained that she was date-raped in college by a man who was now a powerful military general whom she recently had to face—a painful experience—when Frank had to publicly honor him for his service.

She was telling the truth about the general and the rape; the only difference is she didn't become pregnant as a result. "And with a small, maybe irrelevant falsehood, Claire was able to expose a greater, far more important truth: A decorated military general was a rapist. In the context of *House of Cards'* amoral, political spin machine, the end justifies the means," notes Tracie Egan Morrissey in an article for Jezebel.[69] Her revelation emboldened another woman to speak out and admit she was raped by the same man who was her superior in the military. So in Claire's mind, her lie was justified.

In season 6, Claire suddenly finds herself as president of the United States when Frank dies unexpectedly. Once again, she uses the media to take control of her story. Not long after she is sworn in, Claire goes into isolation for three weeks, and a photo of her tear-stained face is leaked to the press causing both Congress and the news media to question her fitness for office. (Hysterical, grieving widows make for terrible presidents, you know.) While Congress debates evoking the Twenty-Fifth Amendment to force her out of office, Claire is quietly arranging for her biggest shocker yet. Her time in seclusion hasn't been to deal with the death of her husband; rather, she's been arranging things so that when she emerges back into the public eye, she can legally fire the entire cabinet she inherited from her husband and replace them with women of her choosing, making hers the first all-female cabinet in U.S. history.

These sly moves all serve to address important feminist issues—rape, bodily autonomy and choice, victim-blaming, sexual harassment, and women's emotions and how they affect their work—but the way Claire goes about it is problematic, even if it is done all the time in real life. In addition, given the fact that the character was only allowed to assume the presidency since Kevin Spacey, who played the president, was fired over sexual misconduct allegations as part of the #MeToo movement, "a woman play[ing] the victim for personal gain"[70] could cast doubt on the validity of the movement, not to mention further call into question the testimony of all victims of sexual violence. This is one of the paradoxes of feminism: women fight to be heard, yet when they are, they are sometimes betrayed by not only their own efforts but also their own sex.

Orphan Black: Agency and Bodily Autonomy

It is a truth universally acknowledged that a show with at least six (depending on how you count them) major female characters must be feminist. And indeed it is. *Orphan Black* is "a sprawling mythos interrogating notions of womanhood, identity, the politics of science, and the prickly notions of autonomy for women, all wrapped in an immensely engaging science-fiction tale about clones."[71]

Above all, *Orphan Black* is about bodily autonomy and the right to make your own choices about how you live your life. The promotional posters and videos for season 3 lay this issue bare by showing each clone making her own declaration of independence. Sarah snarls, "I am not your property"; Helena threatens, "I am not your weapon"; Cosima states, "I am not your experiment"; and Alison asserts, "I am not your toy." "Rebellious Sarah refuses to be controlled, headstrong Alison won't be a pawn in anyone's game, Cosima's resisting being someone else's experiment and Helena is trying to move past her life as a killer," notes Araceli Roach for ScreenRant.[72] In making these declarations, each woman is asserting her individuality and telling Dyad, Neolution—and all those involved in their creation—to fuck off.

But in the political climate in which *Orphan Black* was created—and even today—it is impossible to miss that these words are also a not-so-subtle nod toward supporting feminism and women's reproductive rights. The show is asserting its "feminist ethos, which portrayed women as being so much more than what the men who sought to control them wanted them to be."[73]

For centuries, women have been treated as the chattel of men, even being defined so by law, and it is this Sarah's statement rebels against. Similarly, women's bodies have been used as tools of war from time immemorial (think of how to this day soldiers rape the women of those they are conquering both to weaken morale and assert their dominance), and women's sexual freedom has been used to control them, as Helena reminds us. From the trophy wife and the sugar baby to the mistreatment of sex workers, women have long been seen as playthings only meant for men's sexual pleasure, as Alison notes. Finally, as Cosima points out, women—especially those of color—have been the subject of male scientific and medical experiments from at least the 1800s. For example, in 1844, Black female slaves in Alabama were operated on without their consent and sans anesthesia as a white male doctor raced to be the first to successfully repair vaginal fistulae.[74] Hitler also famously conducted experiments on female concentration camp detainees via the infamous doctors Josef Mengele, Carl Clauberg, and Karl Gebhardt who studied them to effect mass sterilization[75] (similar to the clones being engineered to be sterile) and determine effectiveness of sulfonamide drugs, among many other things.[76] Throughout the United States and the world, the women of the fourth wave are standing up and shouting "never again!"

In creating so many distinct clones—in personality, looks, style, voice, gestures, sexualities, backgrounds, and interests—*Orphan Black* might also be "suggest[ing] that the dull sameness enforced by existing female archetypes needs to die." [77] Look at any typical sitcom and you'll see one type of woman in full force: the beautiful, perky wife/girlfriend (but usually wife) of an oafish, overweight balding man who caters to his every need, even in 2023—just look at *King of Queens*, *According to Jim*, *Still Standing*, *Parks and Recreation*, and even the groundbreaking hit *Modern Family* for prime examples.[78] These women are so dull and lifeless that they are easily ignored and lumped together in viewers' minds, allowing their male counterparts to shine as the stars of the show.[79]

Orphan Black is instead saying, and literally showing, that diversity is not only necessary but also attractive. This philosophy allows women of all shapes, sizes, and races to shine, and crushes the long-held Hollywood standard that, to be the star of a popular show, women must put their bodies through hell to conform to an arbitrary standard. By acknowledging each clone as their own person, they are allowed to take on meaning and become the center of their own stories, which Julia Wick calls "a radical expansion of what women on television can be."[80]

The Equalizer: Intersectional Justice

Fourth-wave feminism is finally allowing BIPOC women into its upper echelons in an integrated manner—to lead like Vice President Kamala Harris and Rep.

Alexandria Ocasio-Cortez, speak out like poet Amanda Gorman and author Roxane Gay, and advocates like Aimee Allison and Kimberlé Crenshaw—and television is finally reflecting this in its shows. While women of color have starred in their own shows since the 1960s (*Julia*, starring Diahann Carroll), those programs have been few and far between and primarily were aimed at audiences of color (*Living Single*, *Girlfriends*) or sitcoms (*The Jeffersons*, *The Cosby Show*, *227*)[81] that didn't regularly focus on serious matters. It wasn't until the 2000s that dramas like *Scandal* and *The L Word* began showing that women of color can carry a serious show. To date, only five Black women have ever led an hour-long prime-time drama.[82]

After so long being considered an afterthought at worst and a separate class at best, women of color finally have their first prime-time, major network show with a female lead who literally kicks ass. The 2020 reboot of *The Equalizer*, starring Queen Latifah, has the same basic premise as the 1980s series of the same name. But this fresh version follows former military and ex-CIA agent Robyn McCall (not Robert McCall as in the original) as she takes justice into her own hands for those who have nowhere to turn and is the "person who is there to help people when the system fails them"[83] or they "can't call 911" and get the police involved.

The reboot of *The Equalizer* is a show for modern life with Robyn (Queen Latifah) balancing her crime fighting with motherhood of daughter Delilah (Laya DeLeon Hayes). *CBS/Photofest*

Executive producers Debra Martin Chase and Queen Latifah are both Black women, which greatly influenced the shape of the new show. "I have been trying for almost 20 years to bring a Black woman who kicks butt to the screen," Chase said in an interview with the *Washington Post*.[84] She pointed out that being a woman of color gives the character more opportunity than a white man would have. "She can dress up and go to the . . . fancy, fancy gala. She can be down in the hood with the boys and still fit in. A savvy woman uses all of that access to her advantage."[85]

By nature, Robyn's feminism is "hood feminism," a term coined by Mikki Kendall in her book of the same name. It is used to reflect how race and gender combine to impact Black women in the criminal justice system,[86] something Robyn McCall is perfectly positioned to do. Despite being raised by a loving family, she fell into a bad way when she was young, was arrested, and experienced the criminal justice system, so she knows what the people she helps are going through. Showrunner Andrew Marlowe told Paramount that it was important to the writers to show "the reality of the world we're living in—a world where people across the political spectrum don't trust the institutions that are meant to protect and defend them. They don't trust the government, the courts, the cops."[87]

This reality makes now an ideal time for someone like The Equalizer who purposefully stays out of and subverts the system. As for the character being a woman, Queen Latifah told TVLine, "I think that Black women have been equalizing for years and years. From Stacey Abrams to Kamala Harris to my mother to my grandmother, seeing a Black woman equalize is not a new thing to me."[88]

But it is new to television audiences, some of whom will struggle with seeing a Black woman in a position of such power. But that is the way of the world now, and *The Equalizer* presents this radical notion in a way "that everybody can access, that has the potential to really live internationally,"[89] Chase said. When it comes down to it, the show is about women's empowerment and justice, two concepts that should be blind to color and gender, or at least treat them equally.

CHAPTER 4

The Real Meaning of Female Strength

Sit still. Smile. Keep your knees together. Be silent. Never curse. Don't raise your voice. And for God's sake, don't ever cry in public.

For centuries, these are the instructions women have been given to mold them into perfect daughters, sisters, wives, and mothers, docile beings meant to please men. As a result, women often had to hide their true selves, dumb themselves down, and shade their light because to do otherwise wouldn't be ladylike.

Even into the 1980s, women on television were rarely allowed to show negative emotions like anger, fear, or a desire for revenge. If they felt these things, they must be demonstrated either in stoic silence or in overdramatic hysterics (think soap opera catfights or bawling jilted lovers) and only to close friends or spouses. They certainly weren't allowed to express these emotions physically, by punching walls—which was par for the course for men—or even pillows. On television as in life, women were expected to remain placid, if not happy, and project a positive image to the world.

But then came along a spate of stories that were willing to break that mold. They allowed women to win physical altercations or at least emerge alive to fight another day without being rescued by a man. At first, these women were what we now refer to as stereotypical "strong female characters," women who could literally beat up the (usually bad) men who opposed them and showed their equality with their fists or their weapons (think Lara Croft or Selene from *Underworld*). They were the polar opposite of the damsel in distress but were often criticized for being drawn as men—but with boobs—or as women "with the gendered behavior taken out."[1] They had something to prove from jump and were defensive about their abilities,[2] as though their mantra was "anything you can do, I can do better."

It was a step in the right direction, but not nearly enough. "No one ever asks if a male character is 'strong.' Nor if he's 'feisty,' or 'kick-ass' come to that.

. . . Sherlock Holmes gets to be brilliant, solitary, abrasive, Bohemian, whimsical, brave, sad, manipulative, neurotic, vain, untidy, fastidious, artistic, courteous, rude, a polymath genius. Female characters get to be Strong," Sophia McDougall complains.[3] Her comment voiced the frustration of a whole generation of women that "even 65 years post–Wonder Woman, female physical strength and mental verve have the vividness of the unfamiliar,"[4] especially when combined because there were so few examples of it in pop culture.

Beginning in the 1990s, a small number of shows went so far as to acknowledge that female strength comes in more than just the ass-kicking variety. Their women were also strong mentally, emotionally, and spiritually. They had agency and controlled their own lives. They were allowed to rage, to kick and scream without being called hysterical, and to rise from the ashes like the phoenixes they were and draw strength from their pain. These were women for whom "'strong' is not an adjective describing that character's physical or emotional or intellectual strength. It is an adjective describing the potency and depth of the character—in the narrative, not moral sense. A strong character is complicated, flawed, compelling. 'Strong is just a synonym here for great.'"[5]

Now, these women are all over our televisions. "Popular representations of feminism in the media sell: whether in music, film, or television, images of independent women appeal to a wide audience," Molly Brost writes in *Americana: The Journal of American Popular Culture*. "Women's 'liberation' is a marketable commodity."[6] But that wasn't always the case and wouldn't be so now if it wasn't for the daring shows that put these women on the screen in the first place and the ones that dared to evolve that depiction into the strong female characters we know and love today.

Buffy and *Charmed*: More Than Just Supernaturally Strong

Buffy the Vampire Slayer and *Charmed* were the matriarchs of the modern fierce female TV show. Both had a cast of strong female characters who could hold their own in a fight, but who were written as well-rounded women who also experienced a full range of emotions, questioned God and the universe, and emerged from their trials stronger than ever before.

While some are quick to point to Buffy Summers as a cliché strong female character, those who do aren't looking deeply enough. "She was too complex, too flawed, too human for that," notes Angelica Bastién.[7] Buffy might have been able to slay vampires and vanquish demons, but she was far from perfect. "She's got a bit of a god complex and has trouble communicating in her romantic relationships," Claire L. Wong points out in *Hollywood Insider*. "But she tries and fails, she learns and grows. Buffy may be a superhuman in a supernatural world, but the depth of her character makes her incredibly real. We can empathize with her and relate to her."[8]

It is those very qualities that make her a strong female character. There are countless examples throughout the series, but perhaps the clearest is season 5, episode 16, "The Body," in which Buffy's mother, Joyce, dies suddenly from a brain aneurysm and Buffy is left to deal with the aftermath. Writing for the website Inverse, Lauren Sarner calls this episode "the best episode of television you can never watch again. Seriously, it will ruin you . . . no show has come close to exploring death so accurately."[9] The episode packs a gut-punch by allowing its characters to explore the harsh realities of death and grief in all their rawness. Buffy, who discovers the body, is at first in denial, reverting to a child-like mewl of "Mommy?" when she realizes her mother isn't responding to her. Then she panics, administering CPR so intensely (keep in mind her Slayer strength) that she breaks one of Joyce's ribs. As the paramedics approach, she goes into shock, vomiting on the floor and then slipping into a mute, zombie-like daze. There is no music in the episode, so the silence is deafening, just as it would have been for Buffy; the few sounds—windchimes outside when Buffy opens the door—are unreal, too loud. It is only when Giles bursts in and Buffy yells "we're not supposed to move the body!" that her own words—"the body," not "my mom,"—startle her into sudden understanding that her mother is really dead and never coming back.

Buffy's friend, Anya, is also given complex emotions as she tries to process not only her own feelings of loss but also the ways in which her friends manifest their grief. One would think that as a vengeance demon, Anya would have plenty of experience with death, but she has clearly never had it affect her so personally before. As such, she is confused and at sea, allowed to ask all the questions about death we think in such situations, but social norms keep us from voicing:

> But I don't understand! I don't understand how this all happens. How we go through this. I mean, I knew her, and then she's, there's just a body, and I don't understand why she just can't get back in it and not be dead anymore! It's stupid! It's mortal and stupid! And, and Xander's crying and not talking, and, and I was having fruit punch, and I thought, well Joyce will never have any more fruit punch, ever, and she'll never have eggs, or yawn or brush her hair, not ever, and no one will explain to me why.

This episode plunges Buffy into adulthood well before she is ready, an experience not uncommon in the real world. The next several episodes show Buffy grieving, while at the same time grappling with her "newfound adult responsibilities like raising her younger sister and paying the bills."[10] The next several episodes show her struggling to accept her loss while at the same time throwing herself into work so that she doesn't have to deal with it. Giles takes Buffy on a vision quest where the first Slayer reaffirms Buffy's mission. Still raw and shaken, Buffy realizes that while she's down and it will take a while to get back up again, she is very much not out. As Shaun Stacy notes on her blog, this resilience is one of the things that makes the show great: *"Buffy the Vampire Slayer* wasn't afraid to show it's [*sic*] female characters defeated, but it never depicted them as victims, either. The show's legacy of powerful female characters continues to draw in new fans, decades after it's [*sic*] original airing."[11]

FRUSTRATION AND OTHER NEGATIVE EMOTIONS

Like *Buffy*, *Charmed* pioneered the way in portraying realistic women with real emotional strength. The most common "negative" emotion expressed in *Charmed* is that of frustration, which Hannah Sanders calls a more culturally acceptable form of (female) anger.[12] The first sign of this emotion is when the sisters get their powers. Piper is frustrated that they have them at all; she never asked for magic and doesn't want it, but is equally helpless to make it go away. Then each of the sisters expresses irritation when they are trying to master their new powers and again when men don't listen to or believe them. Throughout the series, this same emotion is evoked as they try to integrate magic into their lives with some sort of normality—to be everything, just as the second-wave feminism they grew up with promised them they could be.

This is something to which every woman can relate since they are expected to live up to the unrealistic expectation that they can make everyone happy while keeping their lives in balance. In reality, something always has to give, and usually it is women's own desires. What woman hasn't given up the opportunity to do something special with friends to go out with a boyfriend who turned out to be no good? Or had to tend to a child or family member when they were supposed to be on vacation? Sanders elaborates:

> The primacy of frustration [in *Charmed*] highlights the impossibility of this task [doing everything] by demonstrating inevitable sacrifices. The sacrifices are those regarding the sisters' romantic and domestic lives; Weddings are postponed, dates cancelled, and material possessions destroyed. The role of frustration articulates the sisters' desire to be normal individuals, and yet order is restored in every episode's closure, maintaining their focus on each other and consolidating the tension between wanting and having it all.[13]

This frustration manifests in the witches the same way it does in any other woman: tears, anger, or outrage. They yell, scream, fling things across the room (especially Prue, who can use her power to do so), break things, and even question The Elders (like many of us question God). Unlike TV characters of previous generations, they can do this openly, connecting with the audience through this emotion, rather than having to retreat off-camera to a bedroom to lay down and calm themselves. The third wave enabled them to express, rather than repress, that which makes them fully human.

"YOU REMIND ME OF THE BABE . . . THE BABE WITH THE POWER"

Speaking of frustration—it is ridiculous that in 2023 men still find women with power threatening. Or maybe they should. Given the vocal desire to rise up against the patriarchy, some men well may have reason to be scared.

"Women are looking to reclaim their power," says Lisa Lister, a third-generation witch and author. "They can feel that there's something more going on, mainly because of the political and social climate right now. This kind of modern witchcraft is more about female empowerment than it is about casting a spell."[14]

Power is, strictly speaking, an emotion, but it is an often overlooked aspect of female strength. We tend to forget about it because historically women have had so little. A woman without power is helpless and dependent and can only endure, while a woman with it has authority and is free to do as she wishes and has the ability to change her circumstances.

It is not by accident that five of the strongest female characters of the mid-to-late 1990s were witches (four Charmed Ones and Willow on *Buffy*). As explored in the last chapter, witches have always been symbols of women who are not to be trifled with and are feared as purveyors of revenge. (There is a reason the phrase "hell hath no fury like a woman scorned" is still muttered and women still threaten to turn men into toads.)

On *Charmed*, this idea manifests in the sisters' demon-vanquishing abilities. "What I really love [about the show] is the way they fry everybody who tries to hurt them," Jenny Crusie writes enthusiastically. "Prue when she was angry was poetic justice in motion, and once Piper learned to blow things up, it just got better. I'm addicted to that sense of wrongs righted—not only bad guys foiled, but gloating, rude, obnoxious, snotty bad guys, demons that act like every rotten human being I've ever met. . . . Oh, yeah, I love the power."[15]

That power often manifests in the form of ingenuity as well. Solving problems has always been one of a witch's main duties, whether they were tasked with finding the correct herbs to heal, writing the spell to bring love or money, or providing the answer to a thorny issue. "A witch is someone who, when faced with a brick wall, learns to dig a tunnel," writes self-professed witch Anne Theriault for *The Establishment*. "A witch is a survivor and witchcraft is a means of survival in a world that does not always value your life."[16] They don't call witches "cunning women" for no reason.

"A witch is a woman who has power, not a submissive woman. If there's something wrong, she does something about it," says Denise Cush, retired professor of religion and education at Bath Spa University.[17] Women are still seeking answers to seemingly impossible problems: in many areas of the world women don't have equal rights, pay, or representation in government; they're seen as less in traditional religions; they're not taken as seriously in health care, just to name a few concerns. In trying to address these issues, women are taking back their power; in a sense then, all women are witches, regardless of their religion or heritage. Today's feminists don't care who they upset or frighten; in fact, some make men uncomfortable on purpose. "The craze for witchery displays an encouragingly wide understanding that for social change to happen someone has to feel threatened," journalist and activist Laurie Penny wrote in December 2017.[18] Her words ring even truer six years later than they did at the time. Just as television shows are no longer afraid to show women's dark side, fourth-wave feminists are willing to rock the boat by putting the full scope of their emotions on display and taking decisive action against the wrongs they see.

While shows like *Buffy* and *Charmed* aren't teaching women to be witches, they are showing them they have more power than traditional society and media give them credit for. They are giving them role models they can call to mind when threatened or faced with a tough situation and giving them permission to show their strength in nontraditional ways. "We are living in a dunk tank of female rage," writes Kelsea Stahler for *Teen Vogue*, "and this wave of witchiness appears to be a manifestation of that environment. Witchcraft might present itself as the pitch-perfect expression of female rage and frustration."[19]

Nikita: Women Powered by Revenge

When *Nikita* premiered in September 2010, "it did something pretty much unheard of by having not one, not two, but three central female characters who drove every single second of the narrative."[20] Nikita Mears, Alex Udinov, and Amanda Collins represented the good (Nikita and Alex) and the bad (Amanda); the wronged (Nikita and Alex) and the perpetrator (Amanda); the injustice (Amanda) and the redemption (Nikita and Alex).

Nikita and Alex share both a mother/daughter- and sister-type relationship, something neither of them had the opportunity to experience in their own birth families. Nikita often acts as a guardian and caretaker to Alex, helping wean her off drugs, ensuring she doesn't get addicted again, and patching up her physical and emotional wounds. Alex, in turn, rebels against the structure Nikita imposes and often goes off on her own to do what Nikita warns her not to, just like a teen would do to her mother. At the same time, the two are confidantes and friends, providing one another with sisterly support and advice. The complex emotions that accompany these bonds are part of what grounds the characters, giving the audience something more relatable than the "lone wolf" spy of previous generations[21] and reminding both the viewer and themselves "just how messy spycraft can get when personal relationships and past trauma is involved."[22] Indeed, it is the breaking of trust between them that drives the two apart temporarily more than once throughout the series.

In many ways, it is surprising that these two would become so close. Both were on their own when they were arrested and joined Division, with only questionable street family for support. Once inside Division's rigorous training program, they were taught to think as individuals, free from any ties to their past, even their past selves.[23] To Division, love is a weakness that might be exploited; therefore it should not exist in the heart of an agent.[24] Yet it was this forbidden bond that made Nikita and Alex stronger and, ultimately, allowed both of them to find redemption.

As opposed to traditional ideas of female action heroes, Nikita and Alex, while undoubtedly physically strong, are both strong female characters in the truest sense of the phrase, three-dimensional, and not in need of men to survive. They aren't above a roll in the hay or even a love affair or two, but men are the supporting acts in their lives, not the main event. Brittany Frederick, associate editor for TVovermind, asserts that Nikita and Alex "can hold [their] own without the writers feeling the need to show you repeatedly how cool, violent or witty [they are]. The show is called *Nikita* because she is the center of the story, and she proves that she belongs there."[25]

Both Nikita and Alex are motivated by an emotion women are not usually allowed to express: the desire for revenge. This will be discussed at length in chapter 9, so for now it is enough to note that while Nikita's focus remains on Division and those who run it—namely, Percy and Amanda—Alex's changes over time. She is initially driven to avenge her father's murder, but when she finds out Nikita was the perpetrator, she wisely changes tack to kill the person who ordered the hit. Once that is done, she joins Nikita in her quest to end Division and all associated with it, for Division made her as well, even if it was on purpose so she could help Nikita.

Jessica Jones: Bitter Pill

According to showrunner Melissa Rosenberg, when *Jessica Jones* premiered in November 2015, the titular character "was the first and only female super-hero and one of the only flawed, damaged, powerful women onscreen, TV or features."[26] She was also perhaps the most direct depiction of raw negative emotion from a woman in television history. Chelsea Steiner calls the show "a look at female anger and rage through a female lens," something else not seen before on the small screen.[27]

Jessica could be said to be the female equivalent of a tough guy—a heavy, if you will—if that guy also had brains and a smart mouth. She inherited from the hard-boiled PIs of film noir a certain cynicism about life, a love of whiskey, and a take-no-prisoners mentality. But unlike them, she relies upon her "intelligence and investigative muscles just as often as she gets physical with people." Instead of just using her superstrength to get confessions, she works for them.[28]

As this example illustrates, Jessica has a strong sense of right and wrong, a compulsion to help other women, and deep down, a good heart. "[Jessica] kind of represents everything," says Rachael Taylor, who played Jessica's BFF, Trish. "She is male and female. She is strong. She is vulnerable. She is angry. She cries. She is gooey on the inside and hard on the outside. I think that people found her to be pretty refreshing."[29]

Jessica is so complex because of what she has experienced, a trifecta of trauma that would drive anyone to drink. The mental and emotional fortitude it took for her to withstand these experiences and still have her sanity intact dwarfs any physical superpower. When she was young, her whole family was killed in a car crash; unbeknownst to her until it was too late, she was rescued from the crash site only to be subjected to "horrific" experiments that resulted in her superpowers; and then, just when she was recovering, she was preyed upon by Kilgrave, who mentally and sexually abused her, forced her to kill another woman, and then tried to gaslight her into believing she wanted all of it.

As a result, Jessica suffers from severe PTSD, which she manages with copious amounts of alcohol. As the show progresses and she no longer finds the same solace at the bottom of a bottle, she begins to ask "the complex question of what happens when the coping mechanisms we build up over time, like thick skin growing over a blister, stop serving us."[30] How does she begin to deal with all she has been through when she is weak and doubting everything about herself? She is scared to death that she has or will become what Kilgrave wants her to be, even though he is dead and she knows she was strong enough to eventually resist his mind control.

This doubt and fear make her vulnerable, qualities rarely shown in a realistic manner for female characters. While women have been shown as vulnerable to being taken advantage of or seduced by men for years, this is something different, an interior helplessness that throws off Jessica's whole sense of self and leads her deep into an existential crisis from which she fears she will never return. It is only the need to help Trish and her clients that pulls Jessica back from the brink.

MORE THAN A METAPHOR

Jessica's experience, is of course, closely related to those of abused women everywhere. It brings domestic abuse, gaslighting, and rape culture into viewers' homes in a way they can be digested and reflected upon—through the safe, long-distance lens of fiction.

"The narrative . . . has deep feminist understanding of the social structures that allow abuse to flourish," Amanda Marcotte writes for Salon. "[Kilgrave] has magical powers, but [he] also knows to exploit the way women are socialized to be pleasing and submissive to men, even if they find those men repulsive."[31] His mind control is a supernatural version of the mind games real-life abusers play to get their victims to stay; the fact that this is coupled with the illusion of "love" that Kilgrave forces on Jessica makes a powerful statement: many victims are indeed in love with their abusers and reluctant to leave them. Some really do believe "the abuser's claim that no one else cares about them [and] they fear being alone forever if they leave."[32] What's more, Jessica's doubt of herself is a reflection of how "rape culture often puts blame on a victim of sexual assault rather than the abuser, essentially limiting all of the victim's power."[33]

Agent Carter: Backward and in Heels

Agent Peggy Carter is a feminist's feminist, meaning she is the most outspoken of the characters in voicing a desire for equality between the sexes. She almost has to be, for hers isn't the story of the "leading lady who . . . struggles, succeeds and inevitably finds love." No—it is the answer to the question "what happens next?"[34] when that love doesn't survive, a situation many women find themselves in, whether through widowhood, divorce, or a parting of ways.

Unlike many fictional females before her, Peggy doesn't pretend she isn't grieving the loss of the love of her life, Captain America. "This isn't a woman who masked her pain with her pain [*sic*] through armor, but rather a woman who allowed herself to cry, grieve, to feel," writes Gissane Sophia. "She's a woman who's persevered even through her tears. She's a woman who's doubted. She is a woman who's fallen. . . . That's what makes Peggy feel so real, while we admire her for being this extraordinary she falls and questions herself."[35]

Despite her pain, and perhaps just a little because of it, Peggy is more motivated than ever to succeed in a male-dominated world. Every morning she slides her feet into high heels and puts on her bright red lipstick, knowing she will face adversity just because she is a woman. But she isn't simply a stock "strong female character." Yes, "she's independent, capable, intelligent, and excels at her job." Yes, "she takes names and kicks ass without so much as breaking a nail,"[36] but Peggy is also unashamedly human. "She's someone who often allows her heart to do the talking. She gives in to vulnerability," writes Rachel Roth.[37]

Peggy knows the odds are against her, yet she shows up every day anyway, willing to "do anything in her power to earn the respect she knows she deserves."[38] One can almost picture her standing before the men of the agency, her heels digging grooves into the polished floor as she pushes forward while they push back, demanding that she backs down. All the while she is repeating in her mind advice she will one day give to her niece, Sharon: "Compromise where you can, where you can't, don't. Even when the whole world is telling you to move it's your duty to plant yourself like a tree and say, 'no, you move.'"[39]

Every single setback Peggy experiences because she is a woman "only strengthens [her] resolve to do everything she can to ensure fairness and justice."[40] In this show, women are more than just beings who have certain uses to men; they are "people who are proud to be women . . . [and who] refuse to let the misogynistic system determine who they are and what they can achieve."[41]

Some critics argue that this attitude is anachronistic and that all the show is doing is dressing modern characters in period clothing to make a point. Those people, according to actress Hayley Atwell, who played Carter, are missing the point. She told *SciFi Magazine* that in the sixty-nine years between 1946 and when the show premiered in 2015, "we've come a long way, but we've still got a long way to go. I think [the show] parallels with the frustrations that many modern women have. There are still not equal rights for women in terms of the workplace."[42] Still, the misogyny of the period is very real. And the characters were influenced by real women, like Lesley Coffin's grandmother, who served in the Women's Army Corps (WAC) during World War II. Lesley writes:

> There are truths to [Peggy's] character which would have a long lasting impact on the women's movement. For women like my grandmother and her friends, the WAC wasn't just an opportunity to serve their country and help the war effort, it was a chance to embrace a little independence few women were allowed. . . . The young women who escaped homes to serve, gave of themselves out of a sense of war time obligation, but also for the opportunity to assert independence they never experienced. And the women who took that opportunity to turn it into something even bigger so future women could enjoy opportunities they could never have dreamed of.[43]

Peggy Carter was, then, not too far off the truth of a certain portion of the female population. While most women entered peacetime as wives and mothers, and others took traditional jobs as secretaries, a handful of women "carr[ied] the business of the world on [their] shoulders while living up to every cultural standard possible, even the standards that promotors of gender equality set their watches to and live their lives by in the home and workplace."[44] These women, like Peggy, were the stubborn, loudmouthed grandmothers of the third- and fourth-wave feminists who made a show like *Agent Carter* possible.

CHAPTER 5

Female Friendships and Family

Women are, by nature and by culture, communal creatures. For thousands of years, while the men have been off hunting or earning a living, women have depended on multiple generations to raise their families and divvy up the work of running households. They met at the well or the river to trade gossip and life lessons while gathering water or washing; were often secluded from men during worship; bled together in red tents; and used quilting circles as private time to speak of subversive topics that would get them hanged in public. Therefore, it shouldn't come as a surprise that families, whether given by blood or voluntarily chosen, are important in women's lives and that this is reflected by female-led television shows.

FAMILY MATTERS

The nuclear family of parents and children is still the most frequently portrayed relationship on American television. Our relationships with our parents are the first ones we form (or don't) and often affect the rest of our lives. Of the shows covered in this book, *Alias*, *Orphan Black*, and *The Equalizer* have different perspectives on parenthood and family, especially as they relate to women in late twentieth- and early twenty-first-century society.

Several Tough Mothers

As part of her discussion on how Jessica Jones handles the myriad ways in which women's relationships with one another shape them as people, Melanie McFarland of Salon.com writes, "Mothers mold their daughters, and maybe sisters remind us of how we were when the clay was fresh. Friends glue the cracks and shine up the spots created by our stumbles and crashes against a hard and unforgiving world."[1] As this quote implies, mothers are one of the biggest influences on a girl's future development. Their attention, or lack thereof, can affect everything from a girl's self-esteem, how well she does in school, how likely she is to succeed in life to her choice of partner and even how she parents her own children, just to name a few. As the following examples will show, a mother's power should never be underestimated.

ORPHAN BLACK: THREE TYPES OF MOTHERHOOD

Despite having no biological mothers, the clones of *Orphan Black* all have three types of mothers: Susan Duncan, the scientist who created them in a lab; the surrogate who gave birth to them; and the adoptive mother who raised them. Over time, all but Sarah gain a fourth when Mrs. S takes the whole of Clone Club under her wing.

Siobhan Sadler, known affectionately as Mrs. S, is a loving, if strict, mother. She rescued both Sarah and Felix by taking them from London to Canada, where they were considered in "the black," as "undocumented [orphans], out-

Motherhood is a central theme of *Orphan Black*. Shown are Sarah (Tatiana Maslany), her foster mother Siobhan (Maria Doyle Kennedy), and her daughter Kira (Skyler Wexler). *BBC America/Photofest*

side the system," as Mrs. S explains to Sarah in season 1, episode 8, "Entangled Banks." While Felix's exact origins and reason for adoption are a mystery, Sarah was in the black to keep her safe from medical experiments that both Dyad and the Prometheans would conduct on her if they got a hold of her.

Mrs. S's own backstory is never made clear, but some have speculated she was trained by the Irish Republican Army (IRA),[2] which is plausible given her skills evading the law, finding safehouses, and handling all manner of weapons from guns to knives. But the shocking secret that is revealed is that her own mother, Kendall Malone, is the woman whose genes the LEDA and Castor clones were derived from. That means that Kendall is a genetic sister and foster mother and grandmother to the clones, and Mrs. S is actually a half aunt of sorts. When Helena calls Kendall "our original mothersestra," Cosima corrects her, "It's way more accurate for us to call you older sister" (season 3, episode 10, "History Yet to Be Written").

Knowing that Sarah is one half of the special twin clones, Mrs. S dedicates her life to keeping Sarah safe. Sarah, in return, doesn't seem to realize or show any appreciation for her foster mother's sacrifices until Mrs. S explains how they came to be a family in season 1, episode 8. Her love for and commitment to Sarah extends to Kira once Sarah gets pregnant and continues throughout the show until she gives her life to keep Sarah and Felix safe from Ferdinand, a killer ordered by Rachel to eliminate Sarah.

Susan Duncan can be considered the scientific mother of all the clones, as she and her husband, Ethan, were the lead scientists on Project LEDA. She raised Rachel Duncan as her own, and in videos from Rachel's childhood, she is an attentive and loving mother. When Rachel is older, Susan allows members of Neolution to groom Rachel to one day take over Dyad. Rachel believes that Susan died in the fire that destroyed all of the records on Project LEDA, but in season 2, it is revealed that Susan is still alive and successfully created another clone, Charlotte Bowles, whom she wishes to have Rachel raise as her daughter. Charlotte, now eight years old, is kind and well adjusted so Susan must have been a good mother to her as well.

Then there are the clone mothers, Sarah and Helena. As a teenage mom, Sarah is not at first mature enough to parent her baby, so Mrs. S raises her instead. Eight years later, Sarah has shed her rebellious, dangerous lifestyle and wants custody of Kira again, which she gets with Alison's help. Everything Sarah does from there on out is to protect Kira. Like all mothers, she beats herself up for allowing Kira to donate bone marrow (with Kira's consent) to try to save Cosima, whose illness has gotten worse. "What kind of mother am I?" she rages as she watches Delphine insert a long needle into her daughter's hip (season 2, episode 10, "By Means Which Have Never Been Tried"). Later, when Rachel kidnaps Kira from the hospital, Sarah tries to negotiate with Rachel, finally turning herself over to Rachel to free her daughter. Then she makes the heart-breaking choice to send Kira away to live with her father for a while. "It's a really painful decision to make, but it's ultimately one of the most selfless things she's done," Tatiana Maslany told the *Hollywood Reporter* about her character's actions.[3] In season 5, Sarah once again makes a sacrifice for her daughter, this time by going against her own best instinct and allowing Kira to spend time with Rachel, which the girl wants to do (episode 2, "Clutch of Greed").

Helena, for all of her training to be a killer, is surprisingly tender with children. In season 1, she didn't harm the little boy whose home she broke into to have a place to perform surgery on herself after Sarah nearly killed her. In the same way, she never harms Kira, who instinctively trusts her. So when Helena is kidnapped by the Protetheans and her eggs are extracted, fertilized, and frozen for in-vitro, it isn't surprising when she shows motherly compassion to them as well. After she flees her captors, she buries the remaining embryos in Alison's back yard, calling them her "science babies" and telling them she wishes she could keep them, "but I have your twins in my belly. When they are grown, I will tell them about you and our adventures" (season 4, episode 4, "From Instinct to Rational Control"). After Helena gives birth to those twins, Donnie and Art, she has a whole Clone Club of sestras to help raise them.

JESSICA JONES' MOMMY DEAREST

Trish's mother Dorothy is the clearest example of how *not* to parent a well-adjusted daughter. A talent agent with an eye for future stars, Dorothy treated Trish more like a cash cow than a daughter from a very young age. Like so many stage moms before her, Dorothy herded her daughter into television stardom as sugary sweet Patsy without consulting her, dominating and manipulating her and doing whatever was needed to exploit her daughter's fame and image. In fact, her adoption of Jessica after the crash was not motivated by concern for the girl but, rather, by how Trish's role of adoptive sister would foster goodwill among fans and the press.

Not content with Trish finding success as Patsy, Dorothy harassed the young girl into worrying about her weight and looks by calling her Fatsy instead. Not surprisingly, Trish develops bulimia. Seeing an opportunity for more money, Dorothy remakes her child star into a pop icon, and Trish begins taking drugs to cope. As happens with so many real-life stars, she became addicted and suffered a very public breakdown that led to the end of her career and estranged her from her mother.

When *Jessica Jones* begins, Trish has rebuilt her life as a successful talk show host and sometime singer. Dorothy comes back into her life at her engagement

Trish (Rachael Taylor, right) and her mother Dorothy (Rebecca De Mornay) had an often-fraught relationship. *Netflix/Photofest*

party and promptly asks Trish not about herself, her life, or her relationship, but to endorse one of her client's water bottles. Dorothy goes on, in typical fashion, to force Trish into taking a job as a home shopping network host, hawking her own line of products, even though that is the last thing Trish wants to do. Jessica asks Trish why she doesn't just kick her mother to the curb, but she can't. Rachael Taylor, who played Trish, explains: "I think it's just primal, our need as human beings to connect with and need our mothers. I think if there's some kind of fracture in a relationship with someone's mother, that just creates so much deep wounding. . . . But Trish still loves her mom and still needs her mom."[4]

Jessica is well aware of this abuse, as well as Dorothy's disdain for her. In the pilot, Dorothy tells her "taking you in was a mistake," to which Jessica responds, "Thanks, Mom" (season 1, episode 1, "AKA Ladies Night").

By season 3, both women have had enough and cut ties with Dorothy. When Jessica finds evidence that would put serial killer Gregory Sallinger in jail for life, he retaliates by torturing and killing Dorothy. In her eulogy to her mother, Trish reminds herself of her mission as Hellcat:

> Don't give up. She would want you to do everything you can with what you've been given. My mom was intense . . . and aggravating. And she could be mean as hell. But if Dorothy believed that you had

talent, she would move heaven and earth to make damn sure you used it. Mom didn't want to hear about failure. She only wanted to hear three words: "I've got this." (season 3, episode 10, "AKA Hero Pants")

In many ways, Trish's monologue shows that her mother continued manipulating her from beyond the grave. As the constant voice in Trish's head, she motivates Trish to push further and further in her vigilantism, because taking down Sallinger wasn't enough; she still was chasing that image of perfection that Dorothy put into her head at a young age and would keep killing until she finally achieved it and made her mother proud as the perfect superhero. But in doing so, she lost her sense of self and pushed too far, which resulted in her downfall, just as it had in her childhood.

HOMELAND: NOT EVERY WOMAN IS MEANT TO BE A MOTHER

While Dorothy on *Jessica Jones* spent the better part of thirty years making her daughter's life miserable, Carrie Mathison of *Homeland* is smart enough to realize early on that she poses a danger to her daughter, Franny. Even though her job as a spy is dangerous, Carrie chooses to keep her baby when she finds out she is pregnant because Franny is her last remaining piece of Brody, her lover who was brutally executed in the Middle East.

But Carrie, who was already carrying so much on her shoulders—in the last year she lost the job that gave her life meaning; watched her boyfriend be publicly murdered by her enemies; and then found out she was carrying his child—didn't bank on motherhood not working out for her. She doesn't feel the overwhelming wash of love and protectiveness for Franny that mothers are supposed to feel. "Perhaps it's because of her bipolar disorder, perhaps it's because of postpartum depression, perhaps it's because of her incapacitating grief, or, more likely, perhaps it's because of some combination of the three," speculates Libby Hill for *Vox*.[5]

Whatever the reason, this lack of bonding worries Carrie. In the fourth season premiere, she has a break with reality while bathing her daughter that causes her to envision drowning the baby. Then it appears that reality and fantasy merge—we don't really know what happened and what was just in her head—and Carrie holds the baby under the water. Thankfully, she comes to her senses in time to be able to pull Franny out of the water unharmed. Horrified by her actions and scared of what could have happened, Carrie quickly calls her sister and makes arrangements to leave Franny with her for a while.

Carrie was tested by the forces of societal pressure that, despite 175 years of feminism, still views women as potential or current mothers, regardless of what a woman would choose for herself.[6] And she was found lacking in the worst possible way. It is considered natural for a mother and child to magically take to one another, and when that doesn't happen, the mother is to blame, even when she has perfectly valid reasons—mental illness, emotional immaturity or unavailability, addiction, poor judgment, or stress, for example—for this to take place.[7] "Carrie is supposed to love her daughter after not seeing her for months. Period. She's supposed to be thrilled about dropping her dangerous, adventurous, beloved job in the CIA to stroll her baby around a park," Hayley Krischer points out for Salon. "She's not even permitted disappointment."[8]

Hill points out that Franny is "the living, breathing manifestation of all of Carrie's Brody baggage, from the tips of her toes to the top of her ginger-haired head." It could be that subconsciously Carrie was trying to express her sadness and anger over Brody's death and accidently took it out on her daughter. Or, as Hill suggests, she somehow realized that she would never be able to move on as long as the baby was around to reflect Brody back to her every time their eyes met.[9]

Showrunner Alex Gansa told *Entertainment Weekly* that what Carrie did— or imagined doing, she won't tell—happens more often than you might think. "It's not an uncommon thought for parents of newborns whose lives have been turned upside down to contemplate doing something terrible. And of course, it does actually happen too," she said. "I think it shows the extremity of her state. She's in an extreme place emotionally and cut off from her grief, and it's causing her to behave in ways that are upsetting to her."[10]

In a roundabout way, entrusting Franny to her sister's care is the most loving, selfless, motherly thing Carrie could do given her circumstances. Like a woman contemplating putting her baby up for adoption, Carrie is thinking of what is best for the child and her future (granted, Carrie benefits from not being tied down by a baby, too). When her sister, frustrated by being saddled with another child yells, "You bring a life into this world. You take responsibility" (season 4, episode 1, "The Drone Queen"), she doesn't realize that is exactly what Carrie is doing. She is saving her daughter's life by leaving it.

ALIAS: I AM MY FATHER'S DAUGHTER

A spy who frequently works undercover missions is not most people's first thought when it comes to a woman's relationship with her parents, but for Sydney Bristow, espionage is the family business, and her parents are both her greatest allies and worst enemies.

Though she begins the series estranged from her father, Jack, and believing her mother is dead, Sydney comes to find out that her father has been watching over her all along. He is limited in his ability to protect her, given that he is living a double life that is at least partially compromised, but he hasn't forgotten his duty to his daughter and does what he can from the shadows. When he is forced into the light and back into Sydney's life in a more significant way, there is a natural lack of trust. "It's a statement about spy life, but it's really about family life."[11]

While *Alias* had a popular will-they-or-won't-they romance between Sydney and her partner, Vaughn, her most intimate relationship was the one she had with her father. She deliberately chose Jack over her mother as a role model and confidant[12] even though he kept information from her. The merry-go-round of Sydney constantly finding out information Jack hid from her, rejecting him out of anger or hurt, and then later returning to him when she realized he had his reasons, is highly symbolic of the fraught nature between parent and child as the child grows into adulthood to stand no longer behind or beneath their heroic parents, but beside them in equality as mere mortals. Charles Taylor writes for Salon:

Spy Sydney Bristow (Jennifer Garner), surrounded by her family, father Jack Bristow (Victor Garber, to Sydney's left), and coworkers. *ABC/Photofest*

Sydney, because of what she does, is put in the position of constantly experiencing the shock we all do when we discover something heretofore hidden about our parents—and in the position of having to integrate that information into her picture of her father, working to accept him as a flawed human being, which of course means accepting her own adulthood.[13]

The show did them justice by allowing their bond to grow slowly over the course of the series rather than cramming it into a few episodes. By allowing Sydney to take the emotional baby steps she needs—it took her nearly a full season to admit her father was a fantastic spy and she did that in spite of herself—to process that the father she hardly knew kept her at arm's length for her own good, she has the time and space to slowly begin to love him. "Sydney and Jack's story is so emotionally complex and messy, a perfect blend of justified anger, painful regret, and hard-fought second chances," writes Lacy Baugher Milas for *Paste Magazine*. "That the two finally manage to forge a strong and meaningful connection out of the broken pieces between them is the true miracle in a world that's full of near-magical objects and unbelievable coincidences."[14]

Motherhood, on the other hand, is a fraught affair in the world of *Alias*. Sydney's mother, Irina Derevko, was not only secretly a Russian mastermind masquerading as an American but also a pretty terrible mother. From allowing her daughter to think she was dead to flat out telling her she considered killing Sydney at birth, Irina will never win mother of the year. She says to Sydney:

> I never wanted to have a child. The KGB demanded it. They knew it would ensure allegiance. You were simply a means to an end. And then when the doctor put you in my arms and I looked at you, so fragile, all I could think was, how could I have made such a terrible mistake? And at that moment I was sure of one thing. I couldn't be an agent and a mother. I'd either fail at one or both. And I chose to fail at being a mother.

A beat later, the two have this exchange:

> Irina: In time you'll learn . . . you can't do both.
>
> Sydney: Watch me. (season 5, episode 11, "Maternal Instinct")

Sydney faces the prospect of motherhood twice in the series. In a story line eerily similar to Helena's in *Orphan Black*, when Sydney finds out in season 3 she was kidnapped and almost forcibly impregnated by the medieval prophet Rambaldi, she destroys the remaining fertilized embryos so they can't ever be used. "Though it is couched in mysticism, this storyline is, in its own strange way, an abortion-rights parable expressing anxiety over female sexual autonomy—one startling to find in the landscape of post-feminist television," writes Whitney.[15] But is it really that surprising? As a spy, Sydney has to know her lifestyle is far from ideal for raising a child. Her choice to say no to motherhood puts her in direct opposition with her own mother and shows her to be a third-wave feminist demonstrating her right to control what happens to her body. Whitney writes,

> In each scenario, she controls her reproductivity by choice, which is . . . a more promising concept for feminism, since it assesses any choice against a field of possible alternatives rather than proposing that "all choices must be made to signify the same thing." After her baby is born, Sydney continues to work by choice, telling her daughter that "I'm just—trying to make the world safer, so you can grow up and have a regular life. . . . Mama's got to go to work" (5.12, "Sola hay una Sydney Bristow"). Her successful combination of professional and maternal success is a final rebuke to the bad Irina, who views her daughter as "such a terrible mistake."[16]

Later, in the fifth season, when Sydney gets pregnant—along with actress Jennifer Garner—she makes a different choice. This time she wants to be a mother. It alters her ability to do her job, especially in that she doesn't blend in nearly as easily as usual[17] and can't do the death-defying stunts she's known for.[18] But Sydney is more than an action hero; she is a woman of incredible intelligence who can still contribute to the CIA, while allowing her protégée, Rachel, to take the hard knocks.

That season changes her in larger ways, too. Both of her parents die, which can be seen as symbolic of losing her past ties and freeing her to move on. Only through that growth is she able to achieve what neither of her parents had. In the final scene she is free of the CIA and happily married to Vaughn, their daughter, Isabelle, in tow. She may have been her father's daughter once upon a time, but it is now her turn to be the mother hers never was.

THE EQUALIZER: THREE GENERATIONS OF POWERFUL WOMEN

The world has had enough lone wolf men getting even. Enter the 2021 remake of *The Equalizer*, which stars Queen Latifah as Robyn McCall. In this version of the show, three generations of Black women live under the same roof. Vi is a boomer; Robyn is firmly in Gen X; and Delilah is a Gen Zer who thinks the other two are clueless, yet respects their authority.[19] When asked by *Parade* magazine why it was important for Robyn to be a mother, Queen Latifah replied, "We wanted to show how a woman walks the tightrope of the world she's created. Some of those choices can be difficult. So let's see what life is like for a woman who has to balance work and parenthood and herself."[20]

While justice might be the theme of each episode, family is what powers it. Whether Robyn is pursuing the kidnapper of a young boy or helping a teenage girl prove her innocence, Robyn's role and her past experiences urge her forward. In the former, she relates to the situation as a mother, and in the latter, it's as a woman who faced the long arm of the law as a teenager herself.

But unlike the previous men who have held the title of Equalizer, McCall doesn't face the world alone. Vi is there to lend advice and help take care of Delilah when Robyn's work keeps her away from functions she'd like to attend (often to the disappointment of Delilah), and serving as a positive role model for Delilah keeps Robyn from making the rash decisions she'd make if she had only herself to be responsible for. The show is still ongoing, but the grounding influence of Robyn's family doesn't show any sign of weakening; if anything, it gets stronger with each passing episode.

Sisterhood: A Female Bond That Knows No Bounds

When the words "sisterhood" and "feminism" are used in close proximity—as in this book—the image that immediately comes to mind is that of women walking side by side or standing arm in arm in protest. And that is a very valid interpretation. But when it comes to sisterhood on television, there are as many varieties as there are situations. In *Charmed*, for example, the Halliwell sisters are blood related, but in *Jessica Jones*, two foster sisters share a lifelong bond, and in *Orphan Black*, five clones form a bond so close that they rightfully call one another "sestra."

CHARMED: BY BLOOD AND BONE

The importance of sisterhood is made clear in the very first episode of *Charmed* when the Halliwell sisters realize that, to vanquish the demon threatening them, they must do so together. One Charmed One is powerful, but together, they cannot be defeated. As Jenny Crusie writes in the introduction to her book on the show, "They went beyond the Bewitched Brady Bunch into honestly cathartic connection. . . . The outcome of all of that emotional growth was a family of three strong women working together and supporting each other."[21]

That's not to say that every day is rainbows and unicorns for the Charmed Ones—not by far. Brought back together under one roof as adults with established personalities, routines, goals, and preferences, they fight, get on each other's nerves, and sometimes make strangulation tempting just like any real-life siblings. Prue and Phoebe often assume Piper will take care of whatever needs tending; Prue often feels like Phoebe doesn't pull her weight; Phoebe thinks Prue is too demanding; Piper gets tired of making peace between Prue and Phoebe and feels taken advantage of, and so on.

Demons even take advantage of these petty squabbles to amplify their feelings in an effort to turn the sisters against one another and defeat them. And the demon fighting that results, in turn, "metaphorically displays their struggles with each other and the personal struggle of each sister with the concepts of autonomy, communal effort, and connections."[22]

The early episodes of *Charmed* where this dynamic was present were among its best; later seasons tried to recapture the magic with Paige, but never truly succeeded in "generat[ing] that manic energy in service to honest emotion, an unabashed focus on love—of sisters, significant others and humanity—that refuses to be cynical or blasé."[23] Their relationships were "messy and chaotic, a bit like life, but above all [the show] was about women who loved and supported each other, and the power over your circumstances that love can give you."[24]

Potentially losing one another was their collective worst fear, something the show hinted as a possibility many times, for example, in season 1, episode 13, "From Fear to Eternity." In this episode, the demon Barbas takes this fear and uses it against them, trying to literally scare them to death. In season 3, episode 7, "Power Outage," a demon turns the sisters against each other to the point where "they each use their magical powers to harm another. The camera cuts to their magic book, the Book of Shadows; the cover changes, initiating the witches' loss of power. The only way to restore their powers, as Leo states, is 'to try to restore your bond as sisters.'"[25] And when their nightmare is realized in the finale of the third season (episode 22, "All Hell Breaks Loose"), first by Piper's death by gunshot before the demon Tempus resets time, and then again when Prue is killed, her death nearly breaks them.

Season 4, with its introduction of Paige as the long-lost half Halliwell sister, tried particularly hard to recapture the bond the original three sisters had in the first three seasons. But despite statements like Piper's begrudging acceptance of Paige, "no matter what she is my sister, and sisters protect each other" (season 4, episode 2, "Charmed Again, Part One"), the sentiment rings hollow. However, regardless of the strength of their bond, the three must stay together, which they do for four more seasons.

The requirement that the sisters live together to gain the Power of Three makes them a de facto coven. This not only gives them a built-in support system but also harkens back to the very beginnings of witchcraft in literature and art, which portray witches in groups and particularly in family units along the maternal line. Feminist scholar Hannah Sanders writes that this type of matriarchal image—especially when women are shown together around a cauldron—is

> a fearful reminder of the power invoked by unruly women gossiping, laughing, and plotting together. . . . There is considerable weight of cultural connotation behind the depiction of female witches together, defined as sisters through a shared biological heritage and a shared status as "other." A connection can be made to the consciousness raising of second wave feminism but also group female gatherings like Lilith fair and 3rd wave feminism.[26]

This community and the empowerment it brings not only affects the sisters but also the women watching the show. Many women reported watching the show with a female relative like their mother or sister or even a close friend.[27] "In this way, the focus on watching the program as a female 'bonding experience . . .' can be seen to pick up on the theme of female camaraderie that runs throughout the [show] itself."[28]

JESSICA JONES: SISTERS BY CIRCUMSTANCE

When her family is killed in a car accident, Jessica is taken in by her best friend Trish's mom, Dorothy. Already being close and now living together, Trish and Jessica became like sisters, each dealing with their own forms of trauma. Neither of them like how their lives have turned out, so they turn to one another. "These two have each other's backs, they love each other, they protect each other. They speak in the shorthand of lifelong friends. They offer each other support and advice. They argue and disagree. Jessica and Trish personify the strength of friendship. It's a fabulous dynamic that we don't see often enough on our screens," writes critic Virginia DeBolt.[29]

These two women couldn't be more unlikely friends. They are opposites in every way, including looks and personality. Jessica is dark haired and her demeanor screams "go away," while Trish is blonde and outgoing. Jessica doesn't make friends easily, while Trish has legions of adoring fans. "Jessica drinks way too much and her apartment (and her life) are a mess; Trish is successful and seemingly has her life together. Jessica is emotionally distant and unreliable as a friend; Trish is loyal and dedicated."[30] Yet they work well together because their polarities complement each other; what one lacks the other has in spades. By trading strength for strength, they learn to love and trust, something neither excels at because of prior abuse—Jessica at the hands of Kilgrave and Trish from the manipulations of her mother.

Yet for all its strength, Jessica and Trish's friendship has a few dropped stitches and frayed edges, which begin to unravel in season 2. For Trish, this begins when her boyfriend, Will Simpson—who is under the mind control of Kilgrave—nearly kills her. Will, who is addicted to an inhaled government drug that gives him semi-superpowers, becomes completely crazed and goes after Jessica. Desperate to save her foster sister, Trish takes the same drugs Simpson did and, after a long fight, finally kills him.

Trish has tasted the power she's always been jealous of in Jessica and sees an opportunity to level the playing field between them. She could put an end to general feelings of helplessness that plague her, while finally feeling equal to her superpowered sister. Succumbing to temptation, Trish allows herself to become addicted to the drug, and when it runs out, she tracks down disgraced doctor Karl Malus, whose experiments gave Jessica her powers, and asks him to make her like Jessica. "She ignores how Jessica's powers have made life harder, that they came along with the death of her parents, and that for Jessica they are a constant reminder of a life she lost," notes Princess Weekes for the *Mary Sue*.[31]

But instead of bringing the two closer, Trish's powers and her actions because of them drive a wedge into their bond that can never be removed. At the end of season 2, newly empowered Trish takes justice into her own hands for the first time by killing Jessica's mom (who was alive and being held by Dr. Malus), thinking she is doing the right thing. This action, naturally, strains Jessica and Trish's relationship to the point where they don't speak for a long time. Krysten Ritter, who played Jessica, explained the dynamic: "Now we're dealing with her relationship with her best friend, which is as personal as it can get for Jessica. At the core, that's what our show has always been about—that relationship between Jessica and Trish. And Trish really f*cked it up."[32]

This is a major turning point for both characters. Showrunner Melissa Rosenberg described it as Jessica's awakening to independence: "Jessica depended on Trish to be her moral compass, and Trish lived vicariously through her super-powered sister. But that dynamic obviously falls apart, and Jessica becomes her own compass."[33]

Trish tries to mend her ways, but when her mother is murdered, she snaps and begins meting out her own brand of justice, becoming Hellcat—whom the public calls "the Masked Vigilante." Jessica tries to find ways to reason with her and bring her in line. But that is a fruitless effort because Trish doesn't want to be corralled by society's rules. Her powers have gone to her head to the point that she feels she is justified in taking on the roles of judge, jury, and executioner.

Seeing no other alternative, Jessica has her arrested and sent to The Raft, a special prison for superheroes where their powers are stripped away. The final scene between the two—where they share a last look across the parking lot as Trish is loaded into the helicopter that will take her to The Raft—is heartbreaking. It sums up a lifetime of love and an eternity of regret. Jessica's voiceover explains why the rift between them can never be healed: "Some things you look at and you think 'disaster.' You search for exits, escapes. Other things you think, 'maybe I can fix this.' You might ask yourself, 'what's it going to take to make it feel right?' The answer is 'too much.' It'll take too much" (season 3, episode 13, "AKA Everything").

ORPHAN BLACK: SESTRAS IN SCIENCE

The clones of *Orphan Black* may be genetic matches by design, but they chose to become sisters (or "sestras," as Helena calls them). This is even more amazing when you consider that they were all raised believing they were only children; none of them had any experience of what the bond of sisterhood was like, yet they recognized it in one another. Not only that, but they eagerly cultivated it, relying on each other in times of crisis. Angelica Bastién notes that their close-knit family "displays a startling intimacy [not usually seen] in the realm of science fiction"[34] where familial relationships are often portrayed as negative or even lacking altogether.[35]

Sarah doesn't know what to think when she realizes she must be related to Beth Childs somehow. Why else would they share a face? "This could be your story," Felix, Sarah's foster brother, enthuses. "Every foster kid dreams of their lost family. . . . Deep down we all hope that we're special" (season 1, episode 1, "Natural Selection").

Tatiana Maslany plays more than fifteen clones in *Orphan Black*. Pictured from left are Rachel Duncan, Alison Hendrix, Cosima Niehaus, and main character Sarah Manning. *BBC America/Photofest*

That is an interesting choice of words, given that, as a clone, Sarah is both special and not special at all: there are at least 273 copies just like her, but she is also very unique in that she is one of two originals out of the clones from Project LEDA (the only known human cloning project ever to produce female human clones successfully) who can reproduce.

The answers to the questions who they are, why they are, and how they exist are what the clones are after. They are why they formed the initial Clone Club—the girls' lighthearted name for their network of trusted allies—that originally consisted only (that the audience is aware of) of Alison, Cosima, Beth, and Katia. When Katia and Beth are killed and Sarah finds Beth's pink "clone phone," the group shifts to let in Sarah to fill one of the voids. Later Helena joins after being rehabilitated from her murderous ways. Finally, Art and Donnie are made honorary members because they know the truth about them and are helping them. This unlikely group works together to unravel the mystery behind the clones' creation and fight those who would use their existence for evil.

Marcie Casey and Jay Clayton argue that this relationship is a "reconceptualization" or an alternative model to the traditional Western nuclear family. It is a "family of choice," not unlike those seen among the LGBTQIA+ community or single young people in large cities who are estranged from their blood families. Casey and Clayton even go so far as to bring in a scientific tie not unlike the one in *Orphan Black* that includes blood relatives who have previously had no knowledge of one another but found each other through DNA testing sites like Ancestry or 23andMe.[36]

It is interesting, then, that Helena, who is as much of a stranger to the clones as it is possible to be due to her unusual upbringing and training, is the one to "become attached to Sarah and Sarah's daughter Kira as she comes to believe that family is more important to her than what she has been taught her whole life."[37] Just as she started out the show trying to keep the clones separated by death, she ends up being the glue that holds them together. Her pregnancy reminds the clones during times of turmoil and strife that family is what they are really fighting for.

Fans as Family

The idea of family is so strong in *Orphan Black* that it bled over into the show's fandom, who started calling themselves the Clone Club. Just like the show's Clone Club, the fan group was made up of people of all genders, races, and sexualities, something the clones would no doubt applaud. They formed groups online, gathered for in-person and social media meetups, and even began influencing the trajectory of the show, something the creators encouraged. "*Orphan*

Black was innovative in incorporating the responses of its dedicated, cos-playing fans into later episodes of the series, and it featured these extended 'co-creators' in a heart-warming video collage during the credits of the final episode."[38]

Spouses as Family: 'Til Death or Divorce Do Us Part

As we get older and develop our own lives, our relationships with our parents and siblings often lessen as life, location, and competing priorities cause us to drift apart. Often, our spouses take up the place that other family used to occupy—as confidants, helpers, and of course, our main source of love.

For all of their problems, Frank and Claire Underwood are family to one another. They may fight, have affairs, and be cruel, but they always return home to each other. The most intimate gesture for them isn't lovemaking or even just kissing; it is when they share a cigarette while sitting on their windowsill, staring out into the night. "The smoking itself is important, as it signals transgression and trust," writes Caroline Crampton for the *New Statesman*. "Their conversation as they pass the cigarette to each other is even more important, though.

Frank (Kevin Spacey) and Claire (Robin Wright) Underwood are more than spouses in *House of Cards*—they are literally partners in crime. *Netflix/ Photofest*

This is when they plot."[39] Planning their next bit of intrigue is what really bonds them as a couple; scheming is their love language.

For this to work, the Underwoods must have an understanding.

Rule 1: This is no run-of-the-mill political relationship where the man has free rein to do as he pleases while the wife stands by—or, more accurately, stands behind—and supports him. No, Claire and Frank are equals. He may appear to have more power because he is higher ranking, but Claire has a job and ambitions of her own; she is just biding her time. "She isn't just Lady Macbeth, pacing the floor while her husband does the deed. She gets in her own tangles with lobbyists, has her own extra-marital affair, and formulates her own strategies for seizing power," Crampton notes.[40]

Rule 2: They work together to achieve their goals. Deep down, each is as monstrous and diabolical as the other, needing their mate to stay in check as well as to reach their full potential. Claire uses Frank for his contacts, while he uses her to cover his misdeeds. After all, a man with such a respected, successful wife can't possibly be partisan or controversial, no matter what causes he seems to espouse. They may quietly sleep with others, but they are still two dancers in a deadly pas de deux—a dance neither could perform without being in perfect time with the other. And it is that partnership that the public wants to see. Claire knows this, and that is why she threatens to divorce Frank in an election year. In doing so, she reminds him that she can make or break him.[41]

Rule 3: They must always tell one another the truth, even if it is brutal and harsh and not what the other wants to hear. Lies have no place in a conspiracy. As Crampton puts it, "Their relationship may be twisted and dark—Frank declares early on that he loves his wife 'more than sharks love blood'—but it is essential to what they achieve."[42]

However, all good relationships must eventually come to an end. Claire signaled theirs was coming to a close at the end of season 5 when she looked at the camera, and thus at the audience, for the first time. In stealing Frank's signature move, she also took his power. Her words, "My turn," were not just about a change in narrative direction, they signaled she was finally willing to tip the balance of power they had so carefully maintained up until that point and take over the limelight. Even before Kevin Spacey's fall from grace, Claire was going to take what was rightfully hers. His exit simply made it easier. In the show's game of political chess, the king put himself in check, but instead of being taken, the queen ascended the throne.

Buffy and the Slayerettes: Friends as Family

As any teenager, college student, or single adult will tell you, sometimes friends make the best family. And that was certainly the case for Buffy Summers and her friends.

When the show opens, Buffy's father is nowhere to be found, and her mother is too busy with work to do much parenting. As the show goes on, we find out that none of the teenage characters have good relationships with their parents. Willow is the luckiest; her parents are still married, but they are too invested in their academic careers to pay much attention to their daughter. Cordelia's parents conflated love and money, paying her off with expensive gifts rather than affection. Xander's family was abusive, and Tara's father was a misogynist who believed all the women in the family were part demon.

As a result, they banded together into the Scooby Gang—Xander's name for them that is a takeoff on the group of crime-solving friends in the 1970s *Scooby Doo* television show. This group of misfits and outsiders soon became like siblings—confiding in one another, sharing the chores (homework and patrolling for vampires), and loving and fighting in equal measure—all under the semi-parental gaze of Giles, Buffy's Watcher, and Joyce, Buffy's mom who kind of adopted the whole lot. In season 5, episode 16, "The Body," Buffy and all of her friends are seen in a flashback (or fantasy?) all gathered around Joyce's dining table for Christmas dinner, sharing stories and teasing each other like blood siblings. This closeness is part of the reason they are all so affected by Joyce's death later in the episode.

In giving Buffy such a close group of friends to rely on, *Buffy the Vampire Slayer* turned genre conventions on their head. Traditionally those "chosen ones" who save the world from evil do so solo—think The Crow, Spiderman, or Superman—or with a much less important sidekick—think Batman and Robin or Captain America and Bucky Barnes. But long before the X-Men united or the Avengers assembled on the big screen, Buffy and the Scooby Gang worked together to fight each season's Big Bad. "Buffy might've been the one with the heroic destiny, but that didn't mean she had to go it alone," notes Sarah Dobbs for Den of Geek.[43]

This group not only saw Buffy through seven seasons of Big Bads, boyfriends, tests, heartbreak, and even death—twice—but also gave the viewers who, like them, didn't fit in hope that they would someday find their own tribe. And in many ways, they made this happen through fan interactions in real life at conventions and meet and greets and on the burgeoning internet through AOL Instant Messenger, chat rooms, and message boards. Some of these friendships lasted only a few seasons, but others lasted a lifetime.

Father-Figure: Workplace Family in *Homeland*

Carrie Mathison has a strong family bond. At the beginning of the series, viewers see her interacting with her father (who is also bipolar) and her sister, Maggie, who is a psychologist. She relies on both of them, especially Maggie, for support, a need that grows as the series progresses.

Yet, that sororal bond isn't the strongest one Carrie has with the characters on the show. Her closest relationship is with Saul Berenson, her mentor and boss at the CIA. "Carrie has very few people that really understand her life but he does," writes Dana Feldman for *Forbes*.[44] Saul is the one who first saw the potential in Carrie. He recruited her and trained her, so he knows how she thinks better than anyone. "Saul was always a reliable presence who . . . was the only one who could always bring her back from the edge, or push her to it, in the name of world safety," Brian Tallerico points out.[45]

Saul and Carrie very much have a father-daughter type of relationship. Mandy Patinkin, who played Saul, even likened it to the ever-changing relationship he had with his own sons, saying it began as a mentor/parent relationship because Saul saw Carrie as his protégé, the one who would carry on after he was gone.[46] Like a father, Saul advises Carrie and pulls her out of jams, but he isn't afraid to censure and yell at her when needed. Yet he never gives up on her, even

Carrie (Claire Danes) and Saul (Mandy Patinkin) had a close, nearly familial mentor relationship in *Homeland*. Showtime/Photofest

when the rest of the agency has written her off as a loose cannon or a traitor. "Her fearlessness balanced his pragmatism. He reined her in at times, but just as often gave her the encouragement to do whatever was needed to save the day," Tallerico notes.[47]

Their relationship can be seen as reflective of a larger, often unseen (at least by the public) dynamic at play in organizations like the CIA. These people put their lives in each other's hands and rely on their continued honesty to get the job done, so in many ways, they can't help but become close. Patinkin told *The Star*, "In my opinion, family is at the core, the nucleus of the show. . . . [In *Homeland*] family is the system. The family of the CIA and the family of the world at large."[48] That family was tested to the point of death several times throughout the show, but Saul never lost his faith in Carrie, and as Yevgeny says to Carrie, "In the end, who we trust in this life is all that matters" (season 8, episode 12, "Prisoners of War").

CHAPTER 6

The Revolution Will Be Televised: Fighting the Patriarchy

For anyone paying attention to the news over the last decade, there should be no doubt that women are fed up. We've seen #MeToo, #TimesUp, the Women's March on Washington, and more. Why? Because women are tired of being treated as second-class citizens and sexual playthings, and generally being disrespected by men who feel entitled to their time and their bodies.

In addition, the American government is far from equal. In the most gender-equal country, Iceland, women hold nearly 40 percent of parliamentary seats. In the United States, while there are a record number of women serving in Congress, they are still in the minority, with only 27 percent of members being female (24 of 100 seats in the Senate and 120 of 435 seats in the House).[1]

But perhaps most important, the United States is one of only seven United Nations member states that does not have an equal rights law in their constitution (193 countries) or a provision that outlaws discrimination on the basis of sex (115 additional countries). The other six countries without such a law are Iran, Palau, Somalia, South Sudan, Sudan, and Tonga.[2]

Women all over the world are standing up for their rights. The women of Iran have taken to the streets to protest the killing of their own by the country's morality police. Women in India have done the same to shed light on the rape culture that persists in their country. In Argentina, women wearing purple wigs protested violence against women.

We are seeing a "worldwide explosion of female wrath, erupting in response to many lifetimes of putting up with patriarchal crap at all levels—in our homes, at work, in the streets, in the courts, even at the goddamn salon," Melanie McFarland writes for Salon. Half-jokingly, she asks about a first-world problem that reflects a much larger issue, "Why does a woman with short hair pay more than a guy for the same damn haircut? There's still no good answer!"[3]

This female outrage is just the latest manifestation of women on the brink of revolution. Women have been demanding their rights for 175 years (in the United States at least) and addressing wrongs large and small over the airwaves since the 1990s. When women's righteous anger is depicted on television, it is a clarion call to women everywhere to stand up, as well as a reminder that they are not alone in their fight.

Jessica Jones: Speaking Up

Jessica Jones represents the pent-up anger and frustration of women who have gone their whole lives unable (or unwilling) to vent their emotions. She demonstrates, through words and actions, everything women feel about the patriarchy but are constrained by societal pressures or law from saying. Jessica is the woman all feminists would be if they had no more fucks to give. (For those who need proof, simply look at the fact that the second season was released on March 8,

PI Jessica Jones (Krysten Ritter, right) occasionally worked for crooked lawyer Jeri Hogarth (Carrie-Anne Moss). *Netflix/Photofest*

International Women's Day, a sign that the women behind this female-led show are well aware of what they are doing.)

Jessica is "angry, all the time, courtesy of some very deep wrongs that have been done to her and the people she loves—repeatedly, brutally, and committed mostly by men. And it's the ways in which she copes (or doesn't) with her rage, drinks it away or punches it out, avoids it or is shaken awake at night by it, that's turned her into such a compelling icon for the #MeToo age," asserts Khal for Complex.[4]

The story lines and seasonal themes reflect this timeliness. The first season is about abuse and survival: sexual, mental, physical—the mode doesn't matter; it's the scars and trauma left behind and how the characters heal from them that do. Jessica is preyed upon by Kilgrave who seeks to control her; Trish by her mother who uses her for her own gain and the men in the entertainment industry who want her as a sexual plaything; and Jeri by men in the corporate world who would keep her down. "This is a deeply feminist story," writes Amanda Marcotte for Salon, "one that seeks to illuminate these issues and humanize the victims of these crimes."[5]

Season 2 is "about what comes after: namely, anger. [The show] examines feminist rage from a variety of angles . . . [and] the big bad is less clear than it was in Season One, because it's everywhere and nowhere," writes Jenna Scherer for *Rolling Stone*.[6] Jessica faces life without Kilgrave—though he still haunts her memories—and slowly learns to live without the constant fear of him. But then she is dragged into an even more personal fight, to uncover and deal with the violent and invasive experiments that resulted in her superpowers and were really another kind of rape. Trish faces an abusive director from her days as a child star and, feeling helpless because of that situation and so many others her mother put her in, experiences a growing sense of jealousy and injustice that she doesn't have powers like Jessica that might have emboldened her to fight back. And Jeri battles herself when her body turns against her, threatening her self-created sense of power and immortality. She must face that there is one battle that, in the end, her money, status, and willpower can't save her from.

These women's experiences in season 2 are "like an answer to questions that were unvoiced when [the show] first came out. What does sexual assault mean, and what does it do? Why does it leave the wrong person ashamed and everybody silent? . . . [It] marks out the new terrain, where the things that have always been said crash headlong into the things that are never said," Zoe Williams points out in *The Guardian*.[7]

Season 3 is about reckoning. Once you've faced your demons, what comes next? For Jessica, the answer is pain and betrayal as she watches Trish spiral out of control and become the very type of bad guy Jessica has been fighting against. But in experiencing this type of betrayal, she also comes to a certainty about her own sense of right and wrong, a steely resolve that drives her to continue her fight for what she believes in, even if she has to take down her best friend in the process. Trish gives into her misguided sense of justice and, drunk on power, goes on a crime spree disguised as helping victims of crime. When she is finally caught, it isn't until the list of charges against her are read to her that she realizes, "I'm the bad guy" (season 3, episode 13, "AKA Everything"), someone at best on par with the mother she despises, but possibly even worse. This reckoning with her own actions is why she doesn't fight being sent to The Raft. She must atone for her sins. Jeri, meanwhile, finally stops denying her terminal diagnosis and trying to find ways to fix or evade it. Her journey to this point has changed her, and we even see her doing some good. She accepts her own mortality and, while still the entitled bitch we know and love to hate, determines to live her life to the fullest for as long as she can.

Rachael Taylor, who played Trish, says that addressing relevant female concerns as they are happening in real life is "part of the DNA of *Jessica Jones*. We talk about what it's like to be a woman out in the real world in every episode. The fact that our show kind of serves up a mirror for a moment in time, [is] very powerful."[8]

Agent Carter: Breaking Marvel's Glass Ceiling

If you need proof that women have been fighting the patriarchy for a long time, look no further than *Agent Carter*. While, yes, some of the history is questionable, it is true that women faced serious misogyny when their men returned home from the war. Having tasted independence and power while the men were away, women were suddenly expected by a patriarchal society to pretend like none of that had ever happened and go back to their prior roles as happy little homemakers without complaint. But you see, some of them did complain, and they are the ones Peggy Carter represents.

The radio show that is acted out in tandem with some of the scenes in the early episodes of the show serves to drive home the expected role of women, that of the helpless damsel in distress who needs to be rescued by a man. And what's worse is that it seems to be a direct rip-off of Peggy's actual experience. Melissa Leon explains in the Daily Beast, "There's a nurse on the show named Betty Carver who cleans up messes 'while the men fight the war.' She says things like, 'What a *beautiful* day to mend these pants. . . . Oh no, Nazis, again! And they've got me all tied up. If only Captain America were here to save me!!!'"[9] This depiction serves to show that, in the eyes of the world, Peggy Carter is doomed to either be rescued by a man through marriage or die a spinster.

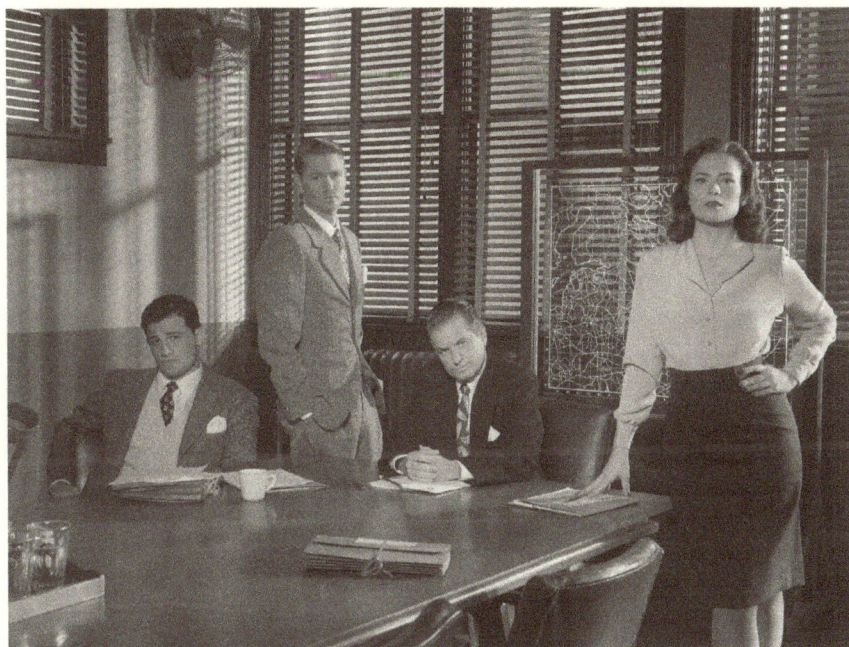

Agent Carter (Hayley Atwell) doesn't back down from the sexism often leveled at her by her fellow spies at the Strategic Scientific Reserve. *ABC/ Photofest*

Not so, answers Peggy, and she does everything she can to prove her worth. But for her, it is a thankless job with little or no recognition. "While Steve Rogers was able to put on a flashy costume and be praised for all of his good deeds on the front page of the newspaper, Peggy Carter's only way to save the day involves having to do something that looks foolish and incompetent to her peers and supervisor, and the need to hide in the shadows," Amy Richau notes in a review of the show.[10] Indeed, this woman "who led an entire secret division of the military [during the war], is reduced to fetching coffee, typing reports and enduring patronizing colleagues,"[11] while scheming ways to conduct her own investigation behind their backs. If they would only take her seriously, it would be so much easier. Instead, she has to endure sexism day in and day out, often in little ways. In the first season, a man asks Peggy, "What's your name, sweetheart?" Her reply, "Agent." Gissane Sophia points out that "a man would never be given a pet name upon introduction, but as a woman, she is immediately objectified [and] thus, repl[ies] in a way to indicate that she deserves respect for the badges she carries."[12]

The confidence it takes to respond with quips like this comes from strong self-esteem, of understanding one's true worth, regardless of what those around you think or say. This is a facet of a strong woman's personality that is rarely talked about and even more rarely displayed in a strong female character on television. This type of confidence is usually hard won, coming as the result of trials, though it can also be shored up by support from parents or other women, especially in settings that prioritize female value like all-girls educational institutions.

Female solidarity is another hallmark of feminism portrayed in the show that isn't shown enough on television, though that is changing as more women influence what makes it to the screen and how. Contrary to popular myth, women don't have to be in competition with one another; there are plenty of men (and other women) and jobs to go around. And for God's sake, female catfights should stay in the 1980s where they belong. Today's women should be able to recognize that such things only serve to divide us and play right into the agenda of the patriarchy.

As the popular saying goes, women should be straightening one another's crowns and reminding other women of their worth, rather than fighting with them. This attitude is shown in *Agent Carter* through Peggy's relationship with other women on the show. Her first roommate, Colleen, while as different from Peggy as could be, was always encouraging her to go out more; Peggy defended Angie at every turn, teaching her how to stand up for herself; and in season 2, Peggy and Ana are friends, even though both have a close relationship with Ana's husband, Jarvis. In most other shows, Ana would be jealous of Peggy, and therefore the two would butt heads. But showrunners Michele Fazekas and Tara Butters didn't want to fall back on that tired trope. "We didn't want to fall into that trap of, oh they're two women, so they're obviously not going to like each other . . . [so] we made her a good person."[13] Ana and Jarvis are so comfortable in their relationship, they're not going to be jealous of other people coming in and out of their lives.

The strength to hold one's ground even the face of opposition was as much a part of the making of *Agent Carter* as it is part of her mindset. Historian Otto L. explained on his blog the masculine-focused culture of Hollywood that the creators had to overcome just to get a woman on screen. When Marvel had been asked previously about why they hadn't yet given audiences a Black Widow or other female superhero, they argued that not only was there no audience for her (by which they meant "men wouldn't watch a movie led by a woman") and no female character was important enough culturally to devote an entire movie to her, much less an ongoing series. Besides, writing female action characters is hard. (Read that last sentence in a whiny voice.)

L. argues that Hollywood perceives writing female characters as difficult because male writers "struggle between *trying* to come up with interesting female characters and still appealing to what is *perceived* as that mythical core audience: young males who are reluctant to see women taking places that once belonged to a masculine status quo. . . . It is as if the *strong female characters* were written as a tool to tackle criticism, rather than being an affirmation of a progressive discourse."[14]

But put *Agent Carter* in the hands of two females—showrunners Tara Butters and Michele Fazekas—and a bevy of female directors, and you get a whole different story. "We're trying to please many people," Butters told *Time* magazine. "But first we wanted to make a show that we would want to watch ourselves."[15] In doing that, Butters and Fazekas broke the glass ceiling at Marvel, allowing for additional female-led hits like *Black Widow*, *WandaVision*, and *Captain Marvel*. That is a legacy that would make Peggy Carter proud.

House of Cards: The Second Lady Becomes the First

By all appearances, *House of Cards* is yet another show about a man's political career: Frank Underwood, his life-changing failure to secure the role of secretary of state, and his plan to defeat each one of his enemies and surpass them all, right into the Oval Office. But lurking in the subtext and secondary story lines is his wife, Claire Underwood, who is biding her time.

Some critics accuse the show of having misplaced priorities in its final season—the one in which Claire finally rises to power. "Rather than focus on the endlessly fascinating question of, 'Who is Claire Underwood, really?' its major arc revolves around the far more trivial question of, 'Who killed Frank Underwood?' . . . Even when men are dead and buried, they're still somehow given more narrative weight than the woman actually on screen," Sophia McDougall argues.[16]

But is that really the case? Claire Underwood has been quietly manipulating the who's who of Washington for five seasons—who's to say the writers weren't manipulating the audience as well? After all, Claire's iconic first words to the audience, "My turn," were written and filmed well before real life interrupted production and forced the writers to rethink season 6.

What did Claire mean by those words at the time they were spoken? Showrunner Melissa James Gibson said it wasn't really all that different than what ended up in the series. Claire's bold move of turning to the audience "immediately created something of a threat for the character of Francis, who had always owned that device. So what was set in motion was a battle for the narrative"[17] and the White House. Had Kevin Spacey's fall from grace not occurred, it would have been a battle between Claire and Frank. "Essentially at the end of Season 5 there's a promise Francis makes, that he's going to own the White House by owning Claire," showrunner Frank Pugliese said.[18] And we all know Claire would never let that happen. So essentially, what the forced change did was speed up a patriarchy-smashing time line that was already in place.

The headline of a magazine held up on the show—"A President Buries a President"—accompanies an image of Claire next to Frank's casket; it is symbolic of Claire's struggle as a woman to step completely out of her husband's shadow. In the lingering questions over his death, Frank manages to continue to represent sexism from beyond the grave by demanding equal attention in the press and reminding everyone—the audience included—that he represented the male power structure, in many ways still owns Claire, and isn't going to make it easy for her "to bury him once and for all."[19]

But that isn't as simple as it may seem. "Claire walks into this White House and instantly everyone is trying to manage her and control her," co-showrunner Melissa James Gibson told the *Hollywood Reporter*. "She just wants to wipe the slate clean of anyone who is trying to prevent her from leading"[20] and assert her own authority.

As real-life elections and the commentary on them have shown, many Americans have trouble being comfortable with women in power, especially when those women dare to look them in the eye and tell them what to think, as real politicians do when addressing the people and Claire does when breaking the fourth wall. That direct confrontation and the uncomfortable feeling it evokes in some viewers is a challenge to the patriarchy in and of itself. It is daring the viewer to acknowledge the speaker as a human being with things to say rather than a nuisance to be ignored.

"Just to be clear," Claire says to the viewer, "it's not that I haven't always known you were there. It's that I have mixed feelings about you. I question your intentions. And I'm ambivalent about attention. But don't take it personally. It's how I feel about most everybody" (season 5, episode 11, "Chapter 63"). Her statement is interesting because she could be projecting the audience's most likely opinion of her back on them. With all we've seen over the last five seasons, of course we have mixed feelings about her. As the popular vote of the 2016 presidential election showed, the majority of Americans are ready for our first female president. But is this woman the right one? We know about her lies, her cunning, and her brutality. Is putting up with those qualities worth finally having a woman in the nation's highest office? What's more, what are her reasons for wanting to be there? Will she help the American people or only herself? As for her comment about attention, the audience is far from used to being the subject of attention from characters on TV shows.

But in addressing the audience, she is also making an implied promise to us, one that is different from the one her husband made. He promised to explain the inner goings-on of Washington, to explain to us who was who and what their motivations were; he never promised to tell us the truth—we just assumed he would. Now, here is his wife already being brutally honest with us. Jackie Strause of the *Hollywood Reporter* posits that "Claire is saying, 'Not only am I going to tell you the truth, but I'm going to let you know how vulnerable I am as well. How scared I am sometimes.' And pose questions to the audience and want their help."[21]

As if she needs it. Claire has been rehearsing for this role for years, honing her underhanded skills like a cat sharpens her claws. And she lets the audience in on her schemes, making us coconspirators with her just like she was with Frank. For example, when a photograph surfaces of Claire looking grief stricken in public, her mascara running, tears pouring from red, puffy eyes, everyone immediately jumps to the same conclusion: this kind of hysteria is why women shouldn't be allowed in positions of power. But in reality, Claire confides in the viewer, the whole thing was carefully orchestrated to throw people off what she was really doing: preparing to replace her entire cabinet with women.

The episode opens with her portraying Lysistrata in what appears to be a high school or college production, hinting at a background in acting that Claire clearly drew upon to stage the photo. She explains,

> It's actually not as easy as it looks. See, in order for me to make that face, I have to imagine the perfect combination of things. Here's the recipe: First, I have to think about all the ways in which men have tried to manage me my whole life. Then, I think of America's worst fear when it comes to a female in the Oval Office. And finally, my biggest regret: Francis J. Underwood. (season 6, episode 5, "Chapter 70")

Her grand reveal finally takes place at a cabinet meeting where the members are planning to invoke the Twenty-Fifth Amendment to declare her unfit for office since she has disappeared (presumably in grief) for weeks in what they assume is dereliction of duty. Claire bursts in unannounced, fires everyone, and invites her all-female cabinet to take their places. Before swearing them in she declares, "Our work begins today. I do solemnly swear to take no prisoners" (season 6, episode 5, "Chapter 70").

Orphan Black: My Body, My Choice

In the United States, the issue most publicly linked with feminism is that of women's reproductive rights. While this is most commonly associated with abortion, it encompasses a host of other issues, including contraception, voluntary sterilization, access to necessary health care, the choice whether or not to have children, and a woman's right to say yes or no to potential sexual partners. These issues are literally and metaphorically portrayed in *Orphan Black* through the clones being owned by the company who created them (and thus they legally have no bodily autonomy) and several organizations trying to experiment on them against their will for scientific and religious purposes.

When *Orphan Black* aired, women in the United States still had a relatively large number of rights, and yet the show's message resonated. However, today it is all the more important with abortion being illegal in many states and ancillary rights being examined by the Supreme Court. Writing about *Orphan Black*, television critic Sadie Gennis noted in 2014:

> At a time when issues surrounding women's bodies and reproductive rights are not just debated, but frequently taken out of women's hands—more often than not, by the government or religious fanatics . . . this is an increasingly relevant discussion to be had. . . . Science-fiction has always been reflective of fears currently plaguing society. And by encasing these issues within the trappings of a sci-fi action-thriller, *Orphan Black* exposes its viewers to radically feminist views without scaring anyone away with the "F" word.[22]

The issues of control and autonomy are addressed in a number of ways throughout the series. Willa Paskin writes in an article for *Slate* that *Orphan Black* "is a show about female bodies being used as objects, products, property. All their lives, without their knowledge, these manufactured women have been closely guarded and monitored. Most of them can't procreate. Do the clones have some purpose beyond being human? Are they freaks, or are they the future? Are they, in their very genetic material, being controlled? Does someone 'own' them?"[23] These are all questions the show attempts to answer.

The topic of ownership is covered most thoroughly in seasons 1 and 3. In season 1, as the clones find out what they are, the genetic manipulation that created them stands in as a symbol for the patriarchy. The clones are so owned by Dyad that they all have tag numbers like lab rats or Holocaust prisoners. What's worse, ownership is literally encoded into their DNA to prevent anyone else from profiting off of their bodies. In season 1, episode 10, "Endless Forms Most Beautiful," Cosima and Delphine decode a part of the clones' synthetic gene sequence and reveal a legal-like hidden message: "This organism and derivative genetic material is restricted intellectual property."

What does this have to do with the patriarchy? It is about control, and women have been fighting to rid themselves of the notion that they are owned by men since the 1800s. At that time both England, and its former colonies, the United States, operated under a system of coverture that legally meant that a woman was "covered" by a man for her entire life (unless she became a widow, but that complexity is beyond the scope of this book, partly because most widows quickly remarried). When a woman was born, she was legally the property of her father, and if he died before she was married, that responsibility passed to her closest male relative, usually either her brother or an uncle or cousin. When a woman got married, she legally became her husband's property until death. This had far-reaching effects on a woman's life, affecting everything from who controlled her wages (the man) and who got custody of her children in the case of divorce or mental impairment (the man) to who decided what she was and wasn't allowed to do (the man). This system began to erode when states began passing Married Women's Property acts in 1839 but didn't become illegal in every state until the 1890s,[24] and even then, vestiges of it remained into the 1970s, when women were finally allowed to open lines of credit without their husband's permission, and the 1980s, when spouses were finally allowed to get divorced without the burden of proving fault.[25] With the shadow of coverture still fresh in their genetic and cultural memories, today's women are justifiably afraid of anything that smacks of its return.

"On *Orphan Black*, denial of choice is tantamount to imprisonment,"[26] Joelle Renstrom writes for *Slate*, unintentionally linking autonomy and physical freedom with the many times the clones are kidnapped throughout the series— an apt point even if she didn't mean to make it. This often happens so that someone can take their eggs or experiment on them without their consent to find out how Sarah (and by extension, Kira) and Helena can procreate. Even setting aside the number of times Sarah or Mrs. S kidnaps Kira for her own safety, the list of times kidnapping is used or threatened is staggering:

- Mrs. S takes Sarah in to prevent her being kidnapped by Dyad, who would experiment on her.
- Rachel kidnaps Kira with the intent of experimenting on her.
- To save Kira, Sarah turns herself in to Rachel, who holds her hostage and plans to take one of her ovaries.
- Helena is kidnapped by the Prolethean pastor who removes her eggs and fertilizes them with his own sperm. Once embryos are created, he surgically impregnates Helena and his own daughter with them.
- Alison is nearly kidnapped by a Neolutionist scientist whose motivation is unknown.
- Helena is kidnapped by Project Castor to obtain blood and tissue samples.
- Kira is kidnapped by P. T. Westmoreland for her eggs.

In another choice-related example, Dr. Virginia Coady, who works with the male Castor clones, uses Sarah as an experiment in rendering the few clones who can procreate sterile. She pumps the blood of one of the Castor clones into Sarah's body, hoping that the genetic defect, which is usually sexually transmitted (as proven by Grace miscarrying Helena's implanted embryo because she previously slept with Mark, who is a Castor clone), will render Sarah sterile as it has others.

This story line has clear real-life reflections, as women have been being forcibly sterilized by powerful men for hundreds of years. One only needs to remember Hitler's law of forced sterilization for German women who may have hereditary diseases as well as females of "undesirable" races like Jewish and Romani to see this practice in action.[27] The United States has a shameful past with this practice as well, having done so to southern and eastern European, Black, Native American, Hispanic, and Latinx women just within the last one hundred years. More recently, female inmates at prisons in California and Georgia[28] have undergone forced sterilization as well, showing that the practice is alive and well, especially in places where women have little to no power or freedom.

"Where other sci-fi shows briefly acknowledge the gender politics at play, *Orphan Black* devotes almost all of its narrative energy towards women working through what it means to be independent," writes Caroline Framke. "They're all desperately trying to hold onto their power. As the obstacles mount up around them, each clone gravitates towards different methods."[29] As reflected in the season 3 promotional materials (see chapter 3), Sarah turns to the brute force that kept her alive on the streets; Cosima to her beloved science; Helena to the only thing she's ever known, violence; Alison to an internal courage she didn't know she had; and Rachel to the power in which she has cocooned herself. Each clone approaches threats in her own way, just as women experience third-wave feminism differently; it is that very feminism that gives them the agency to act as they will.

CHAPTER 7

Women and Sex

Fueled by third-wave feminism that encouraged young women to embrace their sexuality, through things like crop tops, low-rise jeans, sexual music from pop artists like Britney Spears and Christina Aguilera, and even a pole-dancing trend, the '90s and early '00s were some of the most sexually free since the Hippie movement of the '60s. This was, naturally, reflected in the shows of the time.

Ignoring or not understanding this dynamic of feminism, critics argued that female heroines were being hypersexualized—which, of course, they perceived as a bad thing. Some blamed it on the need to appeal to a wide audience, as though the only reason men would watch a television show featuring female main characters was if they could lust after them at the same time—which not only is insulting but also does a disservice to all men. Dawn Heinecken, author of *The Warrior Women of Television*, calls this the "'jiggle' phenomenon," which she defines as female characters who "simultaneously appealed to proponents of the women's movement and served as eye candy."[1]

The origin of this phenomenon lies in both the way TV/movies are made and how the male directors (according to *Variety*, women made up only 17 percent of directors on the top 250 grossing movies in 2021)[2] and male audiences view women on-screen. Collectively, this is referred to as "the male gaze." Film theorist Laura Mulvey says that three male gazes are cast upon every female character: (1) that of the camera (and thus the director), "which is often voyeuristic and presents a patriarchal perspective to the viewer"; (2) that of the male main character "that makes the women the object"; and (3) that of the viewer who interprets these two gazes.[3] Because of this, "women are simultaneously looked at and displayed, with their appearance coded for strong visual and erotic impact so that they can be said to connote to-be-looked-at-ness."[4]

Many shows covered in this book were accused of participating in the "jiggle phenomenon" under the male gaze, but *Buffy* and *Charmed* were cited the most.

In both shows, the main characters are costumed in "skimpy" outfits. Critics called out *Buffy* for fighting vampires in "midriff baring, low-cut tops and tight mini-skirts" as well as "high-heels and tight leather pants," the latter of which became her trademark,[5] rather than in workout clothes, which would have given her greater range of motion; armor, which would have afforded her greater protection; or even tennis shoes, which would have given her more stability. *Charmed* attired its witches similarly in tight, revealing clothing.

The meaning behind these sartorial choices is a double-edge sword. On one hand, yes, they likely were meant to entice male viewers. Fans of *Charmed* noticed the lack of clothing became much more pronounced (and ridiculous) after Constance M. Burge left the show after season 3.[6] Krista Vernoff, a writer and producer on the show left in season 6 because the outfits became more important than the show itself. "I signed on because *Charmed* was a girl-power show," she said to the *Hollywood Reporter*, "and about halfway through [the season] there was an episode where Alyssa Milano comes out in mermaid pasties and there was a huge spike in male viewership. And then every episode after, the question would come from the network, 'How are we getting the girls naked this week?'"[7] This was usually done, she claimed, by writing some sort of supernatural transformation into the script that called for a tiny costume, like a nymph or a goddess.

While these outlandish outfits likely *were* meant to entice male viewers, the characters' normal clothing was also the fashion of the time, something that often gets overlooked in the heat of the sexualization argument. "*Charmed* [was] a contemporary feminist text," writes scholar Rebecca Feasey. "After all, the Halliwell sisters are not only desirable but actively desiring, a position which, we are told, is informed by feminism,"[8] especially that of the third wave, which was incredibly sex-positive.

Similarly, Buffy was a very feminine character who cared about fashion. She generally went on patrol right after school, and what the Charmed Ones wore to vanquish demons was generally whatever they were wearing at the time, whether they were at work, at home, or on a date. These were the same types of clothing their female fans wore daily and might have even been wearing as they watched the show. In fact, Shannen Doherty openly discussed going on "shopping sprees" with costume designer Eilish for her character, Prue,[9] and Rose McGowan used most of her own clothes in season 4 for Paige. In April 2021, shortly after the profile in which Vernoff made her comment about the characters' clothing was published, Holly Marie Combs, who played Piper, tweeted, "We all chose our outfits or lack thereof. 100%. The WB nor [*sic*] our producers ever controlled us or our choices after season 1."[10] Alyssa Milano, who played Phoebe, replied, "I think we gave permission to a generation of women to be themselves and to be strong and own their sexuality. I'm so proud of what this show meant to so many."[11]

Milano touches on another perspective that is often ignored: women of that generation and ones after *want* to look and feel sexy. "Perception of women's sexuality and femininity has changed—and is continuing to change," Brost writes. "For many women, 'femininity' is not opposed to feminism, but is positioned as central to a politics of agency, confidence, and resistance."[12]

Sexpionage: Sex in the Spy Game

Sex and spying go hand in hand in the real world just like they do on the screen. James Bond levels may be a stretch, but there is an actual term for spies who use sex to get what they want, be it information, distraction, or something else: "sexpionage." (Seriously. It even has its own Wikipedia page.) Female spies who used this technique were called "sparrows" or "swallows," and males were called "ravens."[13] Sexpionage was especially popular in Russia but was practiced the world over, even in the United States.

The most blatant modern television example is Carrie Mathison of *Homeland*. In the very first episode she turns on the seduction for her mentor, Saul— with whom she otherwise has a rather paternal mentor-mentee relationship— just because she wants something. Later, she shows absolutely no qualms about having sex with Brody, whom she barely knows and suspects is a POW-turned-terrorist, just to get information. And that isn't the last time she resorts to such tactics. Carrie is intelligent and is arguably the best at her job, but that doesn't stop her from using the oldest trick in the book to get ahead.

Interestingly, when Carrie and Brody have their first encounter (and many thereafter):

> Carrie is not overtly sexualised or presented as a sex symbol whose behaviour is controlled by Brody. Carrie's own physical, emotional and sexual needs are presented as being of equal, if not more importance to those of Brody's. This is a welcome change to the sexualisation of women in television, where female characters are often portrayed only in relation to male protagonists, either as fulfillers or frustrators of male desire.[14]

It is women like Carrie that Kane on *Alias* has in mind when he says to Jack Bristow, "more secrets have been revealed through pillow talk than through torture. If there's a prostitute or a stewardess out there you think may have heard you talking in your sleep, I need to know about it" (season 2, episode 10, "The Abduction"). While we may never know how effective this technique is in real

life, on film at least, female spies who use sex and sexuality are extremely successful because "she can go where no (straight) man can go—into the company of
a man's bedroom. Her treachery is exquisitely personal, and thus devastatingly
effective."[15] Indeed, this is the role Jack's wife, Irina, likely played as she "is far
more overtly sexual and independent than their daughter. She frightens because
she is dangerously free. . . . She holds no alliances or obligations; she feels free to
aid or betray her family, the KGB and others with equal élan."[16]

While Sydney may not be as promiscuous as her mother, her disguises are
often quite sexy, especially compared to the sweatpants and business suits she
wears during her day-to-day life. The most talked about disguise was her 2002
post-Superbowl episode get-up, which was undoubtedly created to lure in male
viewers after the big game. "Cradling a whip and donning black, then red, linge-
rie sets for the pleasure of a drooling mark, [she] rather quickly . . . uses the whip
to disarm both the man and the audience of its voyeuristic pleasures, muttering
about the indignity of it all,"[17] like a good feminist.

However, just because depictions like this draw the male gaze, that doesn't
mean women don't like them as well. To say so ignores the gazes of bisexual
and lesbian women, for one. It also overlooks that some female viewers see
these kinds of women as powerful, as using their sexuality to their advantage,
rather than being exploited by it. Brost notes, "Young women who enjoy such
. . . characters as . . . Sydney Bristow—have different ideas of what it means
to be feminist than previous generations did; they still are interested in watching, listening to, and reading about women that they consider to be strong and
independent,"[18] they just happen to like sexy women as well.

According to scholar Sabrina Calandrón, the women of *Nikita* are similarly
sexualized but in different ways. For them, the visual is not to be found as much
in their clothing (though they do have some truly stunning dresses) as it is in
their interaction with their weaponry. "Images abound in which the protagonist
caresses, brushes gently and brings firearms close to her mouth," she notes. Also,
unlike other spies, Nikita and Alex don't consider their seduction as anything
more than part of their job. "The stake of seduction is not mixed with the sexual
morality of the characters, but contributes to the constitution of their professional morality . . . the administration of seduction games is part of the technical
tools and the most effective use of these resources,"[19] in many ways not much
different than the guns they so lovingly handle.

In opposition to these sensual portraits drawn by the male gaze is Jessica
Jones, who is a direct product of the female gaze. Jessica is a very sexual woman,
but the sex we see her having with Luke Cage—which might be the first time
two superheroes were ever depicted having sex on-screen[20]—is very real, not
romanticized as Hollywood is wont to do. Jessica is shown "like a messy person
in an ordinary body, not someone who is a piece of meat served on a platter,"[21]

Amanda Marcotte observes. Instead of lying submissively in missionary position, she is on top and clearly enjoying herself. This isn't the sex of love, but that of carnal lust, "something which filmmakers and TV production companies often forget women are capable of."[22]

Sex in *Buffy the Vampire Slayer*: Purity Culture Veiled in Myth

In the 1990s, purity culture was all the rage among young Christians. Groups like True Love Waits and Silver Ring Thing promoted abstinence until marriage, especially for girls. Teens would sign "purity pledges" and wear "purity rings" signaling their intention to wait to have sex until their wedding night. In some groups, this meant no kissing or even hand holding before marriage. Some churches would hold formal ceremonies that girls would attend dressed in gowns or wedding dresses and pledge their virginity to their fathers until they gave it to their husbands.[23]

While boys could and did sign the pledge, no such ceremony existed for them because the onus in purity culture—a highly patriarchal system—was on the woman. She was tasked with not only safeguarding her own virginity, but ensuring her boyfriend remained pure as well. This meant dressing modestly and not doing anything that might tempt him to sin. Girls were taught that every time they did something with a boy (especially sexual intercourse) they lost a part of themselves and wouldn't have anything left to give to their husbands. Girls who had sex were compared to a chewed piece of gum or used tissue—something soiled that no one would want to touch, much less marry. This might sound crazy and unhealthy—and it was—but it was popular. A 1994 True Love Waits rally in Washington, DC, drew 25,000 young people, and 210,000 purity pledge cards from around the country were displayed.[24] It is estimated that three million teens signed purity pledges in the United States alone.[25]

It is surprising that something based in religion would make its way onto televisions, albeit mixed with the myth of the show, but it did—in a very insidious and harmful way. "Our favourite witchy 90s shows (especially *Buffy*) roundhouse kicked gender stereotypes, gave us young, powerful female role models, and explored topics which were still taboo at the time, such as teens exploring their sexuality,"[26] wrote Sarah Assenti for *Stylist*, but on *Buffy*, sex always has negative consequences.

Throughout the seven seasons of the show, Buffy only has sex twice, both of which are disastrous. The most famous is when Buffy loses her virginity to Angel, a story line that takes place over season 2's episodes 13 ("Surprise") and

14 ("Innocence"). The mythology around this momentous event is that while most vampires lack souls, Angel was cursed to keep his. The only way for him to lose it—and thus become a dangerous vampire instead of one with a conscience—is to experience a moment of "true happiness." He loves Buffy so much that he experiences that after having sex with her. In a split second he turns evil, going "from being Buffy's main squeeze to that season's Big Bad."[27] He goes on a murderous rampage, and Buffy is forced to make an impossible choice—listen to her feelings for him and let this evil walk the earth or break her own heart by killing him and sending him to hell.

This story line was obviously controversial. When interviewed about it, showrunner Joss Whedon said it was meant to symbolize the common occurrence of men who were previously charming, even kind, suddenly becoming assholes after they have sex with a woman because they've gotten what they wanted.[28] Some have argued this story line also represents the biggest fear of many teenage girls, who could end up pregnant. Most of the time, the man leaves with no repercussions, while the woman is shamed and has to deal with the situation alone.[29] But it also sent a very different message: "female sexuality is dangerous, male sexuality is empowering,"[30] and sex is bad—the very same doctrine being preached by purity culture.

If this had been a one-time occurrence, it could be said that some viewers were reading their own experiences or what they had been taught into the show. But it happened again. In season 4, episode 18, "Where the Wild Things Are," Buffy and her boyfriend, Riley, have a night of hot sex at a fraternity party. Common enough, right? Not in this world. The lovers are unaware that they have woken a dangerous spirit that feeds off of and gains strength from their sexual energy, putting everyone at the party in danger. By tying the spirit to sex, the show makes clear that it wouldn't have woken if Buffy and Riley had kept their hands off one another, not so subtly implying that sex is evil.[31]

It wasn't just Buffy who suffered the consequences of having sex outside of marriage, either. *Buffy* made history with its extremely tolerant depiction of a lesbian relationship between Willow and Tara. It is never explicitly stated that the two are having sex, but the magic the two perform together throughout the sixth season is shown as orgasmic, an artful way to depict what couldn't yet be shown on television—lesbian sex. Both Joss Whedon and Amber Benson, who played Tara, were very clear that they were limited by the network as to what sexual content they could include, so they had to find a way to imply it instead.[32] When Tara was shockingly killed in season 6, episode 19, "Seeing Red," the show joined the "long (and continuing) history of queer women being slaughtered onscreen."[33] If that wasn't bad enough, grief and an overwhelming desire for revenge turns Willow—previously a sweet, unassuming girl—into Dark

In *Buffy the Vampire Slayer*, Willow (Alyson Hannigan, right) and Tara (Amber Benson) broke many taboos by portraying one of the first lesbian relationships on television. *UPN/Photofest*

Willow, a power-crazed witch who became not only a serial killer but also that season's "Big Bad," just like Angel did when he lost his soul and became Angelus.

Collectively, what do these three examples say to viewers? F. R. Kesby, writing for Women's Republic summarizes:

> Sex is bad. Sex brings the pain. It says that if you have sex with him he will leave you. The sex that both Buffy and Angel choose to have is cast in the light of a bad thing Buffy did that she must now deal with. At no point in her guilt about her actions—that are referenced as her choice alone—does anyone sit her down and tell her that it is not her fault. . . . The fact that sex is so demonised in the media prevents young people asking questions they need to be able to have [sex] to [*sic*] safely. Many states in America still teach abstinence-only sex-ed so media is teenagers' main source of information about sex. Telling young girls that having sex will ruin their life is hardly constructive.[34]

Even as women were fighting for greater sexual autonomy and an end to "slut shaming" and other practices that made women feel bad about sex, one of the most popular shows on television among young women was telling them the exact opposite. Given that these episodes were written and/or directed by men, they are clear examples of patriarchy in action.

House of Cards: "Beyond Marriage"

Extramarital affairs are part of the bargain in the Underwood house. Just like every other aspect of their relationship, their sex lives have been negotiated and agreed upon. Because as Frank says, quoting Oscar Wilde, "Everything is about sex. Except sex. Sex is about power" (season 1, episode 9, "Chapter 9"), it has to be handled like any other business matter. They have taken series creator Beau Willimon's personal philosophy so much to heart it's easy to imagine Frank repeating Beau's words to Claire:

> I think that love, even the purest love, is also about power and trans-actional. I don't look at "power" as a bad word, and I don't look at "transactional" as a bad word. Even the phrase "unconditional love" is almost the terminology of contract law. It's saying I am making a bargain with you to make myself completely vulnerable and open, to always be there for you. And I expect that in return. That is transactional.[35]

It is very unusual to see a purposefully nonmonogamous relationship portrayed on television. "Claire and Frank have a high functioning negotiated open/ polyamorous relationship in the form of threesomes together and sex outside of the relationship allowing them both to get their sexual needs met by others, in a way that is not seen to detract from the strength of their marriage," writes clinical psychologist Dr. Karen Gurney.[36]

If Claire and Frank do have sex, they don't derive much pleasure from one another; that is what their affairs are for. Claire's lover, speech writer Tom Yates, lives with them. Frank finds solace in the arms of his former personal trainer, Eric Rawlings.

Following one of their rules of marriage—brutal honesty (see chapter 5), Frank says to Claire about her relationship with Tom, "He can give you things that I can't. . . . But one person—one person cannot give everything to another person. . . . I don't see you the way he sees you. It's not my permission to give, but you'll do what's right for you. . . . And I'll be fine. I mean, if we're gonna go beyond marriage, let's go beyond it" (season 4, episode 11, "Chapter 50").

CHAPTER 8

Diversity's Many Forms

People of color have been on television in major roles since the 1970s,[1] but diversity in the shows we watched wasn't something that most white people or network executives thought much about until the late 1990s. In 1999, the NAACP vilified the four major broadcast networks (there was no streaming at that time) for not including BIPOC (Black, Indigenous, and People of Color) actors in leading or major roles in any of the twenty-six new shows that debuted that fall. As a result, they pledged to do better. (Diversity, of course, isn't just about race. It also includes class, gender, religion, disabilities—including mental health issues—sexuality, and more.) "Officials for all four networks insisted they were concerned and sensitive to the issue of diversity. ABC and NBC acknowledged they 'need to do more,'"[2] but meaningful progress has been slow in coming.

In 2022, the annual Hollywood Diversity Report published by UCLA's Entertainment and Media Research Initiative showed that BIPOC people and women on screen increased over the past year, but on broadcast television these numbers are still far below keeping up with changes in the U.S. population. For example, only 27.4 percent of leading roles in 2022 went to BIPOC actors, yet BIPOC people make up 42.7 percent of the U.S. population. Women had achieved parity with men during the 2011–2013 seasons on network TV but have fallen behind since then; women currently hold 44.3 percent of leading roles.[3] However, on cable and streaming services, they were represented proportionately to the overall population,[4] indicating that these new(er) forms of television are more in tune with public concern for diversity issues.

The report also included signs that could point to an upcoming decline in gender and racial diversity. "The next few years may be a true test of whether Hollywood is truly committed to the changes they promised during the nation's reckoning on race following the murder of George Floyd," said Ana-Christina Ramón, coauthor of the report.[5]

How do the shows in this book stack up? Let's take a look.

The United States Is a Melting Pot, but TV Is "So White"

Eight of the ten shows included in the scope of this book are "blindingly white," to quote Angelica Bastién, even when their characters live in some of the most diverse places in the country: Southern California (*Buffy*), San Francisco (*Charmed*), Los Angeles (*Alias* and *Agent Carter*), New Jersey (*Nikita*), New York City (*Jessica Jones*, *Agent Carter*, and *The Equalizer*), and Washington, DC (*Homeland* and *House of Cards*). Four of these are in the top 20 most diverse cities in the United States.[6] *Orphan Black* takes place in Toronto, Ontario, which is Canada's most diverse city and has been called the world's most diverse city by both the United Nations and the British Broadcasting Corporation (BBC).[7]

Buffy the Vampire Slayer's entire main cast was white. One notable exception was Kendra Young, the Black Slayer called when Buffy temporarily died at the end of season 1. Unfortunately, she was killed off after only three episodes, a common fate of BIPOC characters on the show.[8]

Similarly, *Charmed* was overwhelmingly white, but it did have a Black main character in Lieutenant Darryl Morris who was on the show for seven out of eight of its seasons. Inspector Rodriguez, a demon posing as an SFPD internal affairs agent, was played by actor Carlos Gómez, who is of Cuban American heritage. His character was part of a major plot arc throughout season 2.

Even overtly feminist *Jessica Jones* was extremely Caucasian. The main cast is all white, with the exception of Luke Cage, who is only around for one season. Jessica shows shades of intolerance, too. She uses phrases that separate herself from BIPOC characters, like when she says "you people" to Black women and "call[s] Latino men bigots for being suspicious of a super-powered person. . . . That is levels of tone-deaf that we don't need," asserts Princess Weekes for the *Mary Sue*.[9] Then there is her problematic statement to Malcom when he asks her how she knew he was an ex-con: "People don't usually panic at the sight of cops unless they've ridden in the back of the cruiser."[10] This is a particularly harsh thing to say when BIPOC people are regularly falsely profiled, interrogated, and arrested by law enforcement.

For a show that ran concurrently with the beginning of the fourth wave of feminism, its characters of color are extremely underrepresented and poorly written. "The New York City of *Jessica Jones* is weirdly empty of women of color, at least ones who aren't stereotypes. And those who *are* introduced in more detail are often the victims of cursory, offhand violence," Marykate Jasper points out in an article for the *Mary Sue*.[11] Hannah Collins notes, "It's not that women of color are *horribly* represented on the show as much as we barely see enough notable ones to even properly judge how well they're depicted at all."[12]

Perhaps the best example is Reva Connors, the wife of Luke Cage. She was murdered by Jessica at Kilgrave's command while Jessica was under his control. Then there is Sonia, the ex-wife of Jessica's lover, Oscar, who is a stereotypical Latinx woman, high heels, big hair, loud clothing and all; she's "a one-note, angry mother who Jessica has to rescue her own son from *and* calm down—not the *best* way to avoid stereotyping your sole female Latinx character."[13] The other two Black women are a prison guard and a detective, who, although likeable, were never fleshed out into actual characters.

Cellist Kith Lyonne, Jeri's lover in season 3, was one of only two exceptions, and certainly the only one with a major story line. Played by Sarita Choudhury, who is of English and Indian descent, she was featured in ten episodes before she finally left Jeri. The other is Gillian, Jessica's assistant in season 3, who is South Asian. Gillian appeared in eight episodes, but her part is minor compared to Kith's.

As for the men of the show, Jessica's first-season love interest, Luke Cage, who is Black, is one of two BIPOC male characters who were written without stereotype. Black police chief Brett Mahoney is the other. The other men don't fare as well. Jessica's neighbor, Malcolm Ducasse, was a drug addict who couldn't hold down a job, an all-too-familiar Black stereotype. Even when he got sober and became a professional, he was corrupt. Jessica's second-season building superintendent turned on-again, off-again lover, Latinx Oscar Arocho, is a former felon who makes illegal green cards and cheated on his wife. Pryce Cheng is a calculating professional enemy of Jessica's, and he is also corrupt.

Showrunner Melissa Rosenberg accepted blame for this situation, saying she agreed with critics that characters of color were not handled well, especially the women. She told *Vanity Fair*,

> There aren't enough women of color in meaningful roles. I absolutely agree with them. My focus has always been women, and I think I need to continue to focus on that—but include more women of color, people of color. Eka Darville, who plays Malcolm, has sort of been carrying the flag for us. I think it just sort of happened that our three female leads were all white, and when we were designing the show, it just didn't occur to me.[14]

Jessica Jones' Marvel foremother (or is it fore-grandmother?), *Agent Carter*, also had a very Caucasian cast, especially in season 1. Perhaps that's not as surprising since it takes place in the 1940s, but still. To remedy that, the writers gave Peggy a BIPOC love interest in Dr. Wilkes in season 2. Had that happened in real life in that time period, people would have lost their minds. Even in an open-minded city like Los Angeles, we were still twenty years from the civil rights movement and all the work it took for Black people to finally (officially at least) achieve equal rights.

Showrunners Michele Fazekas and Tara Butters acknowledged this. "When we introduce a character who is African-American, we didn't want to do it and just pretend there's no racism in 1947 and everything's pretty. We wanted to be careful about addressing that and addressing this interracial relationship. . . . He's used to people looking at him and making judgments about him based on what he looks like. And so is Peggy. They connect on that level."[15]

Even *Orphan Black*, a relatively new show compared to *Buffy* and *Charmed*, is pretty white. The clones, while being from many different countries, are still white and of European descent.[16] The only BIPOC main character is Detective Art Bell, Beth's former boss and reluctant member of the Clone Club, who is Black. Minor characters who are BIPOC are Sarah's ex-boyfriend Vic, who is played by Michael Mando, an actor of Latinx heritage; coroner Janis Beckwith, who is Asian; and Carlton (Mrs. S's love interest) and one of Alison's adopted children, both of whom are Black.

It is thought provoking that a show that has so few characters of color—far too often the "others" of the real world—would eventually "other" one of its clones. Rachel losing an eye to Sarah's pencil-gun in season 2, episode 10, "By Means Which Have Never Yet Been Tried," is as close as the show—or any of the shows discussed in this book—comes to portraying a main character with a visible disability. But rather than feel pity for her, the audience feels only justice, thanks to Rachel's past misdeeds.

Rather than go through life with only one eye or with a glass replica, in this world of clones, Rachel is, of course, fitted with a bionic eye. As season 3 progresses, she comes to realize that not only does her new eye save her sight, but it allows someone (later identified as scientific mastermind P. T. Westmoreland) to spy on the clone. When Rachel is sure this is the case, she follows the biblical instructions given by Jesus in Matthew 5:29: "If your right eye causes you to sin, gouge it out and throw it away."[17] In so doing, Rachel is not only getting rid of the physical problem of an interloper seeing through her eyes but also the metaphorical one of her own hatred—which extends to the audience through her.

"With that eye, we were trying to examine how we internalize, for example, classism or racism," writes Devon Maloney for *Vanity Fair*. "We look at the world through how we've internalized them, until the moment we have to pluck out our own eye—'Holy shit. I've held these views and have been perpetuating these particular kinds of views of the world and what I think I deserve from it.' So the eye itself is a metaphor."[18]

If the executives, casting directors, and writers of *Orphan Black* had held that eye up to their own creation (the show) perhaps they would have seen they could have gone further in the racial diversity of their characters. Then again, no one is perfect; if they were, that Bible verse wouldn't have needed to be written.

* * *

The first exception to the unwritten all-white cast rule of the 1990s was *Nikita*. Starring Maggie Q, an actress of Vietnamese descent, *Nikita* was "the highest-profile series role for an Asian actress on a broadcast drama series and the highest-profile CW minority casting in the network's four-year history"[19] as of the show's debut in 2010. In addition, the creative team was diverse; its writing team included women and/or people of color such as Amanda Segel, Kalinda Vazquez, Kristen Reidel, and Albert Kim.[20]

The most recent—and strongest—entry in the diversity category is 2021's *The Equalizer*. Its star, Queen Latifah, is "only the fifth black woman in the history of the medium [of television] to lead an hourlong drama on NBC, CBS, ABC or Fox, following in the footsteps of *Get Christie Love!* star Teresa Graves, *Scandal* lead Kerry Washington and Viola Davis on *How to Get Away with Murder*, and Simone Missick on *All Rise*."[21]

Also in the cast are Robyn's (Queen Latifah's character) Aunt Vi, daughter Delilah, the police chief—all of whom are Black—and her sidekick Melody "Mel" Bayani, who is Asian. The only two white main characters are Mel's husband, hacker Harry Keshegian, and Robyn's former CIA director, William Bishop.

In addition, the show openly confronts issues of race. In season 2, episode 5, "Followers," Aunt Vi is shopping with Delilah in an upscale thrift store when a white woman confronts her about a dress the girl is holding that she wants. Vi is so shocked by this "Karen" that she can't speak, and young Delilah has no idea what to do. The white woman physically fights them for the dress, then calls the police when she fails to secure it. One would think this would be an open-and-shut case in the Black women's favor, but the police demand that Aunt Vi apologize to the "Karen" or they will arrest her. Vi refuses, so the cop starts to cuff her. Delilah then reveals she recorded the whole incident on her phone. She plays the video for the police, who then know the truth; it is now the Karen's turn to apologize.

But things don't end there. Aunt Vi points out to the police that she was assaulted so she is entitled to press charges. The cops sober at the idea that she might take the situation further. "Aunt Vi tells them that she will not press charges because her relationship with policing is not the same as that of the white woman. The police are not a weapon to her," writes Charles Mudede for *The*

Stranger. "Wokeness [is] not so much an idea or program but a mode of survival. Wokeness is about staying alive."[22]

He goes on to note that when Aunt Vi realizes that her life and Delilah's are in danger because of the police presence, "she needs to make a very tough decision: Her dignity or her life. What is of more value at that moment? . . . This is not a situation a black person can sleep on."[23] Is it worth not backing down to teach her niece a lesson of Black strength? No, she decides this situation isn't worth it. White people may have the privilege of fighting one another without consequence, but that is not the case when it is the word of a Black woman against a white woman, even in 2022. And Vi is tired of fighting; she just wants to go home safely with her niece.

That night, Robyn and her daughter have a conversation about what happened that day. This is "probably the first Black parent-child conversation about racism" to appear on a CBS drama. "The Black Lives Matter placard that is shown when the show ends but before the credits is "most definitely the first . . . to appear on a CBS drama."[24] This signals a sure sign of change and progress for a network that back in 1999 didn't have a single Black character in its lineup.

HOMELAND SLAMMED FOR PORTRAYAL OF RACE AND RELIGION

Homeland was heavily criticized for its treatment of Muslims and people from the Middle East throughout its first five seasons. The depiction was so bad that Laura Durkay of the *Washington Post* dubbed it "the most bigoted show on television" and wrote that "since its first episode, *Homeland* . . . has churned out Islamophobic stereotypes as if its writers were getting paid by the cliché."[25] What's more, Pakistani officials were upset that the show defamed a country that is a close ally of the United States.[26]

But the most public flogging came in 2015, when the show hired Arab graffiti artists to add a touch of "realism" to one of their refugee camp sets, supposedly located on the border of Syria and Lebanon. Set designers asked them to make sure whatever they wrote wasn't political but gave them no other instruction. What the artists wrote was الوطن عنصري (*al-watan 'unsuri*), which translates to "*Homeland* is racist."[27] The phrases "*Homeland* is not a series," "There is no *Homeland*," and "*Homeland* is a watermelon"—which translates into the way people say something "is a sham" in Arabic—were written on other walls.[28] The words made it to broadcast, apparently without question, only coming to executives' notice because viewers translated them.[29] Representatives of the show said that because "set decoration had to be completed in two days, the set's designers were 'too frantic to pay any attention' to what the artists were doing."[30] In addition to being a public relations nightmare, this incident fueled criticism against the show.

This repeated attitude is problematic for many reasons, not only because it reinforces fear-based stereotypes of Muslims (which were in decline on television prior to the show's run[31]) but also because it promotes racism and intolerance of innocent people who are just trying to live their lives. Most Americans don't understand that, as *The Guardian* notes, "Palestinians, Iraqis, Saudis all share an agenda regardless of background, culture and history."[32] Instead, they believe what they see on television, which depicts these people as often planning against one another or the United States, sometimes with violence, and always with hatred. The *Washington Post* also points out that, on *Homeland*, people from these countries can only be "terrorists or willing collaborators with U.S. intelligence forces."[33] We don't see any in-depth portrayals of ordinary people, who are usually good, just living their lives. As Heba Amin, one of the graffiti artists on the show, said, shows like *Homeland* endanger real people. "Filled with stereotypes and inaccuracies, *Homeland* poses a threat by not only fueling racism and manipulating perspectives on a mass scale, but further plays a role in American foreign policy and the ways in which politics are conducted in our region," he said.[34]

What caused this situation was not one bad portrayal, but a series of them that hinted at a deeper misunderstanding, or possibly intolerance, of the Middle East and its people. There are hundreds of examples, but one that the *Washington Post* points out is that in season 2, the show completely mischaracterizes the nature of Hamra Street in Beirut. In reality it is a "posh . . . cosmopolitan, expat-filled area near the American University, where Western chains like Starbucks and Gloria Jean's compete for customers and no one would look twice at a blonde, blue-eyed white woman [like Carrie Mathison] with uncovered hair." What the show portrayed was a dirty, crime-ridden area where Carrie was constantly under watchful, disapproving eyes and had to cover her hair and face to avoid being identified as a Westerner.[35]

Another example of implied intolerance can be found in some of the advertising for *Homeland*. In one widely used image for seasons 4 and 5, Claire Danes (Carrie) is dressed in a red headscarf and is glaring suspiciously at the sea of faceless women in black burqas surrounding her. There are many things troubling here. First, not all women in all Middle Eastern countries wear the burqa, which is a common misconception. Second, cladding Carrie in red while everyone around her is in black sends a message of "us vs. them" and paints Carrie as the hero—giving off a "Little Red Riding Hood surrounded by wolves" vibe. Finally, and perhaps most important, the women being faceless dehumanizes them as well as gives a sense that they are something to be feared, which is amplified by the shocked/frightened look on Carrie's face.

This promotional art for season 4 of *Homeland* was seen by some as further evidence of the show's bigotry toward people from the Middle East.
Showtime/Photofest

Reaction to the show's portrayal of Islam has been mixed. On one hand, Durkay writes that the "audience begins to discover that Brody is a terrorist at the same time that Brody's religious conversion to Islam comes to light. *Homeland* links [Brody's] transformation from US Marine to terrorist with his change in religions from Christianity to Islam . . . [and] characterizes Islam as 'sinister and suspicious': Brody secretly prays in his garage to foreboding music."[36] The secrecy of Brody's prayer, however, is explained on the show by Brody's fear that his wife and kids won't be able to handle it—which later proves true. On the other hand, Brian T. Edwards argues that *Homeland* "brings depth to the portrayal of Islam by showing both the comfort that religion brings to Brody and highlighting the prejudiced nature of American thought toward Islam"[37] when people find out he converted.

By season 6, the producers, writers, and directors appear to have begun listening to the negative feedback they were getting. In 2017, they hired Ramzi Kassem, an outspoken critic of the show and director of a legal clinic at City University of New York (CUNY), to advise the show in a role that the *New York Times* quipped was *Homeland*'s "paid conscience consultant."[38] Not coincidently, Carrie began working at the same legal clinic that Kassem directs in real life. They even based the character of Reda Hashem on him. *Homeland* may have learned from its mistakes, but it took far too long for it to do so. In the eyes of many fans—especially Muslims and those of Middle Eastern heritage—it was too little, too late.

Unseen Disability: Mental Illness in *Homeland*

People with disabilities are not often portrayed on television, except for an occasional person with Down syndrome or who uses a crutch or a wheelchair because those are easy to understand through the highly sight-dependent medium of television. But even then, in our ableist society, those characters rarely last more than a few episodes.

Because of this, many Americans don't know that mental illness is also considered a disability and is, therefore, part of the depiction of diversity. Both the Americans with Disabilities Act and the Social Security Administration classify bipolar disorder as a disability[39]—that is, "a physical or mental impairment that substantially limits one or more major life activity."[40] While Carrie Mathison is fairly stable while on her medication, as the show illustrates multiple times, without it she would be unable to function normally.

It is no secret that mental health care in the United States is at best abysmal and, at worst, totally absent. We're getting better at talking about mental illnesses like anxiety, depression, and attention deficit hyperactivity disorder

(ADHD), but less common illnesses like bipolar disorder, which affects an estimated 2.8 percent of the adult female population,[41] are far less likely to be openly discussed or portrayed accurately in film or television. "Generally, the mentally ill are portrayed as inherently dangerous, violent and unpredictable or disabled and incompetent in all forms of the media. . . . People living with bipolar are more frequently depicted as violent," writes Dr. Meron Wondemaghen of the University of Hull in Bristol, England.[42]

This is why a show like *Homeland* is so important. It was "one of the first TV shows to feature a female protagonist living with bipolar disorder—and one many say isn't wholly defined by her illness."[43] It received praise and awards from mental health organizations, the media, and fans who also suffered from bipolar disorder for its realistic portrayal of the disease.[44] In fact, bipolar viewers were concerned early in the series that Claire Danes, who played Carrie, actually "had the disorder herself, such was the authenticity of her performance."[45] Journalist Hannah Jane Parkinson, who has bipolar disorder, wrote in *The Guardian* that she found Danes's performance "accurate and refreshing" and "that the lead protagonist of one of the most popular global television shows—watched by the president of the United States, no less—is intelligent, charming, attractive and just happens to have a serious mental illness is nothing short of a triumph."[46]

Carrie (Claire Danes) purposefully went off her bipolar medication to help with a case because she thought she could think more clearly, which is a myth and very dangerous. *Showtime Networks/Photofest*

The reviews for this story line weren't all glowing, however. Many people, including some bipolar fans, expressed concern that Carrie's willingness to stop taking her medication—which is "a common occurrence in those with the illness"[47]—and use the mania that induces to help her think through problems in her job "dance[s] too closely to the implication that Carrie is such a good spy *because* of her bipolar disorder."[48] They voiced opinions that, in this regard, her mental illness is treated almost like a "superpower" and, "essentially, that those with bipolar and other mental illnesses have a super sense or a heightened genius that—in the case of bipolar—is only at its maximum acuity off medication."[49] This could lead others with the disease to believe they don't need treatment or that they, too, would function better or have more clarity of thought without their medication, which is not only false but also very dangerous.

In addition, once her coworkers at the CIA learn of her illness, it becomes the scapegoat for Carrie's incessant flouting of the rules, lack of impulse control, irresponsibility, and other qualities that often get her in trouble.[50] This, too, is dangerous, because "Carrie's talents and shortcomings have become inseparable in people's minds from the disorder with which she's struggled," writes Nolan Feeney for *The Atlantic*.[51] Rather than seeing Carrie as a woman who is all of those things *and* bipolar, and must face the consequences of her actions like anyone else, the show can fall into a trap of excusing her behavior *because* she is bipolar.

A third opinion is voiced by the National Alliance on Mental Illness, which wrote that in putting Carrie's mental illness in opposition with her career at the CIA, the show "reveals the stigma surrounding mental illness in a job that requires a cool head and a sharp mind—her validity instantly goes out the window. . . . What's crucial about this television series is its realistic portrayal of mental illness as well as real life—how in a matter of days mental illness can turn a life upside down, how peers, loved ones and coworkers can turn on you."[52]

These possible missteps are, however, forgiven in many critics' minds because of the otherwise balanced portrayal of bipolar disorder. Carrie's illness is "not the only storyline she has," notes Dr. Rebecca Beirne of the University of Newcastle in England.[53] And when her illness does act up, both sides of it are shown—"the lack of risk inhibition, the elusiveness of sleep, promiscuity, alienation of friends and family, [and excessive] drinking" of mania, as well as the crushing depression, lack of energy, and insomnia that come after.[54]

The use of electroconvulsive therapy as treatment in Carrie's case was roundly dismissed by critics and bipolar viewers as "quite far-fetched, given that it's often a last resort." Most viewers thought it was likely used for its dramatic visuals and shock value (no pun intended). However, Parkinson notes that "it is extremely effective, and it is still used in bipolar."[55]

Screenwriter Alex Gansa explained the reasoning behind that choice: "Carrie has reached the point . . . where she just can't take the secrecy anymore, can't take the bouts of depression anymore, can't take her thoughts of suicide, can't take how she's certainly negatively affected people's lives around her. She has to wrest control of her life back and decides to do this thing, which also has a certain stigma attached to it, and she voices those concerns."[56]

Another aspect of the story line praised by critics and those who have experienced the illness was the handling of Carrie's recuperation at home with her father and sister after her breakdown. "Anybody who has had to deal with the struggle of a path back to mental health will recognise this stage. . . . The writers could have taken the excuse of a season break to not screen this mundane part of her rehabilitation, but they didn't. It was a decision as responsible as showing the effects of suddenly stopping medication," Parkinson writes.[57]

CREATING AN ACCURATE DEPICTION

Creating Carrie Mathison was a very deliberate action by both the writers and Claire Danes. Everyone involved did extensive research to ensure accuracy. Meredith Stiehm, who wrote many of the episodes dealing with Carrie's bipolar disorder, didn't have to look far from home for hers; her sister, journalist Jamie Stiehm, suffers from the disease.[58] Gansa told the Daily Beast that the writers used *An Unquiet Mind*, a book by mood disorders expert Dr. Kay Redfield Jamison—who has the disease as well—as "their bipolar-illness bible. Kay Jamison is a mental health professional with a mental illness. There was a real parallel, we felt, between a woman in the CIA who had to keep her illness a secret and Kay Jamison, who had to keep her illness a secret from the people that she was practising with because there was this stigma involved."[59]

Danes and the writers understood that what they were doing had never been done before and had the potential to change lives. She told the *Sunday Telegraph*, "Playing someone with bipolar and taking the mystery out of that is a responsibility I don't take lightly. I didn't want to play crazy. That's not bipolar, and it's not Carrie. I wanted to play 'Carrie who occasionally becomes unhinged.'"[60]

Prior to *Homeland*, mental illness was only shown on television on an episodic basis,[61] through what has come to be known as the "very special episode" TV trope from the 1980s and 1990s in which a show, usually a sitcom, gets emotional or even dark for an episode or two to address a serious topic.[62] Before *Homeland*, having an ongoing character or extended arc involving mental illness (especially one where the person who had it wasn't a villain) was practically unheard of.

Homeland received a Voice Award from the Substance Abuse and Mental Health Services Administration and the Center for Mental Health Services (CMHS) for its public education of mental health issues, which include not only Carrie's bipolar struggle but also Agent Peter Quinn's posttraumatic stress disorder in season 6. In speaking about the reasons for the award, Wilma Townsend of the CMHS praised *Homeland* as "a good educational piece for both the general public and people who have a mental illness" because it shows that "a person can have a mental illness and still function."[63]

"Not the Most Interesting Thing about Me": LGBTQIA+ Representation

It takes a strong female character (and not in the butt-kicking way) to push the boundaries of what can be shown on television in regard to sexuality even today, but that was all the more so in the 1990s when many of the shows covered in this book aired. Thanks in large part to the intersectionality and sex-positive nature of third-wave feminism and the increasing efforts in those areas with the fourth wave, shows featuring fierce females were able to depict LGBTQIA+ scenes long before they became commonplace.

TWO GROUNDBREAKING PORTRAYALS: WILLOW'S LESBIAN RELATIONSHIPS ON *BUFFY*

As mentioned in chapter 7, Joss Whedon tangled with the CW Network over the portrayal of Willow's lesbian relationship with Tara. At first, the network wouldn't even let them kiss on screen—even though two years had passed since Ellen DeGeneres broke that television taboo. Another two years would pass before Whedon finally convinced the network to allow the college students to share a smooch visible to viewers in season 5, episode 17, "The Body." "It was a landmark moment in queer representation all the same—and one that progressed and deepened as Willow and Tara's relationship did," Alanna Bennett explains. "This was network television in the very early '00s, after all, and it was rare for same-sex relationships to be afforded the level of intimacy Willow and Tara enjoyed—so rare, in fact, that Whedon famously threatened to quit the show if The WB didn't let the couple kiss onscreen."[64]

In between Willow and Tara's meeting and their on-screen kiss, Whedon masterfully substituted spells for sex to get the idea across that Willow and Tara were lovers without upsetting those in power. This helped contribute to building "a gay relationship that was just as romantic, emotional, and ultimately heartbreaking as any other on the show"[65] [and] "was one of the first depictions of a long-term, loving lesbian relationship on TV."[66]

This relationship was a wonderful (likely) first/early exposure to a lesbian relationship for many of *Buffy*'s young adult viewers. It was sweet and tender and in no way threatening. Michileen Martin for Looper writes,

> We get to watch [their love] from its awkward beginnings and be-
> cause we get to know Willow long before she knows she's gay. It gives
> us a lens through which it's easier to see the two as their friends see
> them—not as a specifically gay couple, but simply a couple. Once
> you accept their love as being nothing but love, it's almost impossible
> to imagine how someone else could fail to do likewise.[67]

Willow would go on to take another television first in season 7, episode 20, "Touched," when she was part of broadcast network TV's first lesbian sex scene with girlfriend Kennedy.[68] By the time that episode aired on May 6, 2003, the show had moved to the more progressive UPN network. "They let us do whatever, and things began to change," Whedon said.[69] With that barrier cleared, the show was free to depict more serious sex acts. Sarah Warn explains the significance of this scene:

> This milestone is important because equal representation of physical
> affection and sexual interaction between women on television is criti-
> cal to desensitizing lesbian sex and portraying lesbian relationships as
> healthy and multi-faceted. The . . . *Buffy* episode does both by treat-
> ing the Willow-Kennedy sex scene matter-of-factly and including it
> alongside the scenes of *Buffy*'s heterosexual couples having sex.[70]

That scene went a long way toward normalizing lesbian sex and even briefly equalizing it as just the same as any heterosexual intercourse. It was a message not lost on fans and contributed to breaking down barriers for people in real life as well as paving the way for future shows to do even more.

LESBIAN, GAY, AND TRANS REPRESENTATION IN *JESSICA JONES*

Jeri Hogarth, the high-powered lawyer who yanks Jessica Jones around like a dog on a leash, is the Marvel Cinematic Universe's first leading gay character. She may be evil, insufferable, and lesbian, but thankfully she isn't the stock "evil gay" character of previous generations. As Jasper points out, Jeri escapes that fate because wealth and a lust for power are what makes her evil, not the fact that she likes women.[71]

"Marvel prides themselves on diversity in their content, and made a big deal out of the nameless gay man who briefly appears in *Avengers: Endgame*. But that nugget of representation pales in comparison to the solid character work that *Jessica Jones* offers," writes Chelsea Steiner for the *Mary Sue*.[72]

The show doesn't shy away from depicting kisses and love scenes between women. Jeri even hires two female prostitutes in season 3, something that is rarely, if ever, shown on television. Jeri's lovers provide representation as well, from her long-suffering wife, Dr. Wendy Ross-Hogarth, and her mistress, Pam, to Kith Lyonne, Jeri's bisexual, polyamorous college paramour, with whom she reunites for most of season 3.

As with Willow and Tara, Jeri just happens to be gay; it is only one part of her character. In fact, if you asked her, she'd name off at least a dozen things she is or has done that are more important than her sexuality.

Smaller characters are part of the LGBTQIA+ community as well. Eddy Costa, the detective we meet in season 3 is gay. A tertiary story line deals with his struggle to adopt a child with his husband, Russell. Though it's never explicitly mentioned, Jessica's quick-witted assistant Gillian is a trans woman and is played by a trans actor. This brings much needed representation and authentic casting from that part of the community to the airwaves, where it is not seen nearly often enough. Actor Aneesh Sheth, who played Gillian, said the lack of specificity in the dialogue about her gender was done purposefully. "I'm transgender, and the character of Gillian is also trans, but there is no mention of her being trans within the show nor kind of a narrative around her identity, which I think is wonderful because trans people exist in the world. It's not always about their narrative. So I think it's just really great to have her exist and see where that story can take us," she said.[73]

While *Jessica Jones* had its issues with characters of color, it is truly a product of the fourth wave of feminism, with its intersectionality and superb drawing of three-dimensional LGBTQIA+ characters. That doesn't mean its other sins can be forgiven, but it does get a point in its favor for this subject.

Complicated Sex(uality): Frank Underwood, *House of Cards*

We've seen plenty of politicians behaving badly in the headlines when it comes to matters of sex. From Bill Clinton's affair with White House intern Monica Lewinsky to more recent issues of unsolicited dick-pics and sugar babies transported over state lines, real life has so many scandals it feels superfluous to make one up. But *House of Cards* aims to give its viewers an (albeit overdramatized) look inside Capitol Hill, so why should this stone remain unturned?

In real life, if a major lawmaker of either party were to be unwillingly outed as gay or bisexual—much less polyamorous—the press, not to mention conservatives in the GOP, would act as if Satan himself appeared on the steps of the Capitol Building. That is the sad reality of the state of our nation.

But it is also the reality for Frank Underwood in *House of Cards*. In season 1, he appears to simply be a philandering politico like so many in Washington, DC. However, over the next two seasons, the sordid reality behind the perfect mask of the Underwoods' marriage comes to light, at least for the viewer. We already know that Frank has extramarital affairs—he proved that by sleeping with Zoe in season 1. But now we find out he sleeps with men as well. Zoe was nothing more than a means to an end—an expression of his "appetite for power through sexual dominance"[74]—and his male affairs appear to be the same until season 4.

That's when we find out just how close he is to Edward Meechum, his bodyguard. In season 2, we see the two engage in a threesome with Claire, something Nathan Darrow, who played Meechum, swears only happened that one time.[75] Yet when Meechum is tragically killed in the attempted assassination of President Underwood, Frank is devastated. His "private mourning indicates that the death of his lover is an emotional loss that reflects the complicated nature of queer loss," writes Jamie Zabinsky for Feministing. "On top of the fact that neither Frank nor Meechum [openly] identified as queer or formally recognized their relationship as anything more than President and Secret Service agent, queer lives are devalued to the point where their loss is rendered invisible."[76] But in this situation, the loss, the totality of their relationship, must remain invisible for Frank to remain in office. As recent political events and hate crimes have shown, the United States is not ready for an LGBTQIA+ president, much less one that is outed while holding office, even if only on television.

Frank, if pressed, would likely call himself queer if he was forced to label himself on the LGBTQIA+ spectrum of sexuality. We see him and Claire having sex only once, in season 2. And later when Claire demanded rough sex, Frank refused, and Claire's unhappiness was clear. This, combined with his affair with Zoe, could well be enough to label Frank as bisexual or maybe pansexual. The problem is, however, that we are never allowed deep enough into his mind—despite all of his fourth-wall breaking, his sexuality is one thing he never discusses with the audience—to know whether or not he is actually attracted to women or is so aroused by the power he finds in his female liaisons that he can have sex with them regardless. So it is possible he is gay in his attraction and in his affections. "He wouldn't be the first person who identifies as straight but has also had gay sex, nor would he be the first person who identifies as gay but has had straight sex," Margaret Lyons points out in a Vulture article.[77]

In some ways, the lack of an answer—Kevin Spacey's abrupt departure before the final season was filmed negated any hope of getting some concrete resolution   makes the whole argument a moot point. But still, the depiction of a very conflicted man on-screen, especially one in power, is representation in and of itself. There are hundreds of thousands of people, if not more, out there who are confused or in denial about their sexuality for a variety of reasons. In that way, Frank's struggle is their own. Perhaps seeing it reflected on-screen will make them feel a little less alone.

Orphan Black: Sexuality and Science

We know so little for sure about human sexuality—even scientists can't agree whether it is genetic or if nurture influences a person's later sexuality, whether it is a choice or as hard coded in us as our eye color, or some combination of both[78]—the question of how it would play out among hundreds of human clones is mind boggling. But that is one of the many questions posed by *Orphan Black*.

"No one watching *Orphan Black* can fail to notice that the show raises profound questions about the origins of sexuality and gender identity. Why, if Leda sisters share the same genes, are some heterosexual, at least one gay or bisexual, and still another transgender? What is the show saying? That sexual orientation is a choice and not biological? Not necessarily," writes Dr. Gregory E. Pence, an international expert on the ethics of human cloning.[79]

To review: Alison, Helena, Beth, and Rachel are straight; Cosima is a lesbian; and Sarah is bisexual/pansexual—in season 4 she has a threesome with a man and a woman and is seen on-screen kissing the woman; Tatiana Maslany, who played the clones, confirms Sarah likes both men and women.[80] (And even though he isn't related to the clones, we can't forget Felix, who is gay.)

Some people question whether the creators of the show really thought through the science behind the clones' sexualities or if they just wanted a variety of characters. Others believe that the reason for the differences is "the Letas are not actually genetically identical and that each contains unique DNA which would likely be the case in real life. The clones themselves probably have bigger genetic differences than just the unique DNA tags Cosima discovers in the final episode of the first season, and sexuality may be one of them," Pence explains.[81]

An official FAQ for *Orphan Black* tackles the question head on:

> Sexual orientation is not determined by simple genetics. This can be seen in the fact that identical twins, who share the exact same DNA, do not necessarily have the same sexual orientation. Instead, sexuality

may be the result of complex "epigenetics"—where certain genes are "switched" on or off during fetal development—as well as childhood experiences and other environmental factors. While all the sisters share DNA, they were carried by different [surrogate] mothers and so would show subtle deviations.[82]

In season 2, episode 8, "Variable and Full of Perturbation," we meet Tony, the only transgender clone on the show. He was part of only one episode, and while many people lauded the show for including a transgender clone, others felt like the show didn't put much effort into creating the character, like they were just checking a diversity box. "The portrayal of Tony seemed to lack poise and detail, and he conforms to stereotypes that aren't what the transgender community generally adhere to," writes Tariq Raouf for Hypable. "Tony Sawicki is incredibly over-sexualized, and his little make-out session with Felix was completely unnecessary."[83] In a world where trans people are frequently misunderstood and LGBTQIA+ people are still sometimes viewed as willing to sleep with anyone of their preferred gender(s), Tony's depiction may have done more harm than good, especially since he didn't have any real story arc and only appeared in that single odd episode.

One thing *Orphan Black* certainly got right was its assertion that, regardless of how you identify, in the words of Cosima, "My sexuality is not the most interesting thing about me" (season 2, episode 2, "Governed by Sound Reason and True Religion"). Statements like this are what prompted Complex to call her "one of the best representations of an LGBT character on television in the modern age."[84] Just as *Charmed* is a show about women who happen to be witches, "*Orphan Black* is a show about women and for women, that happens to be queer."[85] It is only by increasing portrayals of well-rounded characters who happen to be (fill in the blank—people of color, LGBTQIA+, disabled, etc.) that our culture will finally normalize any deviation from the cis-het, rich, white male norm of previous generations.

CHAPTER 9

Redemption Narratives

Redemption is a universal theme that has been affecting female characters from the beginnings of storytelling (think: Eve), but the women of the 1990s through today are not seeking to redeem themselves because they were condemned by God or a priest or shunned by society; they took redemption, the power it bestows, and the strength it requires by their own free will. In this way, they use their need for redemption as a source of agency and, ultimately, a way to help others.

Buffy the Vampire Slayer: Have a Little Faith

Whether you came to *Buffy the Vampire Slayer* from the original movie or the series, the word "Slayer" had a certain connotation: a witty blonde cheerleader, girl-next-door type who just so happened to kill vampires in her off-time. Season 3 introduced audiences to a whole new type of Slayer: dark-haired, bad-ass, sexual Faith who was more likely to be featured in a *Girls Gone Wild* video than be crowned Homecoming Queen. She was Buffy's polar opposite in every way, including her perspective on slaying. While Buffy reluctantly accepts her fate, Faith revels in it: "Slaying is what we're built for," she says. "If you're not enjoying it, you're doing something wrong" (season 3, episode 14, "Bad Girls").

Faith is the last Slayer from the original line, called to her duties when Kendra was killed by Drusilla. Instead of saving the world, Faith was the one who needed saving. Her devil-may-care party girl ways and "want take have" (season 3, episode 14, "Bad Girls") philosophy on life caused her to make some very questionable choices, from theft to murder.

In many ways, Faith is a product of her environment. She didn't have the loving, semi-stable home life that Buffy grew up with (spontaneous sister notwithstanding). Like Xander's, Faith's parents are alcoholics who don't provide much guidance or support, so she has to form her own moral compass. Later, Faith witnesses her first Watcher get killed by a vampire, both of which leave her with trauma. As a result, she develops her carefree attitude as a coping mechanism, hoping that if she closes off her heart to everyone, she won't be hurt again.

While Faith works hard at being a Slayer—"When I'm fighting, the whole world goes away. . . . I only know one thing: I'm going to win and they're going to lose" (season 3, episode 3, "Faith, Hope & Trick")—she parties even harder. Though a minor, she goes out every night, dancing in tight leather clothes, drinking, and having sex with anyone she pleases.

Faith has no one and so tries to ingratiate herself into the Scooby Gang. At first they like her, but then she starts to show her darker side. Buffy has a dislike of Faith—the new Slayer rubs Buffy the wrong way and makes her feel like Faith is trying to replace her in the Scooby Gang—and so Buffy keeps her at arm's length.

In season 3, Faith's recklessness gets out of control, and she accidently kills a human—Deputy Mayor Allan Finch—mistaking him for a vampire. Faith immediately goes into denial and pretends like it doesn't matter, her trauma response activated. Buffy confronts her, wanting to tell Giles about it because he would know what to do, but Faith refuses. Buffy says, "Faith, you don't get it. You killed a man." Faith replies, "No, *you* don't get it. I don't care" (season 3, episode 14, "Bad Girls").

Faith tries to pin the murder on Buffy, but Giles figures out what Faith is doing and has her arrested by the Watcher's Council. She escapes and, embittered against every member of the Scooby Gang, has nowhere left to turn. She then allies herself with the Big Bad of the season, Mayor Richard Wilkins. Faith becomes his new assistant. A lot of people believe he becomes a father figure to her,[1] but regardless of the nature of their relationship, it is clear the two understand and care for one another. Faith finds a purpose beyond slaying in doing things for him and is happier than she's ever been on the show.

But as we all know, happiness doesn't last on television. The day before the mayor's ascension, Buffy and Faith get into a duel in which Buffy stakes Faith in the stomach. Faith's injuries put her in a coma for eight months. When she wakes up, she has a change of heart. Now suicidal, Faith uses a device the mayor gave her on Buffy that allows her to exchange bodies with someone; but rather than start a new life, she's hoping Angel will kill her while she is in Buffy's body. "When she literally takes a walk in Buffy's shoes, she sees how loved and appreciated Buffy is as a person and as the noble Slayer," Claire L. Wong points out in a *Hollywood Insider* article.[2] It is then that she finally learns the difference between right and wrong.

When she gets her own body back, Faith goes to Los Angeles and is hired to kill Angel. He intervenes when Faith tortures her Watcher, Wesley. Faith begs him to kill her, yelling "I know I'm bad" over and over (*Angel*, season 4, episode 13, "Salvage"). Angel refuses, and Faith turns herself in to the police for her crimes.

After serving part of her sentence, Faith breaks out when Wesley tells her she's needed because Angel lost his soul again. "The ease with which she escapes shows she was there because she wanted to be," notes Wong.[3] She confronts Angelus but refuses to kill him because Angel was kind to her when no one else was and refused to give up on her. Now, she refuses to give up on him, trying and failing to restore his soul. Willow later succeeds. Faith and Angel become a team, fighting evil as they both attempt to find redemption for their crimes. Faith returns to Sunnydale to help battle The First, and she and Buffy reconcile, "acknowledging that two Slayers were never meant to exist at once and this was likely the root of their many disagreements."[4]

Faith then continues working with the potential Slayers as part of her rehabilitation. "Through her friendship with Angel in particular, Faith found a new sense of purpose and maturity—it became her goal to keep Slayers not only together, banded together and strong, but help them realize their purpose and keep them from making her old mistakes," Jack Wilhelmi writes in a ScreenRant article on what happened to Faith in the *Buffy* comic books after the series ended.[5]

Nikita: Revenge Served Hot, with a Side of Love

Nikita is a story of revenge and redemption for both Nikita and Alex—technically for Michael as well, but we're focusing on the ladies. They are gunning (literally) for Division and Percy and Amanda, its leaders, but for very different, very personal reasons.

"I'd say [the show is] more redemption than anything." Maggie Q, who played Nikita, said in an interview. "I think it's more about Nikita having to feel human again and wanting to go back and fix the things that she didn't have control over at the time, which is a very hard thing to do."[6]

Nikita explains her motives in the first episode: [Division] "did everything [they could] to make me the best killer I could be. Until I broke one of their rules. . . . I fell in love. From a civilian. [*sic*] His name was Daniel. After three months together, all I wanted was to be with him, have a normal life. But in Division you can't have that, so they killed him and made it look like an accident" (season 1, episode 1, "Pilot").

Nikita is a story of female strength and revenge. *The CW/Photofest*

Yes, there is revenge there, but there is also an element of redemption. In the first season, we see that, behind her tough exterior, Nikita is capable of love. The way she and Birkhoff affectionately call one another "Niki" and "nerd" after she kidnaps him is the first indication that she still has positive feelings for some of her former coworkers. "Love is placed as the cause that unleashes the objective of the search for revenge," writes Sabrina Calandrón about the show. "The hegemonic discourse that the fiction collects points to love as a weakness for women . . . [but] the leading woman manages these gender disqualifications, uses them and turns them into strengths."[7]

It is love, Nikita's last shred of remaining conscience, that motivates her to take Alex in. Yes, Alex is useful to Nikita in infiltrating Division, but she also sees Alex as her younger self, the chance she was never given. There is a bond between them because Nikita understands Alex in a way that no one else can because she has been there. In protecting Alex, she can make up for killing Alex's father, and the work they do together can make up for other transgressions on both of their consciences.

Alex's quest for revenge comes in two parts. First, in season 1, episode 15, "Alexandra," Alex is forced to face Vlad, the man who trafficked her to the United States and made her a sex slave, when one of her former friends in the ring recognizes her and turns her in. After being hooked on drugs again and forced to relive the tragic circumstances that led to her coming to the United States, Alex kills Vlad, exacting her first revenge.

Next, she is on the hunt for Sergei Semak, her father's right-hand man who had him killed so he could gain control of the organization. Over the next two and a half seasons, Alex regains control of her father's organization, Zetrov, and reconciles with Nikita, the second part of her revenge and redemption. Finally, Nikita and Alex work together to expose Amanda as a traitor in revenge for all she put both of them through at Division.

In writing about a lack of female redemption arcs on television, Kate Gardner opines, "Also, give us a female character who gets to join the hero team first as a reluctant ally and then as a trusted friend. It would be a great inversion of the usual redemption stories, where white cishet men get to have the big redemption arcs, while villains who are part of marginalized groups tend to get killed off."[8]

In a way, this is exactly what Nikita does, just backward. Instead of joining an already established "hero team," Nikita takes the initiative to create her own, first with Alex and later with Michael and Birkhoff. Nikita and Michael go from being on opposing sides to allies, friends, and then lovers. It is she and Alex who befriend the men, rather than the other way around. In Nikita's world, she is the hero, and the men are the sidekicks who are called upon when needed for extra strength (Michael) or brains (Birkhoff). But really she would be just fine on her own if it wasn't for that pesky little thing called love—sisterly love for Alex, romantic love for Michael, and brotherly love for Birkhoff—getting in the way.

Jessica Jones: Revenge of the Abused

While the series *Jessica Jones* can be seen as a whole as a story about how three women deal in the present with elements of their past, season 1 in particular is about revenge and redemption. Jessica begins the series haunted by the murder of a woman Kilgrave made her kill when she was under his mind control. She wants more than anything to assuage her guilt and get revenge on him.

"One might wonder why Jessica struggles with these feelings of guilt; after all, it wasn't her choice to murder Reva. But since she broke free from Kilgrave's mind control right after the murder, Jessica begins to wonder whether the *desire* to kill had been inside of her all along. This continually haunts Jessica throughout the series,"[9] only to be made worse when she finds out that the woman she killed was her lover, Luke's, wife. Telling him is what drives the two apart permanently and makes her feel even more horrible about herself.

After Jessica finds out Kilgrave is up to his old tricks, she tries to protect Hope Shlottman, a girl whose fate eerily mirrors her own, as she is also under Kilgrave's control. Unfortunately, Jessica is too late, and Hope murders her parents on Kilgrave's command. Really, Hope is a ruse to draw Jessica out. Kilgrave is still controlling Jessica through Hope, even without using his powers directly on Jessica, and she resents it.

After an extended game of cat-and-mouse, Kilgrave lures Jessica back to her childhood home, where he tells her he wants to show her he has changed and allow her to fall in love with him by her own free will this time. She only agrees to live with him so that he will stop being a threat to her friends. While there, she learns that Kilgrave got his powers from experiments his parents conducted on him. They grew afraid of him and left him to fend for himself, making him use his new powers on people just to survive.

Eventually she devises a way to escape, neutralizing Kilgrave temporarily with an injection. She holds him hostage in a special tank where she can torture him with electric shocks if he tries to use his powers. Both Jeri and Trish are disgusted at the inhumane way Jessica treats Kilgrave and thwart her attempts to get him to confess to his crimes on tape. Jessica goes so far as to track down his parents in an attempt to goad him into confessing; he ends up killing them, mind controlling Trish into nearly killing herself, and escaping.

Jessica follows Kilgrave's trail of victims to the docks where his yacht is ready to set sail. He has a bunch of bystanders, including several cops, under his control. He orders them to attack one another, trying to get Jessica to protect them since they are all innocents like she once was. Jessica pretends to be again under Kilgrave's power, obeys his commands to "smile" and say she loves him (she is really saying it to Trish, who is visible over his shoulder), but then quickly snaps his neck, breaking the control he had over the bystanders. Jessica is arrested, but Jeri comes to her rescue, saying that Kilgrave used his powers on Jessica to make her kill him because he felt guilty over his crimes.

Unlike most redemption narratives, Jessica's doesn't end with Kilgrave's death. He continues to haunt her through hallucinations as Jessica tries to process her feelings about what took place. She is plagued by the idea that she will become a murderer now that she has tasted blood. Her visions of Kilgrave only end when she proves to herself she is nothing like him by sparing the life of the scientist who experimented on her and her mother, giving Jessica the powers she never asked for, even though killing him would be the ultimate revenge. In this way, Jessica finds the redemption she is looking for not in revenge, but in its chosen absence. Similarly, by staying in town when she wants to flee she gains "the confidence and defiance she needs to be able to control the lasting effects of Kilgrave and the rest of her inner demons."[10]

The Equalizer: Righting Wrongs When No One Else Will

When you've done things that haunt you, the best way to silence the voices is by doing good for others. That's what Robyn McCall comes to learn in *The Equalizer*.

But the road to getting there was far from easy. In a former life, she was part of "the Company," an illegal arm of the CIA that did unspeakable things in Venezuela and Afghanistan, among other places. No longer enjoying her work, she leaves them, telling her family she just quit her job at a charity to spend more time with her family. But in reality, she doesn't know what to do with her sudden free time.

One night, she rescues a girl named Jewel from being raped, only to find that she is a suspect in the shooting of a lawyer. The girl protests her innocence even though the police have her on tape committing the crime. Robyn eventually learns that a tech genius doctored the tape because the girl was a witness to a hit he put out. After the cops arrest the tech guy and Jewel is free to go, Robyn realizes this is what she wants to do now: help those who have nowhere else to turn. This will be her penance for what she has done.

Over the course of the first season, she mixes it up with "gentrification profiteers and their hired guns, warmongers and tech magnates, entitled white male murderers and the judges who protect them."[11] Along the way, she snags the attention of Detective Marcus Dante, who knows she is up to something, but not quite what. Her family grows increasingly suspicious, especially her daughter, who finds her stash of guns, wigs, and passports.

As The Equalizer's fame grows, so do Detective Dante's suspicions. With her story unraveling, Robyn considers ending her run as The Equalizer but is pulled back in the game when Dante needs her help. She comes close to being unmasked several times, but she is never in more danger than when a former CIA trainee needs her help and she comes face to face with Mason Quinn. Quinn sends up an electromagnetic charge that crashes the plane Bishop is flying in and he is killed. Robyn is devastated, and her story turns into one balancing her new desire for revenge with her old need for redemption.

At the end of season 2, Robyn is kidnapped by Quinn. By the beginning of season 3, her family, the detective, and some friends all know that Robyn is The Equalizer. It's perfect timing because they need to find her and stop the dirty bomb Quinn is going to frame her for setting off in New York City. Dante and Mel show up just in time to remove the deadly explosives from the bomb before it explodes. Quinn is arrested, only to break free. Robyn shoots him, and he falls from the roof of the building, presumably dead. This is a major step in Robyn's quest because it means she has gotten her revenge for Bishop's death.

After she recovers, Robyn helps find a missing firefighter, works with a motorcycle gang, fends off a "ghost," stops a serial killer, and protects a famous singer. The third season is still airing, and the show has already been renewed for a fourth. While Robyn has done plenty of atoning, we still don't know exactly what sins she is making up for. That is only one of the questions future seasons may answer as she continues her quest for justice and inner peace.

Conclusion

During her presidential campaign, Hillary Clinton often said, "The future is female." This phrase came to be called the motto of the fourth wave of feminism. If recent history and the television shows that reflect it are any indication, they may just be prophetic. Women are tired of more than two thousand years of oppression, and we are fighting back.

Since the mid-1990s, the modern daughters of Athena have been kicking ass both on-screen and off. Most of the actresses who play the amazing, complex characters explored in this book are themselves feminists, further blurring the line between fiction and reality, what is possible only in dreams and what can actually be accomplished. That is one of their lessons, after all—the only limits we have are those we place on ourselves, whether by listening to society or that niggling voice in our heads that tells us we aren't good enough, rich enough, strong enough, or powerful enough to make a difference. Our television heroines show us that those voices lie. The truth is to be found in our hearts and in our collective resistance. Just as they have built upon one another to give us the plethora of female representation we see on television today, so too will we build upon one another to continue to shatter glass ceilings, ensure the rights our foremothers fought so hard to secure are protected, and change the status quo so that we might gain the fundamental parities we now lack.

Hayley Atwell, who played Peggy Carter, once told a story of meeting a young green-eyed woman wearing a hijab at a comics convention in the Middle East. The girl came up to her to get a photo signed and asked, "Can you put 'Women can be heroes, too'?"[1] Atwell said it was in that moment that she really realized what an effect *Agent Carter* had out in the world. She doesn't mention what country this took place in, so it could be that this young girl will have to fight every step of the way against the patriarchy to become a hero, or she might be able to take her first big step the very next day at school. But one thing that is clear is that she left that encounter with Atwell not only having met her hero, but holding inside her the memory of a day that forever altered the trajectory of her life.

That is the power of shows featuring women who stand up against misogyny; they inspire girls and women of all ages to do the same. Women realize it is never too late to speak up or make the first move; their daughters see them taking action and they remember. Their mothers become their heroes just as much as the superpowered or supersmart women on their television screens. And when they are grown, they will look back on those memories to give them strength to fight their own battles. These might be personal—like leaving an abusive partner—or political—like fighting to change laws that prevent women from being treated as equals to men—but regardless of their scope, they will change the world, one act at a time.

This is how women have been fighting oppression from the beginning—looking around at the places where they have influence and acting as they can. In some time periods, this meant they could only influence their husbands from the kitchen or the bedroom; in a rare few instances, until the modern period at least, they declared their rebellion from thrones or in the halls of academia. In some countries, women held literary salons where they discussed ideas and traded contacts to help those in need or passed information during quilting circles that was stitched into the designs or coded in Bible verses. During wartime, women took over for their fathers, brothers, boyfriends, and husbands who were away; in so doing, they realized their own strength and worth, so that when the boys came home, there was no going back. They held up placards and demanded equal treatment in workplaces and under the law. Thirty years ago, their daughters began appearing on our television screens and inspired two new waves of resistance, that while fueled by technology, brought more female-presenting people into the feminist fold than ever before.

Women like me came of age alongside *Buffy* and the Halliwell sisters and idolized Sydney Bristow and Nikita Mears for their ability to fight just as hard as men, outsmart them, and maintain their femininity at the same time. By the time shows like *Jessica Jones* and *Agent Carter* came along, we had daughters of our own to whom we passed on the wide-eyed adoration of the fierce females on our televisions. Alongside these new shows, we introduced our children to our teenage favorites. And as adults, we've had shows like *Orphan Black*, *House of Cards*, and *Homeland* to keep the flame of feminism alive in our souls and remind us that we still have many years of fight left in us. And if we have our moments of doubt amid our youth-obsessed culture, all we have to do is turn on *The Equalizer* to see a woman over fifty putting the patriarchy in its place while upholding justice each week.

For all of their differences, the one thing these shows have in common is a belief in "the inherent value of women's lives and stories."[2] Vampire slayers, witches, spies, private eyes, politicians, and clones sound on the surface like they couldn't possibly offer a coherent message, but they do. They tell us that, whether a woman is called to be strong in mind, body, heart, or spirit, she has the capacity. No matter her background or upbringing, she can find strength in those she considers family, whether given by blood or created by mutual bond. Regardless of how she fights the oppression placed on her and other women—by breaking barriers, championing greater tolerance and inclusion, or daring to express her sensual side—each woman is backed by millions of others who will support her efforts. And for those who have stumbled along the way (and who hasn't?), there is always another chance at redemption; no one is beyond saving, so take the hand extended to you or extend one in return. It is only by working together that our fierceness can have its full impact.

Atwell concluded her story with these words, which are the best possible ending to a book like this: "Whatever happens in the future . . . [our show] and its small impact on young girls are a drop of positivity in our world. . . . For all you little Peggys out there, you are not alone. Go forth and kick ass."[3]

Episode Guide

Narrowing down any show to three "must-watch" episodes is not an easy task. Do you focus on the ones that give a person who has never seen it before the best idea of the plot, or do you recommend your favorite episodes? This list is a mix of both.

I've included the first episode of each because it introduces the characters and sets up the series. For all other episodes, I've given my reasoning for choosing them. These summaries are meant to give the gist of the episode, not a complete recounting, so some subplots may have been omitted. And just for funsies, I've also included my thoughts on how well each show stood the test of time.

Buffy the Vampire Slayer

1. SEASON 1, EPISODE 1: "WELCOME TO THE HELLMOUTH"

In the opening scene, a teenage couple walks around a high school at night, and the viewer is lulled into believing something bad will happen to the girl. But as it turns out, the girl is a vampire and kills the boy. Buffy, newly arrived in Sunnydale, awakes with a start from a nightmare of vampires, graves, and fire. Over the course of her first day of school, Buffy meets everyone who will eventually comprise the Scooby Gang—popular mean-girl Cordelia, awkward Xander, and computer nerd Willow, as well as her new Watcher, Giles. When a dead body is found in a locker—the boy from the opening scene—Giles informs Buffy she is still the Slayer, something Buffy doesn't want to accept. That night at a club, a stranger follows Buffy and tells her she is living on a Hellmouth and that The Harvest is coming. (Buffy doesn't know it yet, but this is Angel, the vampire with a soul.) When Willow leaves the club with a vampire (though she doesn't know that), Buffy senses what he is and tries to follow her, but Cordelia gets in the way. Later, Buffy finds Willow in a crypt at the cemetery and kills the vampire, but another appears and attempts to kill Buffy for The Master, an ancient and powerful vampire who has woken beneath Sunnydale.

2. SEASON 3, EPISODE 14: "BAD GIRLS"

Buffy finds out a new Watcher, Wesley, has been assigned to both her and Faith. He orders Buffy around, but Faith refuses to work with him. Buffy enjoys her night slaying with Faith so much that she can't stop talking about it the next day. The two go dancing and then find a demon named Balthazar that Angel is also looking for. They steal some weapons and get arrested but use their Slayer-strength to escape, causing a car accident. The two slay vampires, but in the process, Faith accidently kills a human, mistaking him for a vampire. They flee but find out Balthazar has both Giles and Wesley held captive. Buffy and Angel go to rescue them, and there is a fight in which Balthazar dies. The next day, Buffy and Faith talk, and Faith says she has already disposed of the body. Buffy tries and fails to get Faith to understand the seriousness of what she has done, but Faith says she doesn't care.

Why This Episode Made the List

It is one of my favorite episodes and really highlights the night-and-day differences between Faith and Buffy. It is also the beginning of Faith's downward spiral and the mayor's rise to becoming the Big Bad who will need to be vanquished at the end of the season.

3. SEASON 4, EPISODE 10: "HUSH"

Buffy has a nightmare about a frightening demonic figure while sleeping in class. Later, Xander and Anya fight about whether or not he really loves her. Willow goes to a Wiccan meeting but leaves disappointed that the girls don't have any real magic. She does, however, meet a shy girl named Tara. That night, the scary figures from Buffy's nightmare meet and open a box that sucks in the voices of everyone in Sunnydale. Everyone wakes up the next morning to find they cannot speak. For the rest of the episode, the characters must find alternative ways of communicating with one another. That night, The Gentlemen roam the town, looking for people to kill. Their first victim is a boy at the UC Sunnydale dorms. Giles figures out who The Gentlemen are: beings who travel to a town with the purpose of collecting seven human hearts. They steal the voices because a scream is the only thing that can kill them. Buffy and Riley go on their respective patrols, while The Gentlemen chase Willow and Tara, hoping for kills two and three. Buffy and Riley fight The Gentlemen's footmen, while Willow and Tara hide. The two witches realize they both have powers and combine them to fight off The Gentlemen. Buffy is captured by The Gentlemen's footmen, but Riley saves her. Buffy sees the box from her dream and gestures for Riley to smash it. When he does, everyone gets their voices back, and Buffy screams, killing The Gentlemen.

Why This Episode Made the List

This is by far the most frightening episode of the series; I still refuse to rewatch it twenty-five years later. The pantomime acting is excellent. But more important, it's where Willow meets Tara. It is also fascinating how this episode plays with the idea of communication and the ways it can go wrong: Xander can't voice his feelings to Anya; the Wiccan girls won't let Tara speak up to agree with Willow; and Buffy and Riley can't reveal their true identities to one another. Ironically, even when they try to talk to each other once their voices have been returned, they can't find the words.

PERSONAL OPINION ON THE SHOW

My favorite seasons were seasons 2 through 6. I felt like the first season was a little slow, and the last one was way too weird for me. If I could recommend additional episodes, I'd include season 5, episode 1, "Buffy vs. Dracula," which is the funniest of the series (in my opinion), and season 4, episode 2, "Restless," because it includes the first Slayer, but mostly because I couldn't write a book that included *Buffy* without including the words of The Cheese Man who haunts Giles, Xander, and Willow's dreams: "I wear the cheese. It does not wear me." Trust me, once you've seen this episode, you'll get it.

How well did *Buffy* stand the test of time? 7/10. In retrospect, Xander often comes off as more sexist than funny, Spike's obsession with Buffy hasn't aged well, and some of the dialogue is cringey given changes in culture.

Charmed

1. SEASON 1, EPISODE 1: "SOMETHING WICCA THIS WAY COMES"

A Wiccan is murdered before the opening credits. Prue and Piper argue over her being late and Prue always having to do everything for her. Piper prepares for her "audition" as a chef the next morning. On the table, the planchette of a Ouija board gifted to the sisters by their deceased mother moves, signaling something supernatural is going to occur. The next day, their youngest sister, Phoebe, returns home jobless and directionless. She finds an old Book of Shadows (spell book to those who don't speak witch) in the attic and reads one of the pages aloud, unknowingly activating their powers. The surge of power draws demons to them, and they have to learn to control their new powers to protect themselves. They find out they are the Charmed Ones, the most powerful witches in history. Through trial and error, they discover they have to work together to perform the spell that is required to vanquish the demons.

2. SEASON 3, EPISODE 9: "COYOTE PIPER"

A female demon with no inhibitions escapes her master and is intent on taking Piper's powers. The demon takes control of Piper on the night of her ten-year high school reunion, which is taking place at Piper's bar, P3. This demon causes Piper to do and say what she really wants, including insulting the high school bully and dancing *Coyote Ugly*–style on the bar, to the amazement of everyone. Prue and Phoebe figure out that Piper is possessed and try to dispossess their sister, but they find out the only way to get the demon out is to kill her. Prue stabs Piper, releasing the demon into Leo's body, and Piper is freed. The three are able to say the spell to release the demon and vanquish the demon. Leo heals Piper the rest of the way.

Why This Episode Made the List

This was my favorite episode because Piper is my favorite and I loved the movie *Coyote Ugly*. But in addition to that, it provides valuable backstory on how the Charmed Ones have grown since high school.

3. SEASON 3, EPISODE 22: "ALL HELL BREAKS LOOSE"; SEASON 4, EPISODE 1: "CHARMED, AGAIN: PART 1"

Season 3, Episode 22: The Charmed Ones are revealed as witches after a TV journalist accidently captures Prue and Piper casting a spell on a demon named Shax live on television. People freak out and start protesting outside their house. Cole convinces Tempus, the demon of time, to turn back time, but the catch is one of the three witches has to die for it to happen. A crazy woman, claiming to be a witch, shoots Piper when the Charmed Ones reject her request to join their coven. Prue bursts through the protesters using her car to get Piper to the hospital, but it is too late; Piper is dead. Phoebe visits Cole in Hell to see if there is any way to bring Piper back. Tempus agrees to help if Phoebe stays in Hell because then essentially one of them is lost, breaking the Power of Three. Time resets to the previous day, but Piper and Prue are still attacked by Shax. Both witches are thrown into the wall and knocked out, with pools of blood forming beneath their heads.

Season 4, Episode 1: A little while after the end of season 3, episode 22, Piper awakens to find out Prue is dead. She tries everything to bring her sister back, but nothing works. They hold her funeral, where they meet a woman named Paige, who has been drawn to them and whom they kind of recognize even though they've never met her. Phoebe has a premonition that Paige will be attacked by Shax, who isn't vanquished because the three weren't together to kill him. Her premonition comes true, but Paige is able to escape the demon using the power of orbing that she didn't know she had—it was instinct. The sisters summon the spirits of their mother and grandmother, who tell them that Paige is their half sister and her powers will be activated when all three are near the Book of Shadows, just like the first time. They bring Paige back to their house and explain everything. Shax reappears, and they are able to finally vanquish him. An overwhelmed and scared Paige walks out. End of part 1.

Why These Episodes Made the List

I listed both of these because they really go together. Season 3, episode 22 is the most emotional episode of the series and is heartbreaking when you don't know what is coming. Season 4, episode 1 is important because it introduces Paige and explains how the show can continue without Prue.

PERSONAL OPINION ON THE SHOW

All othe episodes I've chosen are from the first few seasons because I didn't like Paige and I can't in good faith recommend any episodes beyond the season 4 two-part premiere. Your mileage may vary.

How well did *Charmed* stand the test of time? 5/10. Many of the plots now seem even more outlandish than before, and the skimpier costumes look ridiculous.

Alias

1. SEASON 1, EPISODE 1: "TRUTH BE TOLD"

The episode opens with Sydney (in that iconic red wig) being tortured, then flashes back to the day her boyfriend, Danny, proposed. She tells him about her job as an SD-6 agent, and not long after, he's murdered. That is when Sydney realizes how much of a threat her job is to those she loves. Luckily for her, her father also works at SD-6, but he's a double agent. With this revelation, Sydney comes to understand that SD-6 isn't the covert CIA arm she thought it was but, instead, a dangerous splinter organization and her father is secretly spying on it for the real CIA. Fueled by revenge on SD-6 (much like Nikita will be after her), Sydney follows in her father's footsteps, agreeing to become a double agent as well.

2. SEASON 2, EPISODE 1: "THE ENEMY WALKS IN"

The episode opens with Sydney tied to a chair, waiting to meet "The Man," who is really her mom. When Sydney mouths off, her mother shoots her. After telling her story to a CIA psychiatrist, Sydney meets up with her father, who has Will in tow after rescuing him. They explain who they really are and then concoct a cover story to keep Will safe despite what he now knows. Sydney then bugs a French estate and, on the way out, comes across Vaughn and rescues him from being killed by Khasinau. Jack and Vaughn put his cover as a drug addict into motion. Vaughn holds a press conference telling everyone everything he has written is fiction, even SD-6. In ruining his reputation as a journalist, he is saved being killed by SD-6 and can start over. Sydney and Vaughn trace the operations manual for Irina's organization to Barcelona, where Irina kills Khasinau. She then utters her famous line: "Truth takes time."

Why This Episode Made the List

It is the introduction of Sydney's mother, Irina. With her as an element in the story, the show was forever changed. This episode shows what a chimerical character she was, neither all good, nor all bad, but shifting to suit the needs of her situation. Also, it's another season premiere, and there's another iconic wig—only this time it's periwinkle and Sydney has a cool cybergoth outfit to go with it.

3. SEASON 2, EPISODE 13: "PHASE ONE"

The episode opens with Sydney strutting her lingerie-clad dominatrix stuff for a mark in a private first-class airplane room. She strangles him to get information on Server 47 and knocks him out, but not quite enough. He reappears with a gun just before she can escape via parachute. Flash back to twenty-four hours earlier.

To the delight of fans everywhere, Vaughn confesses his feelings for Sydney. The leader of the CIA tells them about the Alliance of Twelve and tells Sydney and her father to gain the trust of Anthony Geiger, Sloane's replacement. Sydney has a very personal conversation with Geiger and then tells Sark about it. Sark, in turn, tells Sydney about Server 47, which might be what they need to take down SD-6.

That is how Sydney came to be on the plane. The bullet fired by the mark shatters the plane window, causing the plane to depressurize and start to fall. The mark and his bodyguard are sucked out of the plane, but Sydney parachutes to safety. Meanwhile Geiger finds out that Jack and Sydney are double agents and tortures Jack, who refuses to give up any information. The CIA raids SD-6, and Sydney kills Geiger. Sydney and Vaughn kiss, thinking everything is over. Then Sloane, who was thought missing, is shown to be on a beach. He tells Sark that phase 1 is complete, but there is much more to do. In a final shocker, Sydney's best friend, Francie, is seen being shot to death by someone who looks just like her.

Why This Episode Made the List

It's the famous post-Superbowl episode that most people have seen. It's sexy, exciting, and classic *Alias*. In many ways, it sets up a new paradigm for the rest of the series.

PERSONAL OPINION ON THE SHOW

When the show originally aired, I could only watch about half the first season because the show was so intense. Luckily, I built up a tolerance because the intensity still came through strong in 2022. I'm a sucker for all things mystical, so I even liked the strange stuff with Rambaldi, which really bothered some people.

How well did *Alias* stand the test of time? 8/10. Overall, the show has held up well, but the Russian story lines seem a little dated.

Nikita

1. SEASON 1, EPISODE 1: "PILOT"

Nikita provides a synopsis of how she came be a rogue assassin determined to take down Division. Alex's past as a bank robber and how she is recruited into Division (very similarly to Nikita) is shown. Percy assigns Michael to hunt Nikita down and kill her. Nikita visits Daniel's grave and sets a trap for Division. While they are trying to kill an effigy of her, she kidnaps Division's hacker and tech nerd, Seymour Birkhoff, who used to work with her. She eventually returns him to Division. Percy believes Birkhoff's story of what happened with Nikita, but Michael isn't so sure. Meanwhile, Alex tries to adjust to her new life in Division, especially to putting up with Jaden, a fellow recruit determined to make Alex's life miserable. That night, Michael, Percy, and Nikita all attend a black-tie event as part of Operation Broken Arrow. Division is there to kill an ambassador, and Nikita is there to save him. She is successful, and Percy announces that killing her is now their priority.

2. SEASON 1, EPISODE 15: "ALEXANDRA"

Alex is assigned to gain the trust of a Mark Zuckerberg–like tech genius who has developed technology that Division wants to know more about. Her cover is that she met him on a dating site so they go to a club and she steals his phone. While in the bathroom, she meets an Eastern European girl named Irena who is high on drugs. Alex realizes she was one of the girls who was forced into human trafficking with her and later goes back into the club to save her. Irena betrays her to Vlad, the man who forced them into a sex slave ring six years earlier.

While keeping Alex in a cage, Vlad tells Irena the story of Alex's past. She was the daughter of a billionaire who owned a business empire in Ukraine called Zetrov. She was only thirteen when he was killed by Nikita and his whole family—Alex included, or that's how the story goes—died in a fire. Because her body was never found, rumors circulated she was in hiding from her father's enemies who put a price on her head. Nikita tried to save her from that fate, but the man who was supposed to get Alex to safety sold her to Vlad to get money for his family. Alex spent the next several years high on drugs and trapped in a sex slave ring until Nikita rescues her once more.

Michael and Nikita both realize separately who has Alex. After meeting by accident, they work together to try to find her. Vlad gets Alex hooked on the same drugs as before, and she has flashbacks to her father's death. While she is high, Alex tells Vlad about Division and what she can do, not knowing she is being recorded. Nikita frees the women in the brothel. Meanwhile, Irena frees Alex and kills Vlad.

Alex tells Irena to run and that she will have to hunt her down and kill her if she repeats anything she heard. Nikita gives Alex the prototype back, and Michael warns Nikita that Division is on its way. He carries Alex back to Division and gives Percy the technology. Nikita recovers the videotape. Amanda offers to give Alex methadone to ease her withdrawal, but she wants answers first.

Why This Episode Made the List

Alex's past is key to her motivations throughout the rest of the series. It also marks the first time that Nikita and Michael tentatively work together.

3. SEASON 2, EPISODE 9: "FAIR TRADE"

Michael is in London visiting his son. Birkhoff slips a tracker into Senator Pierce's coffee. She is part of Oversight and is determined to take Nikita down. Alex is going to Russia to find the man who killed her father, but is going in disguise as her former self when she was part of the sex ring. Birkhoff helps Nikita sneak into the Oversight meeting, but they are made. Nikita makes it out, but Birkhoff is captured by Amanda and tortured. She crushes one of his hands and then inserts a needle into his nose intending to get a confession or puncture his brain. Nikita offers to trade the black box for Birkhoff. She and Michael discover Sean is the senator's son. Alex frees the other sex slaves she is sent back to Russia with. Nikita hacks the transponder of the cab carrying Birkhoff and Sean and, after getting Birkhoff back, shoots Sean after he destroys the black box.

Why This Episode Made the List

This episode shows the lengths to which Amanda and Alex are both willing to go to get what they want. The extent to which Nikita gets upset when Birkhoff is captured shows how much she cares about him.

PERSONAL OPINION ON THE SHOW

I really loved this show up until about halfway through the third season in the episode where Michael loses his hand. The bionic one he gets in return was too much for me and marked the moment where the show jumped the shark. But because the rest of the show was so good, I'm glad they got a chance to wrap up the series in a way that both made sense and was satisfying.

How well did *Nikita* stand the test of time? 9/10. There isn't much in this show that is so tied to the culture of the time that it seems dated. The whole last season is still outlandish, even for a spy flick, but overall it holds up well.

Jessica Jones

1. SEASON 1, EPISODE 1: "AKA LADIES NIGHT"

Foul-mouthed, hard-drinking Jessica Jones is hired by Bob and Barbara Shlott-man to find their daughter, Hope, a college student at NYU who has gone missing. As Jessica goes about her work, we are introduced to her superpowers. Jessica follows Hope's trail to a restaurant where Kilgrave used to take her when she was under his control. That's when she realizes Kilgrave, whom she thought was dead, is alive and is using Hope to recreate their dating history to get her attention. Fearing he will come after her, Jessica asks her foster sister, Trish, for money so she can run. Jessica accidently finds Hope at a hotel, under Kilgrave's control, and rescues her. When her parents come to take her home, Hope, still under Kilgrave's thrall, kills them in the elevator and tells Jessica to smile, which is a message from Kilgrave.

2. SEASON 3, EPISODE 11: "AKA HELLCAT"

Trish has flashbacks to her childhood throughout the episode, remembering how her mother, Dorothy, abused her. In the present day, Trish goes to her mother's apartment only to find her mother dead in a chair, killed by Gregory Sallinger, as a way to get at Jessica. Trish vows he will pay and heads to Sallinger's apart-ment; the two fight and he sees her face. They keep fighting until Jessica stops them. Jessica takes Trish to clean up, and reality finally hits and Trish breaks down. Meanwhile, Jeri calls a press conference to announce a reward for the identification of the Masked Vigilante. Trish visits Sallinger in the hospital and assures him she will kill him as soon as his police guard is gone. He accuses her of enjoying killing.

That very night she beats a dirty cop to death. The other cops immediately suspect Jessica. Trish doesn't want Jessica to take the fall for her, so she stages a very public event while Jessica has an alibi. Jeri visits Trish and tells her she knows Trish is the Masked Vigilante and that she knows Trish has been using Jeri's files to pick her clients. Jeri offers to destroy her proof if Trish will steal something from Demetri Patseras. Jessica is on the run. Trish beats a guy to death and leaves the dirty cop's badge there to frame him. That moment the power goes to her head, and she decides to keep administering her brand of justice.

Why This Episode Made the List

This is the episode where Trish becomes Hellcat. Her flashbacks explain exactly why Trish does what she does.

3. SEASON 3, EPISODE 13: "AKA EVERYTHING"

Jessica and Jeri agree that Trish needs to be stopped. Jessica tries talking to Trish. Trish apologizes for what she has done to their friendship but says she has to do what she is doing. She tries to get Trish to turn herself in, but Trish refuses because she couldn't keep administering justice behind bars. Jessica is worried Trish is going to do something she can't undo so she tries to take her in but Trish escapes. The public outcry for the arrest and unmasking of the Masked Vigilante grows, even as Trish tries to prove Jessica is wrong about her. Jeri decides that because her clients are in danger, she is going to reveal the identity of the Masked Vigilante, who Jeri claims is far too dangerous to leave out in the streets. In reality, she is planning to help Trish escape to Canada; Jessica reveals Trish's identity before they can escape. Jessica and Trish fight, and Jessica realizes Trish has turned out to be just as vicious as her mother.

Eventually Jessica knocks Trish out and turns her into the police. The Raft claims jurisdiction because Trish has powers. When a police officer reads the charges to Trish, she finally realizes she "is the bad guy." Jessica decides to give Alias Investigations to Malcolm and leave town. Before she leaves she watches as Trish is transferred via helicopter to The Raft. Jessica then heads to the bus station, but turns around when she has a hallucination of Kilgrave, who is encouraging her to give in and leave. Ever defiant, she changes her mind and stays in New York.

Why This Episode Made the List

As the series finale, it ties up a lot of loose ends, but the reason I chose it is because of the strength of the acting. Trish's face while the charges are read to her is heartbreaking, as is the final look between her and Jessica.

PERSONAL OPINION ON THE SHOW

I loved this whole series, but the first season was my favorite because David Tenant played Kilgrave so well.

How well did *Jessica Jones* stand the test of time? 9/10. The only thing I could argue with is that the show needed better-drawn BIPOC characters. But its overall messages still hit hard, and the writing and acting remain top notch.

Agent Carter

1. SEASON 1, EPISODE 1: "NOW IS NOT THE END"

New York, 1946: Peggy Carter, grieving girlfriend of Steve Rogers, returns to work for the Strategic Scientific Reserve (SSR) after World War II ends. She faces strong sexism from her fellow agents despite the respect and notoriety she gained during the war. The SSR investigates her friend, inventor Howard Stark, who is rumored to have sold weapons to enemies of the United States. With no one else to trust, Howard secretly contacts Peggy, asks her to help him prove his innocence, and also tasks her with recovering some of his more dangerous inventions. He tips her off that the sale of the first thing, instructions for how to make molecular nitramine, is going to take place at a club. Howard leaves his butler, Edwin Jarvis, at Peggy's disposal, and the two become reluctant partners. Peggy goes to the club in disguise and overhears that the formula has already fallen into the wrong hands and been made into a small nitramine bomb capable of leveling the city. With Edwin supporting her, Peggy investigates the refinery where the bomb was made. There they meet Leet Brannis, a mute who carjacks a truck full of the nitramine weapons. On his way out, Leet drops one of the bombs, causing the whole refinery to be leveled. Leet and Jarvis get into a car crash, and with the last of his strength, Leet draws a symbol in the dirt, which Peggy finds stands for a company called Leviathan.

2. SEASON 1, EPISODE 7: "SNAFU"

In the past: Dr. Ivchenko uses his powers of hypnosis for the first time during the war to help patients feel no pain when a miliary doctor runs out of anesthesia. He started out good. In the present: Peggy has finally been caught. For six episodes, she's been conducting her own investigations, which is a serious violation of the rules, because no one takes her seriously enough to let her do it as part of the agency. Now she is being interrogated by her own organization. After a while, Jarvis comes in with a confession from Howard Stark, who is willing to surrender if Peggy is released. (What Peggy and SSR don't know is the confession is a fake.) Peggy is fired from the SSR, but when she realizes Dr. Ivchenko was communicating a warning about something terrible coming in Morse Code, she confesses everything that she has done. Realizing he has been made, Dr. Ivchenko hypnotizes Chief Dooley and has him steal a gas cylinder that is one of Howard's weapons from the SSR's labs. The agents later find Dooley wearing a vest Howard created that Dr. Ivchenko strapped to him. Unfortunately, it will explode, and there is no way to deactivate it. To save his agents, Chief Dooley jumps out a window just before the vest explodes, killing him. After meeting up with Dottie, with whom he is working, Dr. Ivchenko takes the gas to a movie theater and sets it off—he leaves and locks the patrons in. The gas in the cinema makes the audience crazy to the point that they attack and kill each other.

Why This Episode Made the List

The shock factor alone makes this episode worth watching. But it also gives Peggy the chance to finally call the agents out on the way they have been treating her. In confessing everything, she can retroactively show what she is capable of doing. Plus, Dr. Ivchenko is one of the best psychological villains—right up there with Kilgrave on *Jessica Jones*.

3. SEASON 2, EPISODE 1: "THE LADY OF THE LAKE"

Chief Jack Thompson and Peggy finally capture Dottie during a failed bank robbery in which she pretends to be Peggy. In Los Angeles, Daniel Sousa has been appointed chief of their branch of the SSR. He works together with LA detective Andrew Henry, who is dealing with a dead woman's body encased in ice that was removed from a semi-frozen lake on the hottest day of the year in LA. When Sousa calls asking for help, Thompson assigns Peggy. In LA, she reunites with Jarvis (who is there to set up a mansion for Howard) and Jarvis's charismatic wife, Ana. Peggy also meets scientist Dr. Jason Wilkes, who explains that the dead body is physicist Jane Scott and her body is frozen from the inside by a material called Isodyne. She was having an affair with Calvin Chadwick, owner of Isodyne Energy. The FBI takes Dottie into custody.

It turns out Detective Henry, who was dying from exposure to Isodyne-contaminated blood, was hired by Calvin to make Jane's body look like she was the victim of the Lady of the Lake killer. He is later killed by a police officer before Peggy can get information out of him.

Why This Episode Made the List

Dottie's capture is immensely satisfying. Plus with the move to LA changing the show so much, watching this one is important for understanding the rest of the season. But more than that, this is where Peggy meets Ana, her new BFF, and Dr. Jason Wilkes, a future love interest.

PERSONAL OPINION ON THE SHOW

It really is a shame that this show had such a short run. There was so much potential for the writers and directors to use the powerful character of Peggy Carter to do and say more. The first and second seasons really had a different vibe. I personally liked the first season better, but the second was good as well.

How well did *Agent Carter* stand the test of time? 9/10. Like *Nikita*, it doesn't date itself and the plot holds up. The only reason I didn't give it a 10 is that no show is perfect.

Homeland

These three episodes are seasons 1 through 3 in a nutshell, so be forewarned.

1. SEASON 1, EPISODE 1: "PILOT"

In flashback, Carrie remembers the day in an Iraqi prison when one of her informants warned her "an American prisoner of war has been turned" just before being executed. Coming back to herself in the middle of a CIA briefing, she finds out Marine sergeant Nicholas Brody, missing and presumed dead for the last eight years, was really a POW and was just rescued during a raid on an al-Qaeda compound. Carrie realizes this could be the P.O.W. the informant warned her about. When she confides in Saul, he says there is no way the CIA can investigate a publicly decorated war hero. Unbeknownst to Brody, his wife was sleeping with his best friend, Mike, assuming Brody was dead. But when she finds out he was found, she rushes to the airport with their kids, promising herself she will ignore her feelings for Mike and be a good wife to Brody. Carrie ignores Saul's advice and hires a friend of hers to illegally install cameras and microphones in Brody's house while the wife and kids are picking him up from the airport. They finish just in time to get out and turn on their side of the surveillance before the family gets home. Carrie watches Brody's every move, following him several places. When Carrie gets back home, Saul is there; he is angry at what she's done and tells her he's going to report her. Later that night she sees news footage of Brody in which he's tapping out a pattern with his fingers. Carrie thinks it is a coded message for a handler or sleeper cell. Saul agrees to let her investigate it.

2. SEASON 1, EPISODE 12: "MARINE ONE"

This episode takes place over the course of three days. Brody records a suicide note explaining that he blew up himself, the vice president, and his advisors, whom he blames for the deaths of eighty-two children during a drone strike in Pakistan, and takes the camera's memory to a drop-off point. Carrie wonders aloud to Saul why Brody turned her in, which makes Saul realize Carrie has fallen in love with Brody. That night, a sniper gets in position for the vice president's upcoming policy summit. Brody's daughter, Dana, catches him praying, and Brody admits he converted to Islam while in captivity. He asks her to keep it a secret. The next morning Brody gets dressed for the summit, hiding an explosive vest under his Marine uniform. Carrie hears about the summit on the radio and heads there. As the lawmakers gather, a gunman opens fire—not a real attack, but a distraction so that the dignitaries will be taken to a secure bunker along with Brody. This puts him in place to conduct the attack.

Carrie contacts Saul and tells him what she suspects (the truth), but Saul believes she is just obsessed with Brody and sends the Secret Service after her. Inside the bunker, Brody presses the detonation button, but nothing happens. He goes to the bathroom and repairs the disconnected wires. Carrie goes to Brody's house and urges his wife and daughter to call Brody and talk him out of blowing everyone up. Thinking Carrie is crazy, his wife calls 911 and Carrie is arrested. Dana, who has her own suspicions, calls him and tells him what Carrie said. Hearing his daughter's voice makes Brody change his mind. The next day, the vice president confirms to Saul that he ordered the drone strike that killed the eighty-two children. Carrie is released into her sister's custody, and Brody reiterates to her that he is not a terrorist and yells at her for harassing his family and him. Carrie finally breaks and starts doubting her own sanity. She asks her sister to take her to the hospital.

That night, Brody tries to get his suicide note back, but the chip is gone. Brody contacts Nazir and explains that his vest malfunctioned, but that maybe it is a good thing that it did, as he is now a trusted ally of the man who is going to be the next president, and will be able to influence him. Nazir agrees. Two days later Saul has found out Carrie hospitalized herself and is preparing for electroconvulsive therapy (ECT) to treat her bipolar disorder. Saul tries to stop her, but Carrie is determined. Saul tells her she was wrong about Brody but right about Abu Nazir; Walden ordered a drone strike that killed eighty-two children, including Abu Nazir's youngest son. Just as the anesthesia is about to take her under, Carrie remembers a key detail that connects Brody with Abu Nazir's dead son. Unfortunately, the ECT will erase that memory.

Why This Episode Made the List

I have never held my breath like I did watching this episode. I genuinely had no idea which way it was going to go. This is television at its finest. Plus, when Carrie breaks, you can really feel it and understand why she goes to the lengths she does to try to "regain" her sanity.

3. SEASON 3, EPISODE 12: "THE STAR"

Brody kills Akbari, steals his gun, and walks out as though nothing has happened. He forces his driver to meet Carrie at a safe house. Majid Javadi tells Saul to abandon Carrie and Brody because their capture would increase Javadi's chances of getting Akbari's job and promises to get Carrie out afterward. Saul refuses and continues with his plans to extract Carrie, involving the military. Dar Adal betrays him, and Senator Lockhart takes command of the CIA, calls off the extraction, and gives the safe house's location to Javadi. Before they get there, Carrie tells Brody she is pregnant. The Iranian military lure Brody and Carrie out and take Brody away, leaving Carrie behind. Brody is given a quick trial and sentenced to be hanged publicly. Carrie attends, pushing her way through the mob; as she looks on, he is hung. Carrie yells to Brody so he knows she is there as he dies. Four months go by. Saul is fired. Carrie decides to keep the baby because she is part of Brody. She is promoted to station chief in Istanbul, making her the youngest station chief in CIA history, plus she is at a prestigious station. Carrie asks if Brody will be given a star at the upcoming CIA memorial along with other fallen agents. He says no, so after the event, Carrie takes a Sharpie and adds a star for Brody to the memorial.

Why This Episode Made the List

This episode is so emotional and well done. While what happens in it was controversial, watching it was truly an experience. It also sets up the motivations for the seasons to come.

PERSONAL OPINION ON THE SHOW

I would recommend the first three seasons of this show to anyone. I seriously couldn't stop watching it—no wonder it won so many awards. The show had a bit of a slump in season 4, and you can skip season 5 and be just fine. The last three are more of a return to the vibe and trajectory of the first ones.

How well did *Homeland* stand the test of time? 5/10. As much as I loved the show, the portrayal of people from the Middle East is hard to ignore, as is the insane number of times Carrie gets away with things she shouldn't.

House of Cards

1. SEASON 1, EPISODE 1: "CHAPTER 1"

Frank Underwood accidently hits a dog with his car. He gets out and suffocates it while explaining to the audience "'how the dog is only suffering pain, not through the kind that makes it strong,' so he is willing to do the unpleasant, but the necessary thing." Inside, Frank and Claire finish getting ready for a gala. Frank turns to the audience again, explaining that the newly elected president, vice president, and White House chief, none of whom Frank really likes, were only elected because of Frank's help and he expects them to reward him by naming him to a higher position than his current one of House Majority whip. The next day, Frank finds out the president won't be naming him secretary of state after all. That night, while they are sharing a cigarette, Frank tells Claire what happened, and she urges him to create a plan for success and how to get revenge. He does, and she likes it.

The following morning, Franks puts it in motion. The next night, Frank and Claire attend the same symphony performance as ambitious reporter Zoe Barnes. Ignored by her editor and fellow journalists at the *Washington Herald*, she is there trying to land a big source. The next morning, a photo appears of Frank checking out Zoe's butt, and she recognizes him as a potential big get. The next night Zoe shows up at Frank's house. When she shows him the picture, Frank invites her in, and she tries to seduce him. Frank ignores her until she mentions she is willing to be his exclusive outlet in the media. After a nasty exchange with Claire, Zoe leaves without coming to an agreement with Frank. The next day, Zoe gets a hold of a partially shredded draft of the education bill that Frank dismissed as too left wing. She writes up an article about it without her boss knowing, and it is released on the front page of the paper. Frank reads it and sees in it evidence that Zoe is as hungry for power as he is.

2. SEASON 1, EPISODE 5: "CHAPTER 5"

Zoe and Frank are having an affair with Frank feeding her the information he wants to get out into the press. Even though she got fired from the *Washington Herald* for her article she is getting all kinds of high-profile job offers. That day, Peter Russo is asked to uphold his campaign promise to stop the closing of a shipyard that would mean twelve thousand people getting laid off. He wants to, but knows he can't because Frank—who is blackmailing him because Frank got Peter's DUI charges to go away—made him take the opposite stance. Back at Zoe's apartment, she allows Frank to take nude photos of her as insurance that she won't betray him. Frank is concerned about a looming teacher's strike that will affect his education bill. He supports Claire when the hotel where she is holding a gala for her NGO refuses to let her in because its employees are unionized and are protesting her in solidarity with the teachers, who are against Frank. The couple scheme to have the gala right outside the hotel instead. The teachers protest the gala, but Frank turns it to his advantage by handing out food to the protesters, a gesture that wins them over. When they get home, Peter is there. He yells at Frank for putting him in a bad position about the shipyard. Frank informs him that Frank is the only person who still believes in him and hands him a razor blade, in case he "wants to take the coward's way out."

Why This Episode Made the List

This show has so many story lines at once that not even half of them are covered in this summary. It is a great example of the way Frank plots, and it shows how far he is willing to go to get his way, both with Zoe and Peter.

3. SEASON 5, EPISODE 11: "CHAPTER 63"

Frank is now president, with Claire as his vice president. Rumors of impeachment and censure are floating around. The next day, Frank finds out that he has a mole in his office who is leaking information. Bob Birch and Terry Womack strongly suggest that Frank consider resigning. Later that day, an article is published that includes a White House source confirming that Frank used sketchy intelligence to close voting centers on election day. One of his staffers, Cathy, agrees to testify in front of the Declaration of War committee.

Why This Episode Made the List

This is the episode where Claire first talks to the audience, and it sets up her rise to power and Frank's eventual downfall.

PERSONAL OPINION ON THE SHOW

This series is a masterpiece of television. The acting is superb, as is the writing. While many have criticized it for taking liberties with how things really work in Washington, most viewers won't know what is true and what isn't, and as a civilian, getting any glimpse behind the government curtain is fascinating.

How well did *House of Cards* stand the test of time? 7.5/10. Setting aside Kevin Spacey's personal issues, the show is still strong. But everything hits differently in a post-Trump world. Some story lines are too much of a reminder of real-world incidents. For some, that might be a plus, but not for me.

Orphan Black

1. SEASON 1, EPISODE 1: "NATURAL SELECTION"

Sarah gets off a subway train only to see a woman who looks just like her step in front of the next one, committing suicide. Shaken, Sarah takes the woman's bag and shoes and flees. Sarah looks through the woman's purse and decides to steal her identity, at least until she can figure out what is going on. At Beth's apartment, Sarah finds out Beth was rich and decides to clean out her bank account to fund her plans to flee with her daughter, Kira. She convinces her foster brother, Felix, to help her fake her own death. Felix goes to the morgue and identifies Beth's body as Sarah. When Sarah is at the bank withdrawing all of Beth's money, she also opens Beth's safe deposit box, where she finds a pink cell phone and birth certificates for Beth and two other women.

As she is walking out, Art, Beth's police partner whose calls Sarah has been dodging, confronts her, thinking she is Beth. Sarah manages to delay an internal affairs hearing Beth was supposed to testify at, but realizes she is going to have to take on Beth's role as a cop even though she has no idea how. Vic, Sarah's abusive ex-boyfriend, shows up at Felix's apartment, and Felix tells him she is dead when he asks where she is. Beth's boyfriend Paul comes home early from a trip while Sarah is there, and Sarah has sex with him to distract him from noticing she isn't Beth. Felix agrees to hold a memorial for Sarah, which Sarah attends. As Sarah is about to get in her car, another woman who looks like her, German Katja Obinger, gets into the back seat and demands to know why she (Beth) didn't meet her as arranged. Katja realizes that "Beth" has no idea who she is. Before she can do anything, Katja is shot in the head through the rear window. Sarah panics and drives away amid a hail of bullets. Katja's cell phone, which is just like the pink one Sarah found in the safe deposit box, starts to ring. When no one answers, Beth's phone starts ringing. They are somehow connected.

2. SEASON 2, EPISODE 4: "GOVERNED AS IT WERE BY CHANCE"

Sarah wakes up in a wrecked car, next to Daniel, who is dead. Cal comes by and helps her get out. All she wants is to flee with Kira, but Cal insists on helping. At the Prolethean farm, Henrik tells Gracie to think of Helena as part of the family, even though he knows Gracie is suspicious and scared of her. They go into the room where Helena is being held. All Helena can remember (she was given a sedative) is that she is wearing a wedding dress, there were a lot of people, and now she is wearing a ring. Alison, too, wakes up in a strange room wearing her theater costume, and her right arm is in a sling. She vomits and finds out she is not in a Dyad facility as she feared, but in rehab. Back at the farm, Gracie tries to smother Helena with a pillow, but Helena knocks her out. Finally free, Helena runs through the halls and finds a laboratory. She has flashbacks to being held down and some procedure happening between her legs. She runs outside and is chased by several men. Cal takes Sarah to the bus station, and she heads to Mrs. S's house, where she runs into Felix.

They find a scrapbook with pictures and newspaper articles that start to paint a picture of how Sarah was fostered and possibly sheds light on the clones' creation. Sarah sneaks into Rachel's apartment and finds more evidence of Rachel's childhood and how she grew up self-aware. She is about to leave when someone comes in—it's Daniel who is not dead after all. He knocks her out. She wakes tied up in the shower and Daniel starts to torture her, but Helena busts in and kills him. Sarah is afraid Helena is going to kill her, too, but she embraces Sarah instead, saying, "I think he took something from inside me," and asking for her help. Back at the farm, Henrik watches through a microscope as cells divide. He has successfully fertilized Helena's eggs with his own sperm.

Why This Episode Made the List

It is a turning point for all of the characters and provides a lot of the backstory that has been missing from the show so far. And it is good to see Sarah and Helena become allies during a time of adversity for both.

3. SEASON 5, EPISODE 10: "TO RIGHT THE WRONGS OF MANY"

In a flashback, we see that Sarah once considered having an abortion when she was pregnant with Kira. In the present, Sarah helps a very pregnant Helena navigate the halls of the Dyad basement amid a blaring alarm. She's trying to help Helena escape, but Helena can't go any farther; her water has broken. Sarah goes for supplies to help Helena give birth and runs into Art, whom she sends back to protect Helena. Dr. Coady gets to her first, and when Art arrives, Coady holds him at gunpoint. Art fakes fainting, mumbling about there being a lot of blood. When Dr. Coady gets close to see what is wrong, Art grabs the gun and Helena stabs her in the throat with a screwdriver she had grabbed. Sarah returns, and amid flashbacks of Sarah in labor with Kira, Sarah and Art deliver Helena's twins. The show jumps forward in time. Alison has converted their garage into an apartment for Helena and the babies.

At Mrs. S's house, Sarah is studying for her GDE, with a cured Cosima as her teacher. Kira leaves for school without a care in the world. Time skips forward again. Alison is setting up her yard for a party; Cosima is making lists of known clones, while Scott and Delphine make doses of the LEDA cure; Sarah is boxing up Mrs. S's house. That afternoon, we find out the party is a belated baby shower for Helena. The clones are all there, along with their family members and kids. Felix gets a call from Rachel, who is nearby but not allowed to join them. He tells her everyone is fine, and she assures him she will keep her promises. She hands Felix a folder and says she wants to make amends.

That night, when the clones are alone, they talk about ways they have failed as mothers and people. Felix joins them and gives them Rachel's gift, a complete list of all 274 LEDA clones with all the information needed to locate and cure them. Helena shares that she has been writing a book called *Orphan Black*. It is the story of all the clones. The last few scenes show all the clones are happy, including Helena, who has finally given the twins real names: Arthur and Donnie, after the only two "real men" she has ever known, and Sarah, who has made Mrs. S's house into her own.

Why This Episode Made the List

As the series finale, it ties up all the story lines of the clones. The beginning of the episode is heart-pounding, not knowing if Helena, Sarah, and Art will live. The birth scene with images from both twins' labors is incredibly emotional and beautiful. The party that Alison hosts is our last chance to see all the clones together before their lives draw them in different directions once again. I found it a wonderful ending to a fantastic show.

PERSONAL OPINION ON THE SHOW

Orphan Black is one of my all-time favorite shows. The first two seasons are my favorites because from there they get progressively stranger. I really think they could have done without the male clones completely. The final season was way too strange for my tastes, but since all is well that ends well, I can deal.

How well did *Orphan Black* stand the test of time? 9/10. It is a pretty recent show, so I don't think it has really had time to age yet.

The Equalizer

1. SEASON 1, EPISODE 1: "THE EQUALIZER"

In a former life, Robyn McCall was part of "the Company," an illegal arm of the CIA that did unspeakable things. No longer enjoying her work, she leaves them, telling her family she just quit her job at a charity to spend more time with her family. She finds out about Jewel, who is a suspect in the shooting of a lawyer. The girl protests her innocence even though the police have her on tape committing the crime. Wanting to help her, but not knowing what to do, she contacts former CIA buddies, a sharpshooter named Melody and her hacker husband, Harry. Robyn eventually learns that a tech genius doctored the tape because the girl was a witness to a hit he put out. He is arrested, and Jewel is freed. Robyn, buoyed by her success, decides she wants to help more people and becomes The Equalizer.

2. SEASON 2, EPISODE 5: "FOLLOWERS"

A woman gets out of bed in the middle of the night because her young son said there was a ghost in his room. Robyn meets with Abe and Rachel, two online true-crime enthusiasts who want her help to find a stalker who is posting videos of a woman without her knowledge, whom he says he will murder in eight hours. They have done their own investigation and have a suspect, Brandon Mackey, but the police won't listen to them. Working with Melody and Harry, they find out that Brandon uses another name on social media, Jason Caldwell. Robyn goes to his house and breaks in, but he's home and points a gun at her. He swears he isn't the stalker and his life is being ruined by the accusation, so he is trying to find the real guy. Harry traces the videos and one of them points to an internet café, so Robyn goes there.

Meanwhile Vi and Delilah are shopping at a clothing store. Vi has a dress in her hands that a white woman wants. When Vi won't give it to her, the two physically fight over it, and the white woman calls the police saying she was assaulted. The police arrive and tell them if they can't work it out, arrests will be made. Delilah reveals she caught the whole thing on video, and once the cops see what happened, they make the white woman apologize, and Vi declines to press charges because she, unlike the other woman, doesn't want to "weaponize the police." Harry and Melody figure out who the woman is who is being stalked. Robyn goes to warn her, only to find that the killer was there, but ran when he heard the knock at the door. He took the woman's son with him. Robyn, Harry, and Melody realize the woman was actually the stalker, not the victim. They find the real mother and son tied up in the basement, and they tell her the stalker's name is Amber. Harry calls and says that a new video just went up, with Rachel as the hostage.

This video is live, and thousands of people are watching. Robyn asks their true-crime group if anyone can tell her where they might be. Someone recognizes the windows, and Robyn calls the police. Just as Amber starts to suffocate Rachel, the police arrive and rescue Rachel. Delilah visits the white woman from the store and tells her she thinks Aunt Vi had a right to be upset over what happened. The woman is rude, so Delilah tells her she just posted video from the incident at the store online.

Why This Episode Made the List

It was intense! But more than that, the subplot about race is very important and thought provoking. Story lines like this are in the headlines all the time but are rarely shown on television, so the fact that this show did it is monumental.

3. SEASON 2, EPISODE 14: "PULSE"

Robyn goes to check on Detective Dante, who turned in his badge after being wrongfully imprisoned and almost killed by corrupt cops. He refuses to talk to anyone about what he went through. His children were traumatized as well because they almost lost their father and are scared of losing him again. While she is there, Robyn gets a call—an emergency signal from an old friend, Marcela. She rushes to Marcela's house to find her friend murdered. Marcela's CIA handler, Griffin, is also there and doesn't want to talk to Robyn, but eventually he says he went to check on her because she hadn't been responding and he found her dead. He revealed Marcela had been working with Chen Ying, a Chinese translator for the United Nations (UN), who offered to trade information for protection. But Chen was recalled to China and killed before she could give them any information. Robyn believes Marcela was killed because of her connection to Chen. She has Harry and Melody investigate and get Robyn into the UN so she can talk with Marcela's friend.

When Robyn finds out Chen gave her friend a bracelet before going back to China, she takes it and finds data stored within that reveals Robyn's old enemy, Mason Quinn, is back in town, thanks to a prisoner exchange. Robyn asks Bishop about it, and he gives her a file and warns her not to open it unless she wants to start down a rabbit hole she may not be able to get out of. But, of course, she opens it, and it makes her think Quinn was involved in Marcela's death. Griffin figures out Quinn was in town to purchase an electromagnetic pulse (EMP) device from a Russian scientist. Robyn and Griffin try to find the weapon, but it was taken out to be used in a demonstration. Quinn kidnaps them both and forces Robyn to watch as he uses the EMP to crash the plane Bishop is on. Quinn plans to kill them both, but Melody shows up and saves them. They seize the weapon, but Quinn gets away on a helicopter. Robyn has the option of using the EMP to take Quinn down, but chooses not to because it would also kill hundreds of innocent people below.

PERSONAL OPINION ON THE SHOW

This show is still airing so I can only evaluate it on the first two and a half seasons. It's a great show that is easy to binge because every episode is so compelling. Queen Latifah infuses such heart into each one. I hope it is renewed for many more seasons.

How well did *The Equalizer* stand the test of time? Ask me in ten+ years. Right now, only the future knows.

Acknowledgments

Believe it or not, this book really began not on the day I wrote its proposal or signed the publishing contract, not even when I wrote the first word; it began on the August afternoon in 1992 when I saw the original *Buffy the Vampire Slayer* movie at the theater with my mom and my cousin, Lisa. All of my television choices since then have been influenced by the kinship I felt with the blonde cheerleader who was brave enough to accept a destiny she couldn't understand and didn't want. In so many ways, that is the connecting thread of all of the shows in this book—women who, each in their own ways, step up when they are called in support of the greater good.

Now that the philosophizing is out of the way, on to the practicalities. Thank you to Bob Bachelor for giving me the opportunity to write this book. Thank you as well to my editor, Christen Karniski, and my copyeditor, Nancy Syrett, for helping me make this book as strong as it can possibly be. Thank you to my agent, Amy Collins, and all of my family, friends, and coworkers for listening to me talk about this book and its contents over the months I wrote and researched it.

My gratitude goes out to the hundreds of people who wrote the books and articles I used as sources for this book. I'm grateful for the work you put in as well as the insights I have quoted in this book. We think about television viewing as a solitary experience, but interpreting the shows we watch is definitely an ongoing dialog. I'm honored to take my place among your ranks.

I'd also like to thank the actors, writers, directors, producers, and others who made these 10 shows possible. Each one influenced (and continues to influence) my life in ways large and small. While being a writer certainly doesn't compare to saving the world—a lot—you are my kin in creativity, and this book is as much yours as it is mine.

Finally, to all who read this book—may you walk away from these pages inspired and motivated to make your own mark on the world.

Notes

Introduction

1. Ryan W. Miller, "Are You a Xennial? How to Tell If You're the Microgeneration between Gen X and Millennial," *USA Today*, December 20, 2018, https://www.usatoday.com/story/news/nation/2018/12/20/xennials-millennials-generation-x-microgeneration/2369230002/.

2. Elizabeth L. Maurer, "Tuning in to Women in Television," National Women's History Museum, September 21, 2016, https://www.womenshistory.org/articles/tuning-women-television.

3. Maurer, "Tuning in to Women in Television."

4. "The History of Working Women, as Seen on TV," TV Professor, October 29, 2021, https://thetvprofessor.com/the-history-of-working-women-as-seen-on-tv/.

5. Maurer, "Tuning in to Women in Television."

6. James Oliver, "Women in Westerns," *Reader's Digest UK*, November 23, 2021, https://www.readersdigest.co.uk/culture/film-tv/women-in-westerns.

7. Maurer, "Tuning in to Women in Television."

8. "Commie Fighters of the '50s," For Your Eyes Only, https://www.for-your-eyes-only.com/Site/Commie_50s.html.

9. "Commie Fighters of the '50s."

10. Thomas Andrae, "Television's First Feminist: 'The Avengers' and Female Spectatorship," *Discourse* 18, no. 3 (1996): 115, http://www.jstor.org/stable/41389423.

11. "The History of Working Women."

12. Kelsie Gibson, "Actresses Who Have Played Catwoman through the Years," *People*, November 28, 2022, https://people.com/movies/actresses-who-have-played-catwoman/#:~:text=Julie%20Newmar%20played%20the%20very.

13. Christina Radish, "Marlo Thomas Talks Makers: Women Who Make America, *That Girl*, and More," Collider, February 26, 2013, https://collider.com/marlo-thomas-makers-women-who-make-america-interview/.

14. Quoted in Maurer, "Tuning in to Women in Television."

15. Herbie J. Pilato, "*That Girl:* The One Who Changed Everything," Television Academy, https://www.emmys.com/news/online-originals/girl-one-who-changed-every thing.

16. Pilato, "*That Girl.*"

17. Radish, "Marlo Thomas Talks Makers."

18. "'The Visionary'—Marlo Thomas as Ann Marie in *That Girl*," Comedy Hall of Fame, https://comedyhalloffame.com/celebrate/the-visionary-marlo-thomas-as-ann -marie-in-that-girl.

19. Pilato, "*That Girl.*"

20. Geoff Hammill, "*The Mary Tyler Moore Show*," Museum of Broadcast Communications, archived from the original on February 1, 2015, https://interviews.television academy.com/shows/mary-tyler-moore-show-the.

21. "The History of Working Women."

22. Patrick Cooley, "Before 'Wonder Woman': How Female Superheroes Evolved," Cleveland.com, June 7, 2017, https://www.cleveland.com/entertainment/2017/06 /before_wonder_woman_how_female.html#:~:text=The%20character%20started%20 to%20evolve%20when%20then%20DC.

23. "The History of the Female Superhero," YouTube, https://youtu.be/JG-AUqE siNE.

24. Tom Foster, "The History and Evolution of Female Superheroes from 1940 to Present," TVovermind, October 6, 2017, https://tvovermind.com/history-evolution -female-superheroes-1940-present/.

25. Anthony Crislip, "Why 'The Bionic Woman' Outshines 'The Six Million Dollar Man,'" Ultimate Classic Rock, https://ultimateclassicrock.com/bionic-woman/.

26. "10 Pioneering Female Superheroes We Saw on Classic TV," Heroes and Icons, August 13, 2021, https://www.handitv.com/lists/10-pioneering-female-superheroes-we -saw-on-classic-tv.

27. "The History of Working Women."

28. "The History of Working Women."

29. Quoted in Jacey Fortin, "That Time 'Murphy Brown' and Dan Quayle Topped the Front Page," *New York Times*, January 26, 2018, https://www.nytimes.com/2018 /01/26/arts/television/murphy-brown-dan-quayle.html.

30. Sarah E. Whitney, "I Can Be Whoever I Want to Be: *Alias* and the Post-Feminist Rhetoric of Choice," Genders 1998–2013, March 1, 2013, https://www.colorado.edu /gendersarchive1998-2013/2013/03/01/i-can-be-whoever-i-want-be-alias-and-post-fem inist-rhetoric-choice.

31. Patrick Hipes, "Streaming TV Series ahead of Broadcast in Featuring Women in Front of and behind Camera, Latest 'Boxed In' Study Finds," Deadline, October 18, 2022, https://deadline.com/2022/10/boxed-in-tv-study-2022-results-streaming-broad cast-series-1235147577/#:~:text=A%20new%20report%20from%20the.

32. GLAAD Media Institute, "Where We Are on TV," GLAAD, 2021–2022, 13, 21, https://www.glaad.org/sites/default/files/GLAAD%20202122%20WWATV.pdf.

Chapter 1

1. Laura Merrill, "Buffyversity: The Real Monster All Along," *Multiversity Comics*, April 6, 2021, http://www.multiversitycomics.com/news-columns/buffyversity-the-real -monster-all-along/.

2. Katharine Schwab, "Why Academics Love 'Buffy the Vampire Slayer,'" *The Atlantic*, October 1, 2015, https://www.theatlantic.com/entertainment/archive/2015/10/the -rise-of-buffy-studies/407020/.

3. F. R. Kesby, "The Problematic Feminism of *Buffy the Vampire Slayer*," Women's Republic, October 15, 2018, https://www.womensrepublic.net/the-problematic-femi nism-of-buffy-the-vampire-slayer/.

4. Schwab, "Why Academics Love 'Buffy the Vampire Slayer.'"

5. Quoted in Sarah Dobbs, "10 Ways *Buffy the Vampire Slayer* Changed the World," Den of Geek, March 10, 2017, https://www.denofgeek.com/tv/10-ways-buffy-the -vampire-slayer-changed-the-world/.

6. Emily St. James and Caroline Framke, "How *Buffy the Vampire Slayer* Transformed TV as We Know It," *Vox*, March 10, 2017, https://www.vox.com/culture/2017/3 /10/14857542/buffy-the-vampire-slayer-explained-tv-influence.

7. St. James and Framke, "How *Buffy the Vampire Slayer* Transformed TV as We Know It."

8. *Scream*, directed by Wes Craven (New York: Dimension Films, 1996), film.

9. Lila Shapiro, "The Undoing of Joss Whedon," Vulture, January 17, 2022, https://www.vulture.com/article/joss-whedon-allegations.html.

10. Shapiro, "The Undoing of Joss Whedon."

11. Shapiro, "The Undoing of Joss Whedon."

12. "Shonda Rhimes Reveals How 'Buffy' Helped Her Rediscover TV," *Hollywood Reporter*, October 8, 2014, https://www.hollywoodreporter.com/news/general-news /shonda-rhimes-reveals-how-buffy-739109/.

13. Shapiro, "The Undoing of Joss Whedon."

14. Shapiro, "The Undoing of Joss Whedon."

15. Rhonda V. Wilcox, "In Memoriam: David Lavery," Association for the Study of Buffy+, https://www.whedonstudies.tv/in-memoriam-david-lavery.html#:~:text=In%20 2008%2C%20David%2C%20Tanya%20R.

16. Rhonda V. Wilcox, "About," Association for the Study of Buffy+, February 22, 2022, https://www.whedonstudies.tv/about.html.

17. "The Slayage Conference," Association for the Study of Buffy+, https://www .whedonstudies.tv/conference.html.

18. Kai Cole, "Joss Whedon Is a 'Hypocrite Preaching Feminist Ideals,' Ex-Wife Kai Cole Says (Guest Blog)," *The Wrap* (blog), August 20, 2017, https://www.thewrap.com /joss-whedon-feminist-hypocrite-infidelity-affairs-ex-wife-kai-cole-says/.

19. Tom Tapp, "Gal Gadot Further Describes 'Justice League' Conflict with Joss Whedon," Deadline, October 18, 2021, https://deadline.com/2021/10/gal-gadot-joss -whedon-shocked-1234858052/.

20. Anthony D'Alessandro, "Ray Fisher Demands WarnerMedia Reveal 'Justice League' Investigation Findings Following CEO Ann Sarnoff's Comments," Deadline, March 23, 2021, https://deadline.com/2021/03/ray-fisher-slames-warnermedia-ann -sarnoff-justice-league-joss-whedon-investigation-1234719795/.

21. Shapiro, "The Undoing of Joss Whedon."

22. Liz Shannon Miller, "What It's like to Be a 'Buffy' Fan in the Wake of These Joss Whedon Revelations," Collider, February 12, 2021, https://collider.com/joss-whedon -charisma-carpenter-allegations-buffy-fans-reaction/.

23. Shapiro, "The Undoing of Joss Whedon."

24. Miller, "What It's like to Be a 'Buffy' Fan."

25. Ailsa Chang, "Joss Whedon Was Once Hailed as a Feminist. Then Came the Stories about His Behavior," St. Louis NPR, January 18, 2022, https://www.npr.org /2022/01/18/1073881791/joss-whedon-was-once-hailed-as-a-feminist-then-came-the -stories-about-his-behavi.

26. Shapiro, "The Undoing of Joss Whedon."

27. Miller, "What It's like to Be a 'Buffy' Fan."

28. Dobbs, "10 Ways *Buffy the Vampire Slayer* Changed the World."

29. Alanna Bennett, "How 'Buffy' Changed Television for a New Generation," BuzzFeed, March 10, 2017, https://www.buzzfeed.com/alannabennett/what-it-means -to-honor-buffy.

30. Billy Nilles, "Ranking TV's Top 20 Badass Female Characters," *E! Online*, April 26, 2020, https://www.eonline.com/news/1143325/ranking-tv-s-top-20-badass-female -characters.

31. Stephen Daisley, "How *Buffy the Vampire Slayer* Transformed Pop Culture," *The Spectator*, March 10, 2017, https://www.spectator.co.uk/article/how-buffy-the-vampire -slayer-transformed-pop-culture/.

32. Claire L. Wong, "Why 'Buffy the Vampire Slayer' Is Still One of the Best TV Shows Ever," *Hollywood Insider*, February 2, 2021, https://www.hollywoodinsider.com/buffy -the-vampire-slayer-success/.

33. Ed Gross, "*Charmed* Creator Spills Show Secrets in Our Decades-Old Interview," *In Touch Weekly*, February 16, 2018, https://www.intouchweekly.com/posts/charmed -cast-secrets-154161/.

34. Isabelle Oderberg, "*Charmed*: Sister Witches Juggle Life and Magic in This Oddly Relatable Late-90s Cult Hit Show," *The Guardian*, August 22, 2021, https://www .theguardian.com/culture/2021/aug/23/charmed-sister-witches-juggle-life-and-magic -in-this-oddly-relatable-late-90s-cult-hit-show.

35. Caroline Preece, "Why *Charmed* Deserves to Be Celebrated," Den of Geek, January 13, 2017, https://www.denofgeek.com/tv/why-charmed-deserves-to-be-celebrated/.

36. Dennis Michael, "*Charmed* Has That Spelling Magic," CNN, archived from the original on September 8, 2014, http://www.cnn.com/SHOWBIZ/TV/9810/23 /charmed/index.html.

37. Sophie Moss, "Culture Throwback: Thinking Back on How *Charmed* Captured Contemporary Feminism," *Luna Luna*, November 23, 2015, http://www.lunalunamaga zine.com/blog/culture-throwback-thinking-back-on-how-charmed-captured-contempo rary-feminism.

38. Matthew Trzcinski, "20 Things That Make No Sense about the Original *Charmed*," ScreenRant, January 10, 2019, https://screenrant.com/charmed-tv-series-original-biggest-plot-holes-no-sense/.

39. Gross, "*Charmed* Creator Spills Show Secrets."

40. Jenny Crusie, "*Totally Charmed*: Introduction," *Jenny's Blog*, 2005, https://jennycrusie.com/excerpts/totally-charmed-introduction/.

41. Preece, "Why *Charmed* Deserves to Be Celebrated."

42. Preece, "Why *Charmed* Deserves to Be Celebrated."

43. Preece, "Why *Charmed* Deserves to Be Celebrated."

44. Rebecca Feasey, "The 'Charmed' Audience: Gender and the Politics of Contemporary Culture," in "A Screen of One's Own," ed. Heather Osborne-Thompson, special issue, *Spectator* 25, no. 2 (Fall 2005): 39–48, https://cinema.usc.edu/assets/097/15720.pdf.

45. Sarah Assenti, "What the Return of *Sabrina* and *Charmed* Says about Feminism in 2018," *Stylist*, October 16, 2018, https://www.stylist.co.uk/long-reads/witchcraft-rebooted-what-the-return-of-sabrina-and-charmed-says-about-feminism-in-2018/231803.

46. Oderberg, "*Charmed*: Sister Witches Juggle Life and Magic."

47. Abdullah Idrees, "The Empowerment of Three: The Halliwell Sisters Charm Televisual Culture," *Studies in Visual Cultures—ENG 705* (blog), April 18, 2018, https://visualculture.blog.torontomu.ca/the-empowerment-of-three-the-halliwell-sisters-charm-televisual-culture/.

48. Oderberg, "*Charmed*: Sister Witches Juggle Life and Magic."

49. Feasey, "The 'Charmed' Audience," 39.

50. Gross, "*Charmed* Creator Spills Show Secrets."

51. Idrees, "The Empowerment of Three."

52. "Prue Halliwell," in *Charmed*, *Charmed* Wiki, https://charmed.fandom.com/wiki/Prue_Halliwell.

53. Oderberg, "*Charmed*: Sister Witches Juggle Life and Magic."

54. Idrees, "The Empowerment of Three."

55. Gross, "*Charmed* Creator Spills Show Secrets."

56. Feasey, "The 'Charmed' Audience," 40.

57. Idrees, "The Empowerment of Three."

58. Caroline Framke, "*Orphan Black* Co-creator Graeme Manson on the Season Finale, a New Threat, and 'Shippers,'" *A.V. Club*, June 21, 2015, https://www.avclub.com/orphan-black-co-creator-graeme-manson-on-the-season-fin-1798280959.

59. Timea, "Here's All of Tatiana Maslany's Clones in *Orphan Black*, Ranked," MovieWeb, January 18, 2022, https://movieweb.com/tatiana-maslany-clones-orphan-black/#:~:text=It%27s%20been%20years%20since%20Orphan.

60. Jill Lepore, "The History Lurking behind 'Orphan Black,'" *New Yorker*, April 16, 2015, https://www.newyorker.com/culture/cultural-comment/the-history-lurking-behind-orphan-black.

61. Ella Mosher, "The Bechdel Test—Encouraging the Conversation about Women in Fiction." Communicator, December 19, 2014, https://chscommunicator.com/42578/opinion/2014/12/the-bechdel-test-encouraging-the-conversation-about-women-in-fiction/.

62. Jessie Commerce, "*Orphan Black*: How the Bechdel Test Helps Us Accurately Analyze Gender Equality," Media Production and Criticism, https://dmillef.wixsite .com/media-criticism/orphan-black.

63. Angelica Jade Bastién, "The Grand Feminist Legacy of *Orphan Black*," Vulture, August 15, 2017, https://www.vulture.com/2017/08/orphan-black-series-review.html.

64. Commerce, " *Orphan Black*: How the Bechdel Test Helps Us Accurately Analyze Gender Equality."

65. Bastién, "The Grand Feminist Legacy of *Orphan Black*."

66. "List of LEDA Clones," *Orphan Black* Wiki, https://orphanblack.fandom.com /wiki/List_of_LEDA_clones#:~:text=There%20are%20at%20least%20274.

67. Caroline Framke, "*Orphan Black* Flips the Sci-Fi Script by Putting Female Agency First," *A.V. Club*, July 18, 2013, https://www.avclub.com/orphan-black-flips-the-sci-fi -script-by-putting-female-1798239300.

68. Tanya Ghahremani, "Why 'Orphan Black' Needs to Kill off Your Favorite Clone," Complex, May 19, 2014, https://www.complex.com/pop-culture/2014/05 /orphan-black-kill-favorite-clone.

69. Framke, "*Orphan Black* Flips the Sci-Fi Script."

70. Devon Maloney, "*Orphan Black* Science Consultant Cosima Herter Breaks down the Series Finale," *Vanity Fair*, August 12, 2017, https://www.vanityfair.com/holly wood/2017/08/orphan-black-series-finale-season-5-cosima-herter-interview.

71. Nicole Nguyen, "How *Orphan Black*'s Cosima Got Her Dreads," Popsugar Tech, July 26, 2014, https://www.popsugar.com/tech/Orphan-Black-Cosima-Hair-35337015.

72. Framke, "*Orphan Black* Flips the Sci-Fi Script."

73. Brian Moylan, "*Orphan Black*: What I Learned Binge-Watching Seasons One and Two," *The Guardian*, April 18, 2015, https://www.theguardian.com/tv-and-radio/2015 /apr/18/orphan-black-bbc-america-seasons-one-and-two.

74. Delia Harrington, "The Orphan Black Legacy: A Galaxy of Complex Women," Den of Greek, August 19, 2017, https://www.denofgeek.com/tv/the-orphan-black -legacy-a-galaxy-of-complex-women/.

75. Framke, "*Orphan Black* Flips the Sci-Fi Script."

76. Bastién, "The Grand Feminist Legacy of *Orphan Black*."

77. Emily Nussbaum, "Cheaper by the Dozen," *New Yorker*, April 21, 2014, https:// www.newyorker.com/magazine/2014/04/28/cheaper-by-the-dozen.

78. Bastién, "The Grand Feminist Legacy of *Orphan Black*."

79. Alicia Lutes, "An Oral History of *Orphan Black* from the Women Who Brought It to Life," Nerdist, August 9, 2017, https://archive.nerdist.com/orphan-black-oral -history-women-bts/.

80. Jennifer Still, "Why Delphine Cormier Is the Unsung Hero of 'Orphan Black,'" *Bustle*, July 28, 2017, https://www.bustle.com/p/why-delphine-cormier-is-the-unsung -hero-of-orphan-black-72939.

81. Caroline Framke, "Orphan Black: 'History yet to Be Written,'" *A.V. Club*, June 21, 2015, https://www.avclub.com/orphan-black-history-yet-to-be-written-1798184133.

82. Still, "Why Delphine Cormier Is the Unsung Hero of 'Orphan Black.'"

83. Still, "Why Delphine Cormier Is the Unsung Hero of 'Orphan Black.'"

84. Dan Solomon, "How Netflix's 'Jessica Jones' Captures the Comic It's Based On—and How It Doesn't," Fast Company, November 24, 2015, https://www.fastcompany.com/3053946/how-netflixs-jessica-jones-captures-the-comic-its-based-on-and-how-it-doesnt.

85. Solomon, "How Netflix's 'Jessica Jones' Captures the Comic It's Based On."

86. Zoe Williams, "*Jessica Jones*: The Timely Return of a Feminist Superhero," *The Guardian*, February 24, 2018, https://www.theguardian.com/culture/2018/feb/24/jessica-jones-mind-control-and-redemption-the-timely-return-of-a-feminist-superhero.

87. Greg Kennedy, "Female Super Empowerment: *Jessica Jones* Is Back." *The National*, March 5, 2018, https://www.thenationalnews.com/arts-culture/television/female-super-empowerment-jessica-jones-is-back-1.710419.

88. Kennedy, "Female Super Empowerment."

89. Quinn Keaney, "What Exactly Did Trish 'Take' Away from Jessica Jones? The Answer Is Pretty Grim," Popsugar Entertainment, June 21, 2019, https://www.popsugar.com/entertainment/What-Did-Trish-Take-From-Jessica-Jessica-Jones-46258146.

90. Amanda Marcotte, "Before Binge-Watching *Jessica Jones*, Read *Alias*, the Feminist Comic It's Based On," Salon, November 20, 2015, https://www.salon.com/2015/11/19/before_binge_watching_jessica_jones_read_alias_the_feminist_comic_its_based_on/.

91. Jenna Scherer, "'Jessica Jones': We Finally Have a Superhero Icon for the #TimesUp Era," *Rolling Stone*, March 9, 2018, https://www.rollingstone.com/tv-movies/tv-movie-news/jessica-jones-we-finally-have-a-superhero-icon-for-the-timesup-era-127314/.

92. Chelsea Steiner, "*Jessica Jones* and Its Legacy of Female Anger," *Mary Sue*, February 19, 2019, https://www.themarysue.com/rip-jessica-jones/.

93. J. M. Tyree, "The Good Paranoia: Notes on *Jessica Jones*," *Michigan Quarterly Review*, July 31, 2019, https://sites.lsa.umich.edu/mqr/2019/07/the-good-paranoia-notes-on-jessica-jones%EF%BB%BF/.

94. Tyree, "The Good Paranoia."

95. Sophie Gilbert, "The Villainous Women of 'Jessica Jones,'" *The Atlantic*, March 15, 2018, https://www.theatlantic.com/entertainment/archive/2018/03/jessica-jones-season-2-review-netflix/555395/.

96. Marykate Jasper, "Jeri Hogarth: Jessica Jones and Female Capitalist Success," *Mary Sue*, March 13, 2018, https://www.themarysue.com/jeri-hogarth-jessica-jones-season-2/.

Chapter 2

1. June Thomas, "Secret Agent Woman," *Slate*, November 17, 2011, https://slate.com/culture/2011/11/covert-affairs-homeland-why-are-there-so-many-female-spies-on-television.html.

2. Sarah E. Whitney, "I Can Be Whoever I Want to Be: *Alias* and the Post-Feminist Rhetoric of Choice," Genders 1998–2013, March 1, 2013, https://www.colorado

.edu/gendersarchive1998-2013/2013/03/01/i-can-be-whoever-i-want-be-alias-and-post
-feminist-rhetoric-choice.

3. Lacy Baugher, "Twenty Years after *Alias*, TV Still Needs More Sydney Bristows,"
Den of Geek, September 29, 2021, https://www.denofgeek.com/tv/twenty-years-after
-alias-tv-still-needs-more-sydney-bristows/.

4. Baugher, "Twenty Years after *Alias*."

5. Whitney, "I Can Be Whoever I Want to Be."

6. Mark Cotta Vaz, "Internal Memorandum," in Alias *Declassified: The Official
Companion* (New York: Bantam Books for Young Readers, 2002), n.p.

7. A. J. Black, "*Alias* (Series Overview + Reviews)," We Made This, April 9, 2018,
https://wemadethisnetwork.com/2018/04/09/alias-series-overview-reviews/.

8. J. J. Abrams, introduction to Alias *Declassified: The Official Companion*, by Mark
Cotta Vaz (New York: Bantam Books, 2002), n.p.

9. Billy Nilles, "Ranking TV's Top 20 Badass Female Characters," *E! Online*, April
26, 2020, https://www.eonline.com/news/1143325/ranking-tv-s-top-20-badass-female
-characters.

10. Whitney, "I Can Be Whoever I Want to Be."

11. Charles Taylor, "'Alias' Grace," Salon, January 12, 2005, https://web.archive.org
/web/20140821014601/http://www.salon.com/2005/01/12/alias_2/.

12. Baugher, "Twenty Years after *Alias*."

13. Karl Hodge, "The Lazy Geek's Guide to *Alias*," Den of Geek, January 25, 2011,
https://www.denofgeek.com/tv/the-lazy-geeks-guide-to-alias/.

14. Mark Cotta Vaz, Alias *Declassified: The Official Companion* (New York: Bantam
Books for Young Readers), 61.

15. Baugher, "Twenty Years after *Alias*."

16. Caroline Preece, "Why *Nikita* Will Be Missed," Den of Geek, January 15, 2014,
https://www.denofgeek.com/tv/why-nikita-will-be-missed/.

17. Johnny Brayson, "Why Nikita Is the Deadliest Woman in Pop Culture,"
CHARGE!, July 10, 2019, https://watchcharge.com/why-nikita-is-the-deadliest-woman
-in-pop-culture/.

18. Melissa Leon, "Marvel's 'Agent Carter' Stomps on the Patriarchy," Daily Beast,
January 7, 2015, https://www.thedailybeast.com/marvels-agent-carter-stomps-on-the
-patriarchy.

19. Meg Dowell, "We Need a New Agent Carter Series Now More Than Ever,"
Culturess, August 13, 2019, https://culturess.com/2019/08/13/need-new-agent-carter
-series-now-ever/.

20. Kaitlin Thomas, "Before 'WandaVision,' There Was 'Agent Carter,' and It Was
Marvel's Best Show," Salon, January 31, 2021, https://www.salon.com/2021/01/31
/agent-carter-wandavision-marvel-tv-shows-disney-plus/.

21. Thomas, "Before 'WandaVision,' There Was 'Agent Carter.'"

22. Mikey O'Connell, "'Homeland' Declassified: Battles, Backlash, CIA Meetings
and a Secret Call with Edward Snowden," *Hollywood Reporter*, January 16, 2020, https://
www.hollywoodreporter.com/movies/movie-features/homeland-declassified-battles
-backlash-cia-meetings-a-secret-call-edward-snowden-1269957/.

23. Meredith Blake, "President Obama Names His Favorite Show of 2015—and No, It's Not 'Homeland,'" *Los Angeles Times*, December 9, 2015, https://www.latimes.com/entertainment/la-et-st-president-obama-favorite-tv-show-the-knick-20151209-story.html#:~:text=Back%20in%202012%2C%20he%20was.

24. Emily Nussbaum, "'Homeland': The Antidote for '24,'" *New Yorker*, November 29, 2011, https://www.newyorker.com/culture/culture-desk/homeland-the-antidote-for-24.

25. Matt Brennan, "Yes, 'Homeland' Is Still On: It's the Most Adaptable Show on Television," *Los Angeles Times*, February 7, 2020, https://www.latimes.com/entertainment-arts/tv/story/2020-02-07/homeland-showtime-claire-danes-mandy-patinkin-final-season.

26. "Homeland," Television Academy, https://www.emmys.com/shows/homeland.

27. Nilles, "Ranking TV's Top 20 Badass Female Characters."

28. "Homeland," Emmys.com, archived from the original on September 27, 2012, https://www.emmys.com/shows/homeland.

29. Vanessa Thorpe, "Claire Danes: Getting under the Skin of *Homeland*'s Troubled CIA Agent," *The Observer*, March 3, 2012, https://www.theguardian.com/tv-and-radio/2012/mar/03/homeland-claire-danes-carrie-mathison.

30. Mary Hartnett, "The Powerful Portrayal of *Homeland*'s Carrie Mathison," *TN2 Magazine*, March 31, 2017, https://www.tn2magazine.ie/the-powerful-portrayal-of-homelands-carrie-mathison/.

31. Emily St. James, "*Homeland*'s Carrie Mathison Is the Most Influential TV Character of the 2010s," *Vox*, November 11, 2015, https://www.vox.com/2015/11/11/9715382/homeland-season-5-claire-danes.

32. Nilles, "Ranking TV's Top 20 Badass Female Characters."

33. June Thomas, "Queen Latifah Makes the Impossible: A CBS Cop Show for the Black Lives Matter Era," *Slate*, February 7, 2021, https://slate.com/culture/2021/02/equalizer-queen-latifah-cbs-black-lives-matter-super-bowl.html.

34. Charlene Badasie, "The Fate of Queen Latifah's Equalizer Has Been Decided," Giant Freakin Robot, May 10, 2022, https://www.giantfreakinrobot.com/ent/queen-latifah-equalizer-fate.html.

35. Mike Hale, "'The Equalizer' Review: Queen Latifah on the CBS Assembly Line," *New York Times*, February 4, 2021, https://www.nytimes.com/2021/02/04/arts/television/the-equalizer-queen-latifah-review.html.

36. Andrew Marlowe and Terri Miller, "Updating 'The Equalizer' for a New Era," Paramount, February 11, 2021, https://www.paramount.com/news/content-and-experiences/updating-the-equalizer-for-a-new-era.

37. Candice Frederick, "*The Equalizer* Season 2 Review: Queen Latifah Masterfully Flips the Script on Tired Procedural Dramas," *TV Guide*, October 8, 2021, https://www.tvguide.com/news/the-equalizer-season-2-review-queen-latifah-masterfully-flips-the-script-on-tired-procedural-dramas/.

38. Badasie, "The Fate of Queen Latifah's Equalizer Has Been Decided."

39. Badasie, "The Fate of Queen Latifah's Equalizer Has Been Decided."

40. Marlowe and Miller, "Updating 'The Equalizer' for a New Era."

41. Doreen St. Félix, "Queen Latifah Obliterates Trumps N' Musks in 'The Equalizer,'" *New Yorker*, March 5, 2021, https://www.newyorker.com/magazine/2021/03/15/queen-latifah-obliterates-trumps-n-musks-in-the-equalizer.

42. Frederick, "*The Equalizer* Season 2 Review."

43. Yohana Desta, "Kevin Spacey Is Seeking 'Evaluation and Treatment' after Allegations," *Vanity Fair*, November 2, 2017, https://www.vanityfair.com/hollywood/2017/11/kevin-spacey-evaluation-treatment-allegations.

44. Jess Joho, "How 'House of Cards' Season 6 Fails Its Madam President," Mashable, November 7, 2018, https://mashable.com/article/house-of-cards-season-6-review-feminism-metoo.

45. Brian Stelter, "Netflix Does Well in 2013 Primetime Emmy Nominations," *New York Times*, July 18, 2013, https://archive.nytimes.com/artsbeat.blogs.nytimes.com/2013/07/18/watching-for-the-2013-primetime-emmy-nominations/.

46. "House of Cards," Golden Globes, July 7, 2016, https://www.goldenglobes.com/tv-show/house-cards.

47. Joho, "How 'House of Cards' Season 6 Fails Its Madam President."

48. Amanda Marcotte, "*House of Cards* Goes Full Feminist in Its Second Season," *Slate*, February 18, 2014, https://slate.com/human-interest/2014/02/house-of-cards-season-2-goes-full-feminist-the-show-has-unflinching-honest-story-lines-about-rape-and-abortion.html.

49. Joho, "How 'House of Cards' Season 6 Fails Its Madam President."

50. Jackie Strause, "How 'House of Cards' Pulled off That Timely, Feminist Coup," *Hollywood Reporter*, November 8, 2018, https://www.hollywoodreporter.com/tv/tv-news/house-cards-final-season-claire-underwood-cabinet-twist-explained-1159290/.

51. Marcotte, "*House of Cards* Goes Full Feminist in Its Second Season."

Chapter 3

1. Deborah Sontag, "Anita Hill and Revitalizing Feminism," *New York Times*, April 26, 1992, https://www.nytimes.com/1992/04/26/nyregion/anita-hill-and-revitalizing-feminism.html.

2. Quoted in Sontag, "Anita Hill and Revitalizing Feminism."

3. Quoted in Jennifer Baumgardner and Amy Richards, *Manifesta: Young Women, Feminism, and the Future* (New York: Farrar, Straus & Giroux, 2000), 77.

4. Su-Lin Yu, "Reclaiming the Personal: Personal Narratives of Third-Wave Feminists," *Women's Studies* 40, no. 7 (October 2011): 873–89, https://doi.org/10.1080/00497878.2011.603606.

5. Alanna Bennett, "How 'Buffy' Changed Television for a New Generation," BuzzFeed, March 10, 2017, https://www.buzzfeed.com/alannabennett/what-it-means-to-honor-buffy.

6. Chris Jenkins, "10 Surprising Ways 'Buffy the Vampire Slayer' Influenced Modern Culture," Listverse, May 16, 2015, https://listverse.com/2015/05/16/10-surprising-ways-buffy-the-vampire-slayer-influenced-modern-culture/.

7. Stephen Daisley, "How *Buffy the Vampire Slayer* Transformed Pop Culture," *The Spectator*, March 10, 2017, https://www.spectator.co.uk/article/how-buffy-the-vampire-slayer-transformed-pop-culture/.

8. Jenkins, "10 Surprising Ways 'Buffy the Vampire Slayer' Influenced Modern Culture."

9. Patricia Pender, "Buffy Summers: Third-Wave Feminist Icon," *The Atlantic*, July 31, 2016, https://www.theatlantic.com/entertainment/archive/2016/07/how-buffy-became-a-third-wave-feminist-icon/493154/.

10. Caroline Preece, "Why *Charmed* Deserves to Be Celebrated," Den of Geek, January 13, 2017, https://www.denofgeek.com/tv/why-charmed-deserves-to-be-celebrated/.

11. Daisley, "How *Buffy the Vampire Slayer* Transformed Pop Culture."

12. Sophie Moss, "Culture Throwback: Thinking Back on How *Charmed* Captured Contemporary Feminism," *Luna Luna*, November 23, 2015, http://www.lunaluna magazine.com/blog/culture-throwback-thinking-back-on-how-charmed-captured-con temporary-feminism.

13. Moss, "Culture Throwback."

14. Victoria Harris, "Witches on Surfboards: How Witch Media Has Ridden the Waves of Feminism for the Classroom," *Cardinal Compositions* 4 (2020): 37, https:// ir.library.louisville.edu/cgi/viewcontent.cgi?article=1007&context=cardcomp.

15. Anne Theriault, "The Real Reason Women Love Witches," *The Establishment*, October 24, 2017, https://medium.com/the-establishment/the-real-reason-women-love-witches-647d48517f66.

16. Pam Grossman, "Waking the Witch: The Feminist History of Spiritualism." *Ms.*, October 29, 2019, https://msmagazine.com/2019/10/29/waking-the-witch-the-feminist-history-of-spiritualism/.

17. Ann Braude, *Radical Spirits: Spiritualism and Women's Rights in Nineteenth-Century America* (Bloomington: Indiana University Press, 2020), 153.

18. Quoted in Grossman, "Waking the Witch."

19. Kelsea Stahler, "Thank Hecate! Witches Are Here to Save the World," *Teen Vogue*, November 14, 2018, https://www.teenvogue.com/story/witches-pop-culture-sabrina-ahs-charmed-real-world.

20. Stahler, "Thank Hecate!"

21. Sarah Assenti, "What the Return of *Sabrina* and *Charmed* Says about Feminism in 2018," *Stylist*, October 16, 2018, https://www.stylist.co.uk/long-reads/witchcraft-re booted-what-the-return-of-sabrina-and-charmed-says-about-feminism-in-2018/231803.

22. Stahler, "Thank Hecate!"

23. Quoted in Laurie Penny, "Witch Kids of Instagram," *The Baffler*, December 13, 2017, https://thebaffler.com/war-of-nerves/witch-kids-of-instagram.

24. Penny, "Witch Kids of Instagram."

25. Penny, "Witch Kids of Instagram."

26. Assenti, "What the Return of *Sabrina* and *Charmed* Says about Feminism in 2018."

27. Stahler, "Thank Hecate!"

28. Sarah E. Whitney, "I Can Be Whoever I Want to Be: *Alias* and the Post-Feminist Rhetoric of Choice," Genders 1998–2013, March 1, 2013, 163, https://www.colorado

.edu/gendersarchive1998-2013/2013/03/01/i-can-be-whoever-i-want-be-alias-and-post
-feminist-rhetoric-choice.

29. Mark Makela, "Transcript: Donald Trump's Taped Comments about Women,"
New York Times, October 8, 2016, https://www.nytimes.com/2016/10/08/us/donald
-trump-tape-transcript.html.

30. Tim Wallace and Alicia Parlapiano, "Crowd Scientists Say Women's March
in Washington Had 3 Times as Many People as Trump's Inauguration," *New York
Times*, January 22, 2017, https://www.nytimes.com/interactive/2017/01/22/us/politics
/womens-march-trump-crowd-estimates.html.

31. Courtney Weaver, Joe Rennison, Lindsay Whipp, and Nicole Bullock, "Trump
Reacts to Mass Protests with Conciliatory Tweet: More Than 2.5m People Gather
around the World to Take Part in Women's March," *Financial Times*, January 22, 2017.

32. "This Is What We Learned by Counting the Women's Marches," *Washington
Post*, February 24, 2019.

33. Mary Bowerman, "There's Even a Women's March in Antarctica." *USA Today*,
January 21, 2017, https://www.usatoday.com/story/news/politics/onpolitics/2017/01
/21/womens-march-on-washington-antarctica/96882184/.

34. "The Women's March, 2017," National Museum of American History, March 2,
2020, https://americanhistory.si.edu/creating-icons/women%E2%80%99s-march-2017.

35. Jodi Kantor and Megan Twohey, "Harvey Weinstein Paid off Sexual Harassment Accusers for Decades," *New York Times*, October 5, 2017, https://www.nytimes
.com/2017/10/05/us/harvey-weinstein-harassment-allegations.html.

36. Tonya Mosley, "'Me Too' Founder Tarana Burke Says Black Girls' Trauma
Shouldn't Be Ignored," NPR, September 29, 2021, https://www.npr.org/2021/09
/29/1041362145/me-too-founder-tarana-burke-says-black-girls-trauma-shouldnt-be
-ignored.

37. "Women Have Paid the Price for Trump's Regulatory Agenda," Center for American Progress, September 10, 2020, https://www.americanprogress.org/article/women
-paid-price-trumps-regulatory-agenda/.

38. Patty Housman, "*Roe v Wade* Overturned: What It Means, What's Next,"
American University, June 29, 2022, https://www.american.edu/cas/news/roe-v-wade
-overturned-what-it-means-whats-next.cfm.

39. Greg Kennedy, "Female Super Empowerment: *Jessica Jones* Is Back," *The National*, March 5, 2018, https://www.thenationalnews.com/arts-culture/television/female
-super-empowerment-jessica-jones-is-back-1.710419.

40. Chelsea Steiner, "*Jessica Jones* and Its Legacy of Female Anger," *Mary Sue*, February 19, 2019, https://www.themarysue.com/rip-jessica-jones/.

41. Eric Deggans, "'Jessica Jones' Struggles in Life—but Triumphs on Screen."
NPR, November 20, 2015, https://www.npr.org/2015/11/20/456812993/jessica-jones
-struggles-in-life-but-triumphs-on-screen.

42. Virginia DeBolt, "Friends and Lovers on Marvel's *Jessica Jones*," Old Ain't
Dead, December 3, 2015, https://oldaintdead.com/friends-and-lovers-on-marvels
-jessica-jones/.

43. Sophie Gilbert, "The Villainous Women of 'Jessica Jones,'" *The Atlantic*, March 15, 2018, https://www.theatlantic.com/entertainment/archive/2018/03/jessica-jones-season-2-review-netflix/555395/.

44. Sam Stone, "*Jessica Jones*: Why You Should Have Sympathy for Trish Walker, Villain," CBR, June 22, 2019, https://www.cbr.com/jessica-jones-defense-trish-walker/.

45. Gilbert, "The Villainous Women of 'Jessica Jones.'"

46. Marykate Jasper, "Jeri Hogarth: *Jessica Jones* and Female Capitalist Success," *Mary Sue*, March 13, 2018, https://www.themarysue.com/jeri-hogarth-jessica-jones-season-2/.

47. Jasper, "Jeri Hogarth: *Jessica Jones* and Female Capitalist Success."

48. Kadeen Griffiths, "Jessica and Trish's Relationship in 'Jessica Jones' Season 3 Will Be Complicated but Not Unfixable, according to Actor Rachael Taylor," *Bustle*, March 9, 2018, https://www.bustle.com/p/jessica-trishs-relationship-in-jessica-jones-season-3-will-be-complicated-but-not-unfixable-according-to-actor-rachael-taylor-8450629.

49. Kaitlin Thomas, "Before 'WandaVision,' There Was 'Agent Carter,' and It Was Marvel's Best Show," Salon, January 31, 2021, https://www.salon.com/2021/01/31/agent-carter-wandavision-marvel-tv-shows-disney-plus/.

50. Oliver Sava, "*Agent Carter*'s Excellent Season Premiere Changes More Than Just the Scenery," *A.V. Club*, January 20, 2016, https://www.avclub.com/agent-carter-s-excellent-season-premiere-changes-more-t-1798186282.

51. Sava, "*Agent Carter*'s Excellent Season Premiere Changes More Than Just the Scenery."

52. Otto L., "The *Black Widow* Effect, or Marvel and the Hidden Gem Called Peggy Carter," Medium, April 2, 2016, https://medium.com/@vivarium/the-black-widow-effect-or-marvel-and-the-hidden-gem-called-peggy-carter-bde6813bc140.

53. L., "The *Black Widow* Effect."

54. "Hayley Atwell's Machine Gun Fun," *Belfast Telegraph*, May 18, 2011, https://www.belfasttelegraph.co.uk/entertainment/film-tv/news/hayley-atwells-machine-gun-fun-28618734.html.

55. Gissane Sophia, "Character Deep Dive: Peggy Carter," Marvelous Geeks Media, December 18, 2020, https://marvelousgeeksmedia.com/2020/12/18/character-deep-dive-marvels-peggy-carter/.

56. Rebecca Even, "Proud to Be a Woman: *Agent Carter*," *Cornell Daily Sun*, February 11, 2016, https://cornellsun.com/2016/02/10/proud-to-be-a-woman-agent-carter/.

57. Elizabeth Staszak, "A Fantasy from a Fantasy: A Review of ABC's *Agent Carter*," CBE International, February 18, 2015, https://www.cbeinternational.org/resource/fantasy-fantasy/#_ednref1.

58. Michelle Esteban, "Major FBI Milestone: This Year Marks 50 Years of Women Serving as Special Agents," KOMO, May 9, 2022, https://komonews.com/news/local/major-fbi-milestone-2022-marks-50-years-of-women-serving-as-special-agents.

59. Jessica M. Goldstein, "The CIA Is Trying to Recruit Gen Z—and Doesn't Care If They're All over Social Media," *Washingtonian*, November 9, 2021, https://www.washingtonian.com/2021/11/09/how-gen-z-and-the-tiktok-generation-are-becoming-spies/.

60. Emma Newburger, "Women Head the Top Three CIA Directorates for the First Time in History," CNBC, January 16, 2019, https://www.cnbc.com/2019/01/16/women-head-the-top-three-cia-directorates-for-the-first-time.html.

61. Amy Oliver, "The Real-Life Carrie from *Homeland*: CIA Drama Back on Screens Tonight," *Mail Online*, October 6, 2013, https://www.dailymail.co.uk/femail/article-2445871/Meet-real-life-Carrie-Homeland-CIA-drama--screens-tonight--reads-like-Valerie-Plames-amazing-life-story-But-does-think-plots-fact-fiction.html.

62. Inkoo Kang, "Maya vs. Carrie—Comparing the Feminism of 'Zero Dark Thirty' and 'Homeland,'" Yahoo, December 17, 2012, https://www.yahoo.com/entertainment/news/maya-vs-carrie-comparing-feminism-zero-dark-thirty-144513423.html.

63. Robert Windrem, "Hunting Osama bin Laden Was Women's Work," NBC News, November 14, 2013, https://www.nbcnews.com/news/world/hunting-osama-bin-laden-was-womens-work-flna2D11594091.

64. Windrem, "Hunting Osama bin Laden Was Women's Work."

65. Windrem, "Hunting Osama bin Laden Was Women's Work."

66. Windrem, "Hunting Osama bin Laden Was Women's Work."

67. Windrem, "Hunting Osama bin Laden Was Women's Work."

68. Jess Joho, "How 'House of Cards' Season 6 Fails Its Madam President," Mashable, November 7, 2018, https://mashable.com/article/house-of-cards-season-6-review-feminism-metoo.

69. Tracie Egan Morrissey, "*House of Cards*' Claire Underwood Is a Feminist Warrior Antihero," Jezebel, February 17, 2014, https://jezebel.com/house-of-cards-claire-underwood-is-a-feminist-warrior-1524425272.

70. Joho, "How 'House of Cards' Season 6 Fails Its Madam President."

71. Angelica Jade Bastién, "The Grand Feminist Legacy of *Orphan Black*," Vulture, August 15, 2017, https://www.vulture.com/2017/08/orphan-black-series-review.html.

72. Araceli Roach, "'Orphan Black' Season 3 Character Posters: I'm Not Just One, I'm a Few," ScreenRant, March 22, 2015, https://screenrant.com/orphan-black-season-3-character-posters/.

73. Bastién, "The Grand Feminist Legacy of *Orphan Black*."

74. Rachel Zellars, "Black Subjectivity and the Origins of American Gynecology," AAIHS, May 31, 2018, https://www.aaihs.org/black-subjectivity-and-the-origins-of-american-gynecology/.

75. "Carl Clauberg," Auschwitz-Birkenau Memorial and Museum, https://www.auschwitz.org/en/history/medical-experiments/carl-clauberg/.

76. Blanka Konopka, "Horror Experience of Women Subjected to Bestial Experiments at WWII Concentration Camp Retold in Powerful New Exhibition," *FirstNews*, September 23, 2021, https://www.thefirstnews.com/article/horror-experience-of-women-subjected-to-bestial-experiments-at-wwii-concentration-camp-retold-in-powerful-new-exhibition-24909.

77. Lili Loofbourow, "The Many Faces of Tatiana Maslany," *New York Times*, April 2, 2015, https://www.nytimes.com/2015/04/05/magazine/the-many-faces-of-tatiana-maslany.html?ref=magazine&_r=2.

78. Alexis Soloski, "Kevins Can Score Improbably Attractive TV Wives," *New York Times*, June 9, 2021, https://www.nytimes.com/2021/06/09/arts/television/kevin-sitcom-attractive-wife.html.

79. Julia Wick, "Subverting Female Archetypes with the Clones of 'Orphan Black,'" Longreads, April 13, 2015, https://longreads.com/2015/04/13/subverting-female-arche types-with-the-clones-of-orphan-black/.

80. Wick, "Subverting Female Archetypes with the Clones of 'Orphan Black.'"

81. S. Fambul, "17 Shows That Changed the Game for Black Women on TV," *Glamour*, August 6, 2020, https://www.glamour.com/gallery/tv-shows-that-changed -the-game-for-black-women.

82. Bethonie Butler, "Why the Success of 'The Equalizer' Is Bigger Than the Show Itself," *Washington Post*, May 21, 2021, https://www.washingtonpost.com/arts-entertain ment/2021/05/21/the-equalizer-queen-latifah/.

83. Butler, "Why the Success of 'The Equalizer' Is Bigger Than the Show Itself."

84. Butler, "Why the Success of 'The Equalizer' Is Bigger Than the Show Itself."

85. Butler, "Why the Success of 'The Equalizer' Is Bigger Than the Show Itself."

86. Ericka Taylor, "'Hood Feminism' Is a Call for Solidarity in a Less-Than-Inclusive Movement," NPR, February 26, 2020, https://www.npr.org/2020/02/26/808943234 /hood-feminism-is-a-call-for-solidarity-in-a-less-than-inclusive-movement.

87. Andrew Marlowe and Terri Miller, "Updating 'The Equalizer' for a New Era," Paramount, February 11, 2021, https://www.paramount.com/news/content-and-experi ences/updating-the-equalizer-for-a-new-era.

88. Mekeisha Madden Toby, "Queen Latifah: 'Black Women Have Been Equalizing for Years and Years, from Hatshepsut to Kamala Harris,'" TVLine, February 21, 2021, https://tvline.com/2021/02/21/the-equalizer-queen-latifah-black-women-interview-cbs -reboot/.

89. Butler, "Why the Success of 'The Equalizer' Is Bigger Than the Show Itself."

Chapter 4

1. Heather M. Porter, "In Search of the Complete Female Character in Marvel's Cinematic Universe," in *Marvel's* Black Widow *from Spy to Superhero: Essays on an Avenger with a Very Specific Skill Set* (Jefferson, NC: McFarland, 2017), 24–25.

2. Sophia McDougall, "I Hate Strong Female Characters," *New Statesman*, June 10, 2021, https://www.newstatesman.com/culture/2013/08/i-hate-strong-female-characters.

3. McDougall, "I Hate Strong Female Characters."

4. Zoe Williams, "*Jessica Jones*: The Timely Return of a Feminist Superhero," *The Guardian*, February 24, 2018, https://www.theguardian.com/culture/2018/feb/24 /jessica-jones-mind-control-and-redemption-the-timely-return-of-a-feminist-superhero.

5. Chuck Wendig, "On the Subject of the 'Strong Female Character,'" Terrible-minds, March 8, 2013, http://terribleminds.com/ramble/2013/03/08/on-the-subject-of -the-strong-female-character/.

6. Molly Brost, "Spy Games: *Alias*, Sydney Bristow, and the Ever Complicated Gaze," *Americana: The Journal of American Popular Culture (1900–Present)* 6, no. 1 (Spring 2007), https://www.americanpopularculture.com/journal/articles/spring_2007 /brost.htm.

7. Angelica Jade Bastién, "The Enduring Legacy of *Buffy the Vampire Slayer*," Vulture, October 25, 2021, https://www.vulture.com/2021/10/buffy-the-vampire-slayer-twenty-years-greatest-legacy.html.

8. Claire L. Wong, "Why 'Buffy the Vampire Slayer' Is Still One of the Best TV Shows Ever," *Hollywood Insider*, February 2, 2021. https://www.hollywoodinsider.com/buffy-the-vampire-slayer-success/.

9. Lauren Sarner, "'Game of Thrones' and 'Jessica Jones' Owe Buffy's Success 15 Years Ago," Inverse, January 16, 2016, https://www.inverse.com/article/9852-game-of-thrones-and-jessica-jones-owe-buffy-s-success-15-years-ago.

10. Wong, "Why 'Buffy the Vampire Slayer' Is Still One of the Best TV Shows Ever."

11. Shaun Stacy, "'Buffy' at 25: How the Show Changed Pop Culture Forever," GurlCulture, January 10, 2022, https://gurlculture.com/2022/01/09/buffy-at-25-how-the-show-changed-pop-culture-forever/.

12. Hannah E. Sanders, "Living a Charmed Life: The Magic of Post-Feminist Sisterhood," in *Interrogating Postfeminism Gender and the Politics of Popular Culture*, ed. Diane Negra, Lynn Spigel, and Yvonne Tasker (Durham, NC: Duke University Press, 2007), 86.

13. Sanders, "Living a Charmed Life," 87.

14. Quoted in Theresa Harold, "Witchcraft Is More Popular Than Ever—but Why?," *Stylist*, March 1, 2017, https://www.stylist.co.uk/life/spells-in-the-city-why-an-increasing-number-of-women-are-practicing-witchcraft-digital-spiritual-modern/69261.

15. Jenny Crusie, "*Totally Charmed*: Introduction," *Jenny's Blog*, 2005, https://jennycrusie.com/excerpts/totally-charmed-introduction/.

16. Anne Theriault, "The Real Reason Women Love Witches," *The Establishment*, October 24, 2017, https://medium.com/the-establishment/the-real-reason-women-love-witches-647d48517f66.

17. Quoted in Harold, "Witchcraft Is More Popular Than Ever—but Why?"

18. Laurie Penny, "Witch Kids of Instagram," *The Baffler*, December 13, 2017, https://thebaffler.com/war-of-nerves/witch-kids-of-instagram.

19. Kelsea Stahler, "Thank Hecate! Witches Are Here to Save the World," *Teen Vogue*, November 14, 2018, https://www.teenvogue.com/story/witches-pop-culture-sabrina-ahs-charmed-real-world.

20. Caroline Preece, "Why *Nikita* Will Be Missed," Den of Geek, January 15, 2014, https://www.denofgeek.com/tv/why-nikita-will-be-missed/.

21. Kayti Burt, "*The Protege* Is a Reminder of Just How Good *Nikita* Was," Den of Geek, August 26, 2021, https://www.denofgeek.com/movies/the-protege-review-nikita-comparison/.

22. Burt, "*The Protege* Is a Reminder of Just How Good *Nikita* Was."

23. Sabrina Calandrón, "Feminidad y uso de la fuerza: La fabricación de una heroína a partir de la serie de televisión *Nikita*," Academia, September 21, 2016, 170, https://www.academia.edu/35765353/Feminidad_y_uso_de_la_fuerza_la_fabricaci%C3%B3n_de_una_hero%C3%ADna_a_partir_de_la_serie_de_televisi%C3%B3n_Nikita.

24. Calandrón, "Feminidad y uso de la fuerza," 170–71.

25. Brittany Frederick, "10 Reasons 'Nikita' Doesn't Need Changing," TVovermind, October 14, 2010, https://tvovermind.com/10-reasons-nikita-changing/.

26. Chancellor Agard, "'Marvel's *Jessica Jones* Boss Breaks down Trish and Jessica's Series Finale Fates," *Entertainment Weekly*, June 18, 2019, https://ew.com/tv/2019/06/18/marvels-jessica-jones-series-finale-jessica-trish-fate/.

27. Chelsea Steiner, "*Jessica Jones* and Its Legacy of Female Anger," *Mary Sue*, February 19, 2019, https://www.themarysue.com/rip-jessica-jones/.

28. Khal, "'Jessica Jones' Is Marvel at Its Most Daring," Complex, November 17, 2015, https://www.complex.com/pop-culture/2015/11/jessica-jones-netflix-review.

29. Kadeen Griffiths, "Jessica and Trish's Relationship in 'Jessica Jones' Season 3 Will Be Complicated but Not Unfixable, according to Actor Rachael Taylor," *Bustle*, March 9, 2018, https://www.bustle.com/p/jessica-trishs-relationship-in-jessica-jones-season-3-will-be-complicated-but-not-unfixable-according-to-actor-rachael-taylor-8450629.

30. Jenna Scherer, "'Jessica Jones': We Finally Have a Superhero Icon for the #TimesUp Era," *Rolling Stone*, March 9, 2018, https://www.rollingstone.com/tv-movies/tv-movie-news/jessica-jones-we-finally-have-a-superhero-icon-for-the-timesup-era-127314/.

31. Amanda Marcotte, "Before Binge-Watching *Jessica Jones*, Read *Alias*, the Feminist Comic It's Based On," Salon, November 20, 2015, https://www.salon.com/2015/11/19/before_binge_watching_jessica_jones_read_alias_the_feminist_comic_its_based_on/.

32. Williams, "*Jessica Jones*: The Timely Return of a Feminist Superhero."

33. Sierra Isley, "'Jessica Jones' Is the Feminist Show You Should Be Watching," @dolescent, July 5, 2018, https://www.adolescent.net/a/jessica-jones-is-the-feminist-show-you-should-be-watching.

34. Esther Bergdahl, "The Kick-Ass Female Superhero We've Been Waiting for Is Finally Here," *Mic*, January 6, 2015, https://www.mic.com/articles/107766/marvel-s-agent-carter-promises-us-the-heroine-we-deserve.

35. Gissane Sophia, "Character Deep Dive: Peggy Carter," Marvelous Geeks Media, December 18, 2020, https://marvelousgeeksmedia.com/2020/12/18/character-deep-dive-marvels-peggy-carter/.

36. David Caballero, "Peggy Carter, First Lady of the MCU," Digital Trends, May 6, 2022, https://www.digitaltrends.com/movies/peggy-carter-hayley-atwell-first-lady-of-mcu/.

37. Rachel Roth, "*Agent Carter*: Why ABC Canceled the Marvel TV Series," CBR, November 29, 2020, https://www.cbr.com/why-marvel-agent-carter-canceled/.

38. Roth, "*Agent Carter*: Why ABC Canceled the Marvel TV Series."

39. Corey Latta, "Introduction: Part 2," in *Titans: How Superheroes Can Help Us Make Sense of a Polarized World* (Eugene, OR: Cascade Books, 2017), xxvi.

40. Rebecca Even, "Proud to Be a Woman: *Agent Carter*," *Cornell Daily Sun*, February 11, 2016, https://cornellsun.com/2016/02/10/proud-to-be-a-woman-agent-carter/.

41. Even, "Proud to Be a Woman: *Agent Carter*."

42. Kathie Huddleston, "Modern Day Hero," *SciFi Magazine*, February 2015, 35.

43. Lesley Coffin, "Women like Marvel Agent Carter Very Real Part of History," *Mary Sue*, January 6, 2015, https://www.themarysue.com/real-women-history-marvel-peggy-carter/.

44. Elizabeth Staszak, "A Fantasy from a Fantasy: A Review of ABC's *Agent Carter*," CBE International, February 18, 2015, https://www.cbeinternational.org/resource /fantasy-fantasy/#_ednref1.

Chapter 5

1. Melanie McFarland, "'Jessica Jones' Tells Every Woman's Origin Story," Salon, March 17, 2018, https://www.salon.com/2018/03/17/jessica-jones-tells-every-womans -origin-story/

2. "Siobhan Sadler," *Orphan Black* Wiki, https://orphanblack.fandom.com/wiki /Siobhan_Sadler.

3. Marisa Roffman, "'Orphan Black's' Tatiana Maslany on Sarah's 'Selfless' and 'Painful' Decision," *Hollywood Reporter*, April 25, 2015, https://www.hollywoodreporter.com /tv/tv-news/orphan-black-spoilers-sarah-kira-791147/.

4. Kadeen Griffiths, "Jessica and Trish's Relationship in 'Jessica Jones' Season 3 Will Be Complicated but Not Unfixable, according to Actor Rachael Taylor," *Bustle*, March 9, 2018, https://www.bustle.com/p/jessica-trishs-relationship-in-jessica-jones-season -3-will-be-complicated-but-not-unfixable-according-to-actor-rachael-taylor-8450629.

5. Libby Hill, "A Shocking, Horrifying Act on *Homeland* Aims to Build Empathy for the Indefensible," *Vox*, October 6, 2014, https://www.vox.com/2014/10/6/6900651 /homeland-carrie-drowns-baby.

6. Hill, "A Shocking, Horrifying Act on *Homeland*."

7. Hill, "A Shocking, Horrifying Act on *Homeland*."

8. Hayley Krischer, "Why the Bathtub Scene on Last Night's 'Homeland' Was So Uniquely Disturbing," Salon, October 6, 2014, https://www.salon.com/2014/10/06 /why_the_bathtub_scene_on_last_nights_homeland_was_so_uniquely_disturbing/.

9. Hill, "A Shocking, Horrifying Act on *Homeland*."

10. James Hibberd, "'Homeland' Showrunner Explains That Shocking Premiere Scene," *Entertainment Weekly*, October 5, 2014, https://ew.com/article/2014/10/05 /homeland-premiere-interview/.

11. Molly Brost, "Spy Games: *Alias*, Sydney Bristow, and the Ever Complicated Gaze," *Americana: The Journal of American Popular Culture (1900–Present)* 6, no. 1 (Spring 2007), https://www.americanpopularculture.com/journal/articles/spring_2007 /brost.htm.

12. Sarah E. Whitney, "I Can Be Whoever I Want to Be: *Alias* and the Post-Feminist Rhetoric of Choice," Genders 1998–2013, March 1, 2013, https://www.colorado .edu/gendersarchive1998-2013/2013/03/01/i-can-be-whoever-i-want-be-alias-and-post -feminist-rhetoric-choice.

13. Charles Taylor, "'Alias' Grace," Salon, January 12, 2005, https://web.archive.org /web/20140821014601/http://www.salon.com/2005/01/12/alias_2/.

14. Lacy Baugher Milas, "TV Rewind: How Spy Drama *Alias* Gave Us Television's All-Time Best Father/Daughter Duo," *Paste Magazine*, August 26, 2021, https://www .pastemagazine.com/tv/streaming/alias-tv-show-sydney-jack/.

15. Whitney, "I Can Be Whoever I Want to Be."

16. Whitney, "I Can Be Whoever I Want to Be."

17. Stephen M. Silverman, "Jennifer Garner's Baby Makes TV History," *People*, October 6, 2005, https://people.com/celebrity/jennifer-garners-baby-makes-tv-history/.

18. Todd Peterson, "Garner's Pregnancy Becomes Storyline," *People*, July 25, 2005, https://people.com/celebrity/garners-pregnancy-becomes-storyline/.

19. Charles Mudede, "The Karen Episode of Queen Latifah's *The Equalizer* Shows All That Is Wrong with the Current Anti-woke Movement," *The Stranger*, November 22, 2021, https://www.thestranger.com/slog/2021/11/22/63036726/the-karen-episode-of-queen-latifahs-the-equalizer-shows-all-that-is-wrong-with-the-current-anti-woke-movement.

20. Mara Reinstein, "Queen Latifah Explains How She Got Her Royal Name and Why Women Love Her as 'The Equalizer,'" *Parade*, September 30, 2022, https://parade.com/tv/queen-latifah-the-equalizer-season-3.

21. Jenny Crusie, "*Totally Charmed*: Introduction," *Jenny's Blog*, 2005, https://jennycrusie.com/excerpts/totally-charmed-introduction/.

22. Hannah E. Sanders, "Living a Charmed Life: The Magic of Post Feminist Sisterhood," in *Interrogating Postfeminism Gender and the Politics of Popular Culture*, ed. Diane Negra, Lynn Spigel, and Yvonne Tasker (Durham, NC: Duke University Press, 2007), 79.

23. Crusie, "*Totally Charmed*: Introduction."

24. Caroline Preece, "Why *Charmed* Deserves to Be Celebrated," Den of Geek, January 13, 2017, https://www.denofgeek.com/tv/why-charmed-deserves-to-be-celebrated/.

25. Sanders, "Living a Charmed Life," 86.

26. Sanders, "Living a Charmed Life," 79.

27. Rebecca Feasey, "The 'Charmed' Audience: Gender and the Politics of Contemporary Culture," in "A Screen of One's Own," ed. Heather Osborne-Thompson, special issue, *Spectator* 25, no. 2 (Fall 2005): 42, https://cinema.usc.edu/assets/097/15720.pdf.

28. Feasey, "The 'Charmed' Audience," 43.

29. Virginia DeBolt, "Friends and Lovers on Marvel's *Jessica Jones*," Old Ain't Dead, December 3, 2015, https://oldaintdead.com/friends-and-lovers-on-marvels-jessica-jones/.

30. Anita Sarkeesian, "Some Thoughts on *Jessica Jones*," Feminist Frequency, December 1, 2015, https://feministfrequency.com/2015/12/01/some-thoughts-on-jessica-jones/.

31. Princess Weekes, "Alright, Let's Talk about Trish Walker," *Mary Sue*, March 21, 2018, https://www.themarysue.com/season-two-trish-walker/.

32. Caitlin Gallagher, "Why Jessica and Trish's Relationship on 'Jessica Jones' Is the Show's Real Love Story," *Bustle*, June 13, 2019, https://www.bustle.com/p/why-jessica-trishs-relationship-on-jessica-jones-is-the-shows-real-love-story-17992114.

33. Chancellor Agard, "'Marvel's *Jessica Jones* Boss Breaks down Trish and Jessica's Series Finale Fates," *Entertainment Weekly*, June 18, 2019, https://ew.com/tv/2019/06/18/marvels-jessica-jones-series-finale-jessica-trish-fate/.

34. Angelica Jade Bastién, "The Enduring Legacy of *Buffy the Vampire Slayer*," Vulture, October 25, 2021, https://www.vulture.com/2021/10/buffy-the-vampire-slayer-twenty-years-greatest-legacy.html.

35. James Pyles, "Where Are the Families in Science Fiction?," Powered by Roots, March 25, 2021, https://poweredbyrobots.com/2021/03/24/where-are-the-families-in-science-fiction/.

36. Marcie Casey and Jay Clayton, "Queer Kinship: Privacy Concerns in *Orphan Black*," *Journal of Literature and Science* 14, no. 1/2 (2021–2022): 123, https://www.literatureandscience.org/wp-content/uploads/2022/07/8.-CASEY-CLAYTON-Final.pdf.

37. Jessie Commerce, "*Orphan Black*: How the Bechdel Test Helps Us Accurately Analyze Gender Equality," Media Production and Criticism, https://dmillef.wixsite.com/media-criticism/orphan-black.

38. Casey and Clayton, "Queer Kinship," 128.

39. Caroline Crampton, "Strong, Interesting Female Characters Are the Secret of *House of Cards*' Success," *New Statesman*, February 14, 2014, https://www.newstatesman.com/culture/2014/02/strong-interesting-female-characters-are-secret-house-cards-success.

40. Crampton, "Strong, Interesting Female Characters Are the Secret of *House of Cards*' Success."

41. Jamie Zabinsky, "Politics, Power and Queerness in 'House of Cards' Season 4," Feministing, May 31, 2016, https://feministing.com/2016/05/31/politics-power-and-queerness-in-house-of-cards-season-4/.

42. Crampton, "Strong, Interesting Female Characters Are the Secret of *House of Cards*' Success."

43. Sarah Dobbs, "10 Ways *Buffy the Vampire Slayer* Changed the World," Den of Geek, March 10, 2017, https://www.denofgeek.com/tv/10-ways-buffy-the-vampire-slayer-changed-the-world/.

44. Dana Feldman, "'Homeland' Ends on a High Note with Carrie and Saul in Cahoots," *Forbes*, April 27, 2020, https://www.forbes.com/sites/danafeldman/2020/04/27/homeland-ends-on-a-high-note-with-carrie-and-saul-in-cahoots/?sh=2e794cbd134b.

45. Brian Tallerico, "*Homeland*'s End Brings the Show's Defining Relationship Full-Circle," Vulture, April 26, 2020, https://www.vulture.com/2020/04/homeland-finale-carrie-saul-partnership-ending.html.

46. *Los Angeles Times*, "'Homeland's' Mandy Patinkin Describes the Dynamic between Saul and Carrie," YouTube, June 5, 2018, https://www.youtube.com/watch?v=O_6AkiBsI_0.

47. Tallerico, "*Homeland*'s End Brings the Show's Defining Relationship Full-Circle."

48. Rob Salem, "Mandy Patinkin Says *Homeland* Is a Show about Choices and Family," *The Star*, March 6, 2013, https://www.thestar.com/entertainment/television/2013/03/06/mandy_patinkin_says_homeland_is_a_show_about_choices_and_family.html.

Chapter 6

1. Carrie Blazina and Drew Desilver, "A Record Number of Women Are Serving in the 117th Congress," Pew Research Center, January 15, 2021, https://www.pew

research.org/fact-tank/2021/01/15/a-record-number-of-women-are-serving-in-the -117th-congress/.

2. "International Women's Rights," Equal Means Equal, https://equalmeansequal .com/international-womens-rights/.

3. Melanie McFarland, "'Jessica Jones' Tells Every Woman's Origin Story," Salon, March 17, 2018, https://www.salon.com/2018/03/17/jessica-jones-tells-every-womans -origin-story/.

4. Khal, "'Jessica Jones' Is Marvel at Its Most Daring," Complex, November 17, 2015, https://www.complex.com/pop-culture/2015/11/jessica-jones-netflix-review.

5. Amanda Marcotte, "Before Binge-Watching *Jessica Jones*, Read *Alias*, the Feminist Comic It's Based On," Salon, November 20, 2015, https://www.salon.com/2015/11/19 /before_binge_watching_jessica_jones_read_alias_the_feminist_comic_its_based_on/.

6. Jenna Scherer, "'Jessica Jones': We Finally Have a Superhero Icon for the #TimesUp Era," *Rolling Stone*, March 9, 2018, https://www.rollingstone.com/tv-movies /tv-movie-news/jessica-jones-we-finally-have-a-superhero-icon-for-the-timesup -era-127314/.

7. Zoe Williams, "*Jessica Jones*: The Timely Return of a Feminist Superhero," *The Guardian*, February 24, 2018, https://www.theguardian.com/culture/2018/feb/24 /jessica-jones-mind-control-and-redemption-the-timely-return-of-a-feminist-superhero.

8. Ashley Boucher, "Why 'Jessica Jones' Is the Superhero TV Show We Need in the #MeToo Era," *The Wrap*, March 10, 2018, https://www.thewrap.com/jessica-jones -superhero-tv-show-we-need-in-metoo-era/.

9. Melissa Leon, "Marvel's 'Agent Carter' Stomps on the Patriarchy," Daily Beast, January 7, 2015, https://www.thedailybeast.com/marvels-agent-carter-stomps-on-the -patriarchy.

10. Amy Richau, "Agent Carter Season 1 Episode 3 Review—'Time and Tide,'" Flickering Myth, January 14, 2015, https://www.flickeringmyth.com/2015/01/agent -carter-season-1-episode-3-review-time-tide/.

11. Esther Bergdahl, "The Kick-Ass Female Superhero We've Been Waiting for Is Finally Here," *Mic*, January 6, 2015, https://www.mic.com/articles/107766/marvel-s -agent-carter-promises-us-the-heroine-we-deserve.

12. Gissane Sophia, "Character Deep Dive: Peggy Carter," Marvelous Geeks Media, December 18, 2020, https://marvelousgeeksmedia.com/2020/12/18/character-deep -dive-marvels-peggy-carter/.

13. Quoted in Sydney Bucksbaum, "'Agent Carter' Bosses Discuss How 'Doctor Strange' Tie-In Impacts Peggy's Love Life," *Hollywood Reporter*, January 19, 2016, https:// www.hollywoodreporter.com/tv/tv-news/agent-carter-how-doctor-strange-857229/.

14. Otto L., "The *Black Widow* Effect, or Marvel and the Hidden Gem Called Peggy Carter," Medium, April 2, 2016, https://medium.com/@vivarium/the-black-widow -effect-or-marvel-and-the-hidden-gem-called-peggy-carter-bde6813bc140.

15. Quoted in Eliana Dockterman, "'Agent Carter' Creator on the Pressures of Creating Marvel's First Female Project," *Time*, January 15, 2015, https://time.com/3654883 /agent-carter-creator-marvel-female/.

16. Sophia McDougall, "I Hate Strong Female Characters," *New Statesman*, June 10, 2021, https://www.newstatesman.com/culture/2013/08/i-hate-strong-female-characters.

17. Liz Shannon Miller, "'House of Cards': What the Final Season Would've Looked like If Kevin Spacey Hadn't Been Fired," IndieWire, October 26, 2018, https://www.indiewire.com/2018/10/house-of-cards-season-6-if-kevin-spacey-hadnt-been-fired-1202015443/.

18. Miller, "'House of Cards.'"

19. Emma Dibdin, "'House of Cards' Says Time's up as Final Season Exposes Fears about Women in Power," *Hollywood Reporter*, November 4, 2018, https://www.hollywoodreporter.com/tv/tv-news/house-cards-season-6s-all-female-cabinet-reveal-1157946/.

20. Jackie Strause, "How 'House of Cards' Pulled off That Timely, Feminist Coup," *Hollywood Reporter*, November 8, 2018, https://www.hollywoodreporter.com/tv/tv-news/house-cards-final-season-claire-underwood-cabinet-twist-explained-1159290/.

21. Jackie Strause, "'House of Cards': Robin Wright on Final Season's 'Vulnerability and Insecurities,'" *Hollywood Reporter*, November 2, 2018, https://www.hollywoodreporter.com/tv/tv-news/house-cards-premiere-claire-underwood-speaking-camera-explained-1154454/.

22. Sadie Gennis, "TV's Most Important Political Debate Is Happening Right Now on *Orphan Black*," *TV Guide*, June 5, 2014, https://www.tvguide.com/news/orphan-black-feminist-reproductive-rights-1082607/.

23. Willa Paskin, "Nine Lives, at Least," *Slate*, April 18, 2014, https://slate.com/culture/2014/04/season-2-of-orphan-black-starring-tatiana-maslany-reviewed.html.

24. *Encyclopædia Britannica Online*, s.v., "Coverture | Law," October 8, 2007, https://www.britannica.com/topic/coverture.

25. Allison Anna Tait, "The Return of Coverture," *Michigan Law Review*, January 28, 2016, https://michiganlawreview.org/the-return-of-coverture/.

26. Joelle Renstrom, "*Orphan Black* Was Never about Cloning," *Slate*, August 13, 2017, https://slate.com/technology/2017/08/orphan-black-was-never-about-cloning.html.

27. Kurt Nowak, "Coercive Sterilization in Nazi Germany," Museum of Tolerance, https://www.museumoftolerance.com/education/archives-and-reference-library/online-resources/simon-wiesenthal-center-annual-volume-4/annual-4-chapter-14.html.

28. Robyn Schickler, Michelle Whittum, Nicole Fanarjian, Rachel Rapkin, and Brian T. Nguyen, "The History of Female Surgical Sterilization: A Social and Ethics Perspective," *Journal of Gynecologic Surgery* 37, no. 6 (December 1, 2021): 465–69, https://doi.org/10.1089/gyn.2021.0102.

29. Caroline Framke, "*Orphan Black* Flips the Sci-Fi Script by Putting Female Agency First," *A.V. Club*, July 18, 2013, https://www.avclub.com/orphan-black-flips-the-sci-fi-script-by-putting-female-1798239300.

Chapter 7

1. Dawn Heinecken, *The Warrior Women of Television: A Feminist Cultural Analysis of the New Female Body in Popular Media* (Salzburg, Austria: Peter Lang, 2003), 23.

2. Brent Lang, "Number of Female Directors on Top Hollywood Films Declines in 2021," *Variety*, January 2, 2022, https://variety.com/2022/film/news/number-of-female-directors-on-top-hollywood-film-2021-1235145889/.

3. Theresa Carilli and Jane Campbell, eds., *Women and the Media: Diverse Perspectives* (Lanham, MD: University Press of America, 2005), 6.

4. Molly Brost, "Spy Games: *Alias*, Sydney Bristow, and the Ever Complicated Gaze," *Americana: The Journal of American Popular Culture (1900–Present)* 6, no. 1 (Spring 2007), https://www.americanpopularculture.com/journal/articles/spring_2007/brost.htm.

5. Katie Brown, "*Buffy the Vampire Slayer* and *Charmed*: The Re-feminization of Female 'Superheroes,'" *The Artifice*, February 4, 2015, https://the-artifice.com/buffy-the-vampire-slayer-charmed-feminization/.

6. Brown, "*Buffy the Vampire Slayer* and *Charmed*."

7. Lacey Rose, "Krista Vernoff on Overcoming Her Past, Overhauling 'Grey's Anatomy' and (Finally) Emerging from Shonda's Shadow," *Hollywood Reporter*, April 1, 2021, https://www.hollywoodreporter.com/tv/tv-news/krista-vernoff-on-overcoming-her-past-overhauling-greys-anatomy-and-finally-emerging-from-shondas-shadow-4158013/?utm_medium=social&utm_source=twitter.

8. Rebecca Feasey, "The 'Charmed' Audience: Gender and the Politics of Contemporary Culture," in "A Screen of One's Own," ed. Heather Osborne-Thompson, special issue, *Spectator* 25, no. 2 (Fall 2005): 46.

9. Charmed Lover, "Shannen Doherty Talks about Her Clothes on *Charmed*," YouTube, https://www.youtube.com/watch?v=t31rlqzeGIg.

10. Holly Marie Combs (@H_Combs), "Also we all chose our outfits . . .," Twitter, April 1, 2021, https://twitter.com/H_Combs/status/1377721365185273860.

11. Alyssa Milano (@Alyssa_Milano), "Well, this absolutely broke my heart," Twitter, April 1, 2021, https://twitter.com/Alyssa_Milano/status/1377699635838521346.

12. Brost, "Spy Games: *Alias*, Sydney Bristow, and the Ever Complicated Gaze."

13. Michael Dobbs, "Sexpionage: Why We Can't Resist Those KGB Sirens," *Washington Post*, April 12, 1987, https://www.washingtonpost.com/archive/opinions/1987/04/12/sexpionage-why-we-cant-resist-those-kgb-sirens/900e1e59-1a7b-455f-93cf-22e67394512b/.

14. Mary Hartnett, "The Powerful Portrayal of *Homeland*'s Carrie Mathison," *TN2 Magazine*, March 31, 2017, https://www.tn2magazine.ie/the-powerful-portrayal-of-homelands-carrie-mathison/.

15. Sarah E. Whitney, "I Can Be Whoever I Want to Be: *Alias* and the Post-Feminist Rhetoric of Choice," Genders 1998–2013, March 1, 2013, https://www.colorado.edu/gendersarchive1998-2013/2013/03/01/i-can-be-whoever-i-want-be-alias-and-post-feminist-rhetoric-choice.

16. Whitney, "I Can Be Whoever I Want to Be."

17. Whitney, "I Can Be Whoever I Want to Be."

18. Brost, "Spy Games: *Alias*, Sydney Bristow, and the Ever Complicated Gaze."

19. Sabrina Calandrón, "Feminidad y uso de la fuerza: La fabricación de una heroína a partir de la serie de televisión *Nikita*," Academia, September 21, 2016, 169–70, https://www.academia.edu/35765353/Feminidad_y_uso_de_la_fuerza

_la_fabricaci%C3%B3n_de_una_hero%C3%ADna_a_partir_de_la_serie_de_televisi
%C3%B3n_Nikita.

20. Jenna Scherer, "'Jessica Jones': We Finally Have a Superhero Icon for the
#TimesUp Era," *Rolling Stone*, March 9, 2018, https://www.rollingstone.com/tv-movies
/tv-movie-news/jessica-jones-we-finally-have-a-superhero-icon-for-the-timesup-era
-127314/.

21. Amanda Marcotte, "Before Binge-Watching *Jessica Jones*, Read *Alias*, the Feminist
Comic It's Based On," Salon, November 20, 2015, https://www.salon.com/2015/11/19
/before_binge_watching_jessica_jones_read_alias_the_feminist_comic_its_based_on/.

22. Kayleigh Dray, "*Jessica Jones*: How a PTSD Survivor Came to Be the Greatest
Feminist Superhero of Our Time," *Stylist*, February 19, 2019, https://www.stylist.co.uk
/people/jessica-jones-ptsd-survivor-rape-feminist-superhero-comic-netflix/28808.

23. Leah MarieAnn Klett, "Purity Culture Harmed Thousands of Evangelical Teens;
What Did the Church Get Wrong about Sex?," *Christian Post*, May 20, 2019, https://
www.christianpost.com/news/purity-culture-harmed-thousands-of-evangelical-teens
-what-did-the-church-get-wrong-about-sex.html.

24. Caitlin Harrison, "The Negative Effects of Purity Culture and How to Start to
Heal," Kindman & Co., January 31, 2022, https://www.kindman.co/blog/the-negative
-effects-of-purity-culture-and-how-to-heal.

25. True Love Waits, "Three Million Teens Sign 'True Love Waits' Pledge," Oregon
Faith Report, February 9, 2012, https://oregonfaithreport.com/2012/02/three-million
-teens-sign-true-love-waits-pledge/.

26. Sarah Assenti, "What the Return of *Sabrina* and *Charmed* Says about Feminism
in 2018," *Stylist*, October 16, 2018, https://www.stylist.co.uk/long-reads/witchcraft-re
booted-what-the-return-of-sabrina-and-charmed-says-about-feminism-in-2018/231803.

27. Michileen Martin, "How *Buffy the Vampire Slayer* Changed TV and No One
Noticed," Looper, June 18, 2019, https://www.looper.com/155959/how-buffy-the
-vampire-slayer-changed-tv-and-no-one-noticed/?utm_campaign=clip.

28. Emily VanDerWerff, "How *Buffy the Vampire Slayer* Transformed TV as We
Know It," *Vox*, March 10, 2017, https://www.vox.com/culture/2017/3/10/14857542
/buffy-the-vampire-slayer-explained-tv-influence.

29. F. R. Kesby, "The Problematic Feminism of *Buffy the Vampire Slayer*," Women's Republic, October 15, 2018, https://www.womensrepublic.net/the-problematic-feminism
-of-buffy-the-vampire-slayer/.

30. Brown, "*Buffy the Vampire Slayer* and *Charmed*."

31. Brown, "*Buffy the Vampire Slayer* and *Charmed*."

32. Sarah Warn, "'Buffy' to Show First Lesbian Sex Scene on Broadcast TV," After
Ellen, April 3, 2003, https://afterellen.com/buffy-to-show-first-lesbian-sex-scene-on
-broadcast-tv/.

33. Alanna Bennett, "How 'Buffy' Changed Television for a New Generation,"
BuzzFeed, March 10, 2017, https://www.buzzfeed.com/alannabennett/what-it-means
-to-honor-buffy.

34. Kesby, "The Problematic Feminism of *Buffy the Vampire Slayer*."

35. Eliana Dockterman, "*House of Cards* Creator Beau Willimon: Love Is 'Transactional,'" *Time*, February 16, 2015, https://time.com/3724484/house-of-cards-beau-willimon-season-3/.

36. Karen Gurney, "Sex Lives of the Underwoods," Havelock Clinic, London, May 31, 2017, https://thehavelockclinic.com/bed-underwoods-sex-lives-frank-claire/.

Chapter 8

1. "Breaking Barriers," Pioneers of Television, https://www.pbs.org/wnet/pioneers-of-television/pioneering-programs/breaking-barriers/#:~:text=Gradually%2C%20people%20began%20to%20push.

2. Greg Braxton, "TV Networks Pledged to Improve Diversity in 1999: Will This Time Be Any Different?" *Los Angeles Times*, July 27, 2020, https://www.latimes.com/entertainment-arts/tv/story/2020-07-27/tv-networks-diversity-pledge-naacp-boycott-1999.

3. "Hollywood Diversity Report 2022," UCLA Entertainment and Media Research Initiative, October 27, 2022, https://socialsciences.ucla.edu/wp-content/uploads/2022/10/UCLA-Hollywood-Diversity-Report-2022-Television-10-27-2022.pdf.

4. Christy Piña, "Study: Diversity in TV Casting Increasing, More Lead Roles for Women," *Hollywood Reporter*, October 27, 2022, https://www.hollywoodreporter.com/tv/tv-news/ucla-hollywood-diversity-report-tv-2022-1235249634/.

5. Piña, "Study: Diversity in TV Casting Increasing."

6. Dana Hanson, "The 20 Most Diverse Cities in the U.S. in 2022," Money Inc., September 26, 2022, https://moneyinc.com/most-diverse-cities-in-the-u-s-in-2022/.

7. "Why Toronto Is the Most Multicultural City in the World," Study Abroad Foundation, November 8, 2022, https://www.studyabroadfoundation.org/blogs/why-toronto-most-multicultural-city-world#:~:text=Recognized%20by%20both%20the%20United.

8. Claire L. Wong, "Why 'Buffy the Vampire Slayer' Is Still One of the Best TV Shows Ever," *Hollywood Insider*, February 2, 2021, https://www.hollywoodinsider.com/buffy-the-vampire-slayer-success/.

9. Princess Weekes, "'Jessica Jones' Has a Problem with How It Handles Race and Gender," *Mary Sue*, March 13, 2018, https://www.themarysue.com/jessica-jones-race-gender-superpowers/.

10. Weekes, "'Jessica Jones' Has a Problem with How It Handles Race and Gender."

11. Marykate Jasper, "*Jessica Jones* Is Great at Examining Trauma—unless It Happens to Women of Color," *Mary Sue*, March 14, 2018, https://www.themarysue.com/jessica-jones-women-of-color/.

12. Hannah Collins, "Ultimately, *Jessica Jones'* Feminism Fails Women of Color," CBR, March 25, 2018, https://www.cbr.com/jessica-jones-feminism-no-women-of-color/.

13. Collins, "Ultimately, *Jessica Jones'* Feminism Fails Women of Color."

14. Nicole Sperling, "*Jessica Jones* Creator Melissa Rosenberg on Power and Pitfalls of Female Rage," *Vanity Fair*, March 21, 2018, https://www.vanityfair.com/holly wood/2018/03/jessica-jones-season-2-netflix-marvel-melissa-rosenberg-krysten-ritter.

15. Sydney Bucksbaum, "'Agent Carter' Bosses Discuss How 'Doctor Strange' Tie-In Impacts Peggy's Love Life," *Hollywood Reporter*, January 19, 2016, https://www.holly woodreporter.com/tv/tv-news/agent-carter-how-doctor-strange-857229/.

16. Marcie Casey and Jay Clayton, "Queer Kinship: Privacy Concerns in *Orphan Black*," *Journal of Literature and Science* 14, no. 1/2 (2021–2022): 136, https://www.lit eratureandscience.org/wp-content/uploads/2022/07/8.-CASEY-CLAYTON-Final.pdf.

17. Matt. 5:29 (New International Version).

18. Devon Maloney, "*Orphan Black* Science Consultant Cosima Herter Breaks down the Series Finale," *Vanity Fair*, August 13, 2017, https://www.vanityfair.com/holly wood/2017/08/orphan-black-series-finale-season-5-cosima-herter-interview.

19. Nellie Andreeva, "Maggie Q to Star as CW's 'Nikita,'" *Hollywood Reporter*, February 18, 2010, https://www.hollywoodreporter.com/business/business-news/maggie-q -star-cws-nikita-20855/.

20. Kayti Burt, "*The Protege* Is a Reminder of Just How Good *Nikita* Was," Den of Geek, August 26, 2021, https://www.denofgeek.com/movies/the-protege-review-nikita -comparison/.

21. Melanie McFarland, "A Queen Becomes 'The Equalizer': What It Means When Black Women Take on Legacy Superhero Roles," Salon, February 7, 2021, https://www .salon.com/2021/02/07/the-equalizer-super-bowl-queen-latifah-cbs/.

22. Charles Mudede, "The Karen Episode of Queen Latifah's *The Equalizer* Shows All That Is Wrong with the Current Anti-woke Movement," *The Stranger*, November 22, 2021, https://www.thestranger.com/slog/2021/11/22/63036726/the-karen-episode -of-queen-latifahs-the-equalizer-shows-all-that-is-wrong-with-the-current-anti-woke -movement.

23. Mudede, "The Karen Episode of Queen Latifah's *The Equalizer*."

24. June Thomas, "Queen Latifah Makes the Impossible: A CBS Cop Show for the Black Lives Matter Era," *Slate*, February 7, 2021, https://slate.com/culture/2021/02 /equalizer-queen-latifah-cbs-black-lives-matter-super-bowl.html.

25. Laura Durkay, "'Homeland' Is the Most Bigoted Show on Television," *Washington Post*, October 2, 2014, https://www.washingtonpost.com/posteverything/wp/2014 /10/02/homeland-is-the-most-bigoted-show-on-television/.

26. Matt Brennan, "Yes, 'Homeland' Is Still On: It's the Most Adaptable Show on Television," *Los Angeles Times*, February 7, 2020, https://www.latimes.com/entertain ment-arts/tv/story/2020-02-07/homeland-showtime-claire-danes-mandy-patinkin-final -season.

27. Brian T. Edwards, "Moving Target: Is 'Homeland' Still Racist?," *Los Angeles Review of Books*, March 31, 2017, https://lareviewofbooks.org/article/moving-target-is -homeland-still-racist/.

28. Sara Yasin, "Graffiti Artists Write '*Homeland* Is Racist' in Arabic on the Show's Set in Berlin," BuzzFeed News, October 14, 2015, https://www.buzzfeednews.com /article/sarayasin/graffiti-artists-homeland.

29. Edwards, "Moving Target: Is 'Homeland' Still Racist?"

30. Yasin, "Graffiti Artists Write '*Homeland* Is Racist' in Arabic on the Show's Set in Berlin."

31. Peter Beaumont, "*Homeland* Is Brilliant Drama: But Does It Present a Crude Image of Muslims?" *The Guardian*, December 19, 2017, https://www.theguardian.com /tv-and-radio/2012/oct/13/homeland-drama-offensive-portrayal-islam-arabs.

32. Beaumont, "*Homeland* Is Brilliant Drama."

33. Durkay, "'Homeland' Is the Most Bigoted Show on Television."

34. Yasin, "Graffiti Artists Write '*Homeland* Is Racist' in Arabic on the Show's Set in Berlin."

35. Durkay, "'Homeland' Is the Most Bigoted Show on Television."

36. Durkay, "'Homeland' Is the Most Bigoted Show on Television."

37. Edwards, "Moving Target: Is 'Homeland' Still Racist?"

38. Liz Robbins, "He Didn't like 'Homeland': Now He's Advising It," *New York Times*, March 12, 2017, https://www.nytimes.com/2017/03/12/nyregion/he-didnt-like -the-show-now-hes-advising-it.html.

39. Stephanie Watson, "Is Bipolar a Disability? Your FAQs," Healthline, March 4, 2021, https://www.healthline.com/health/bipolar-disorder/is-bipolar-a-disability #takeaway.

40. ADA, "What Is the Definition of Disability under the ADA?," National Network, 2019, https://adata.org/faq/what-definition-disability-under-ada.

41. "Bipolar Disorder," National Institute of Mental Health, 2022, https://www .nimh.nih.gov/health/statistics/bipolar-disorder.

42. Meron Wondemaghen, "*Homeland*, Carrie Mathison and Mental Illness on Television," The Conversation, October 24, 2014, https://theconversation.com/homeland -carrie-mathison-and-mental-illness-on-television-33458.

43. "The New Normal: Actress Claire Danes, *Homeland* and Hollywood's New Take on Mental Illness," National Alliance on Mental Illness, March 6, 2012, https://www .nami.org/Blogs/NAMI-Blog/March-2012/The-New-Normal-Actress-Claire-Danes -Homeland-and-H#:~:text=Showtime%27s%20original%20series%20Homeland %20is.

44. Jim Mitchell, "How 'Homeland' Became a Pioneer in the Portrayal of Mental Illness," SBS, February 11, 2018, https://www.sbs.com.au/guide/article/2018/02/12 /how-homeland-became-pioneer-portrayal-mental-illness.

45. Mitchell, "How 'Homeland' Became a Pioneer in the Portrayal of Mental Illness."

46. Hannah Jane Parkinson, "Does *Homeland* Sensationalise Carrie Mathison's Bipolar Disorder?" *The Guardian*, December 1, 2014, https://www.theguardian.com /commentisfree/2014/dec/01/homeland-carrie-mathison-bipolar-disorder-claire-danes.

47. Parkinson, "Does *Homeland* Sensationalise Carrie Mathison's Bipolar Disorder?"

48. Emily St. James, "*Homeland's* Carrie Mathison Is the Most Influential TV Character of the 2010s," *Vox*, November 11, 2015, https://www.vox.com/2015/11/11/9715382 /homeland-season-5-claire-danes.

49. Mitchell, "How 'Homeland' Became a Pioneer in the Portrayal of Mental Illness."

50. Wondemaghen, "*Homeland*, Carrie Mathison and Mental Illness on Television."

51. Nolan Feeney, "*Homeland*: The Case against Calling Carrie a Bipolar 'Superhero,'" *The Atlantic*, October 7, 2013, https://www.theatlantic.com/entertainment

/archive/2013/10/-em-homeland-em-the-case-against-calling-carrie-a-bipolar-super hero/280321/.

52. "The New Normal."

53. Mitchell, "How 'Homeland' Became a Pioneer in the Portrayal of Mental Illness."

54. Parkinson, "Does *Homeland* Sensationalise Carrie Mathison's Bipolar Disorder?"

55. Parkinson, "Does *Homeland* Sensationalise Carrie Mathison's Bipolar Disorder?"

56. Jace Lacob, "'Homeland' and 'Shameless': Television Tackles Bipolar Disorder with Realism," Daily Beast, April 10, 2012, https://www.thedailybeast.com/homeland -and-shameless-television-tackles-bipolar-disorder-with-realism.

57. Parkinson, "Does *Homeland* Sensationalise Carrie Mathison's Bipolar Disorder?"

58. Mitchell, "How 'Homeland' Became a Pioneer in the Portrayal of Mental Illness."

59. Lacob, "'Homeland' and 'Shameless': Television Tackles Bipolar Disorder with Realism."

60. Quoted in Lacob, "'Homeland' and 'Shameless.'"

61. St. James, "*Homeland*'s Carrie Mathison Is the Most Influential TV Character of the 2010s."

62. "Very Special Episode," TV Tropes, https://tvtropes.org/pmwiki/pmwiki.php /Main/VerySpecialEpisode.

63. Wondemaghen, "*Homeland*, Carrie Mathison and Mental Illness on Television."

64. Alanna Bennett, "How 'Buffy' Changed Television for a New Generation," BuzzFeed, March 10, 2017, https://www.buzzfeed.com/alannabennett/what-it-means -to-honor-buffy.

65. Sarah Dobbs, "10 Ways *Buffy the Vampire Slayer* Changed the World," Den of Geek, March 10, 2017, https://www.denofgeek.com/tv/10-ways-buffy-the-vampire -slayer-changed-the-world/.

66. Wong, "Why 'Buffy the Vampire Slayer' Is Still One of the Best TV Shows Ever."

67. Michileen Martin, "How *Buffy the Vampire Slayer* Changed TV and No One Noticed," Looper, June 18, 2019, https://www.looper.com/155959/how-buffy-the -vampire-slayer-changed-tv-and-no-one-noticed/?utm_campaign=clip.

68. Dobbs, "10 Ways *Buffy the Vampire Slayer* Changed the World."

69. Quoted in Sarah Warn, "'Buffy' to Show First Lesbian Sex Scene on Broadcast TV," AfterEllen, April 3, 2003, https://afterellen.com/buffy-to-show-first-lesbian-sex -scene-on-broadcast-tv/.

70. Warn, "'Buffy' to Show First Lesbian Sex Scene on Broadcast TV."

71. Marykate Jasper, "Jeri Hogarth: *Jessica Jones* and Female Capitalist Success," *Mary Sue*, March 13, 2018. https://www.themarysue.com/jeri-hogarth-jessica-jones-season-2/.

72. Chelsea Steiner, "*Jessica Jones* Delivers Marvel's Best LGBTQ+ Representation," *Mary Sue*, June 25, 2019, https://www.themarysue.com/jessica-jones-lgbtq-representa tion-season-three/#:~:text=Jeri%20Hogarth%20(Carrie-Anne%20Moss.

73. Steiner, "*Jessica Jones* Delivers Marvel's Best LGBTQ+ Representation."

74. Jamie Zabinsky, "Politics, Power and Queerness in 'House of Cards' Season 4," Feministing, May 31, 2016, https://feministing.com/2016/05/31/politics-power-and -queerness-in-house-of-cards-season-4/.

75. Jason Guerrasio, "The 'House of Cards' Star Who Plays Meechum Remembers the Show's Most Notorious Sex Scene," Insider, https://www.businessinsider.com /house-of-cards-meechum-sex-episode-2016-3.

76. Zabinsky, "Politics, Power and Queerness in 'House of Cards' Season 4."

77. Margaret Lyons, "*House of Cards* Has a Frank-and-Claire Problem," Vulture, March 3, 2015, https://www.vulture.com/2015/03/house-of-cards-frank-claire.html.

78. "Both Nature and Nurture Contribute to Signatures of Socioeconomic Status in the Brain," ScienceDaily, May 18, 2022, https://www.sciencedaily.com/releases /2022/05/220518140703.htm.

79. Gregory E. Pence, "Sexuality, Gender Identity and *Orphan Black*," in *What We Talk about When We Talk about Clone Club: Bioethics and Philosophy in* Orphan Black (Dallas, TX: BenBella Books, 2016), 145.

80. "Sarah Manning," American Institute of Bisexuality, https://bi.org/en/bi-charac ters/sarah-manning.

81. Pence, "Sexuality, Gender Identity and *Orphan Black*," 145.

82. "*Orphan Black* (TV Series 2013–2017)," IMDb, https://www.imdb.com/title /tt2234222/faq/.

83. Tariq Raouf, "'Orphan Black' and Trans Representation: Where They Went Wrong," Hypable, May 3, 2016, https://www.hypable.com/orphan-black-trans-repre sentation/.

84. Tanya Ghahremani, "Why 'Orphan Black' Needs to Kill off Your Favorite Clone," Complex, May 19, 2014, https://www.complex.com/pop-culture/2014/05 /orphan-black-kill-favorite-clone.

85. Audrey Jane Black, "Sisterhood, Science, and Surveillance in *Orphan Black*," in *Fourth Wave Feminism in Science Fiction and Fantasy*, vol. 2, *Essays on Television Representations, 2013–2019*, ed. Valerie Estelle Frankel (Jefferson, NC: McFarland, 2020), 31.

Chapter 9

1. Jack Wilhelmi, "What Faith Did after *Buffy the Vampire Slayer* Ended," Screen-Rant, April 4, 2020, https://screenrant.com/buffy-vampire-slayer-faith-after-finale -ending/.

2. Claire L. Wong, "An Analysis: Female Villain Redemption Arcs That Paved the Way for Villanelle in 'Killing Eve,'" *Hollywood Insider*, January 14, 2021, https://www .hollywoodinsider.com/female-villain-redemption-arcs-tv/.

3. Wong, "An Analysis: Female Villain Redemption Arcs That Paved the Way for Villanelle in 'Killing Eve.'"

4. "Faith Lehane," Buffyverse Wiki, https://buffy.fandom.com/wiki/Faith_Lehane.

5. Wilhelmi, "What Faith Did after *Buffy the Vampire Slayer* Ended."

6. Matt Richenthal, "*Nikita* Spoilers: A Free Woman . . .," TV Fanatic, January 15, 2011, https://www.tvfanatic.com/2011/01/nikita-spoilers-a-free-woman/.

7. Sabrina Calandrón, "Feminidad y uso de la fuerza: La fabricación de una heroína a partir de la serie de televisión *Nikita*," Academia, September 21, 2016, 170–71,

https://www.academia.edu/35765353/Feminidad_y_uso_de_la_fuerza_la_fabricaci
%C3%B3n_de_una_hero%C3%ADna_a_partir_de_la_serie_de_televisi%C3%B3n
_Nikita.

8. Kate Gardner, "Why Do Women Rarely Get Redemption Arcs?," *Mary Sue*, August 6, 2018, https://www.themarysue.com/female-characters-redemption-arcs/.

9. Corey Patterson, "*Jessica Jones*: Freedom and Guilt," Pop Culture and Theology, March 9, 2018, https://popularcultureandtheology.com/2018/03/09/jessica-jones-free
dom-and-guilt/.

10. "Kilgrave," Marvel Cinematic Universe Wiki, https://marvelcinematicuniverse
.fandom.com/wiki/Kilgrave#cite_ref-JJ313_16-0.

11. Doreen St. Félix, "Queen Latifah Obliterates Trumps N' Musks in 'The Equalizer,'" *New Yorker*, March 5, 2021, https://www.newyorker.com/magazine/2021/03/15
/queen-latifah-obliterates-trumps-n-musks-in-the-equalizer.

Conclusion

1. Hayley Atwell, foreword to *Marvel's* Agent Carter*: Season One Declassified* (New York: Marvel Entertainment, 2015), n.p.

2. Esther Bergdahl, "The Kick-Ass Female Superhero We've Been Waiting for Is Finally Here," *Mic*, January 6, 2015, https://www.mic.com/articles/107766/marvel-s
-agent-carter-promises-us-the-heroine-we-deserve.

3. Atwell, foreword to *Marvel's* Agent Carter, n.p.

Bibliography

Abrams, J. J. Introduction to Alias *Declassified: The Official Companion,* by Mark Cotta Vaz. New York: Bantam Books for Young Readers, 2002.

ADA. "What Is the Definition of Disability under the ADA?" National Network, 2019. https://adata.org/faq/what-definition-disability-under-ada.

Agard, Chancellor. "Marvel's *Jessica Jones* Boss Breaks down Trish and Jessica's Series Finale Fates." *Entertainment Weekly,* June 18, 2019. https://ew.com/tv/2019/06/18 /marvels-jessica-jones-series-finale-jessica-trish-fate/.

Andrae, Thomas. "Television's First Feminist: 'The Avengers' and Female Spectatorship." *Discourse* 18, no. 3 (1996): 112–36. http://www.jstor.org/stable/41389423.

Andreeva, Nellie. "Maggie Q to Star as CW's 'Nikita.'" *Hollywood Reporter,* February 18, 2010. https://www.hollywoodreporter.com/business/business-news/maggie-q -star-cws-nikita-20855/.

Assenti, Sarah. "What the Return of *Sabrina* and *Charmed* Says about Feminism in 2018." *Stylist,* October 16, 2018. https://www.stylist.co.uk/long-reads/witchcraft-rebooted -what-the-return-of-sabrina-and-charmed-says-about-feminism-in-2018/231803.

Atwell, Hayley. Foreword to *Marvel's* Agent Carter: *Season One Declassified.* New York: Marvel Entertainment, 2015.

Badasie, Charlene. "The Fate of Queen Latifah's Equalizer Has Been Decided." Giant Freakin Robot, May 10, 2022. https://www.giantfreakinrobot.com/ent/queen-latifah -equalizer-fate.html.

Bastién, Angelica Jade. "The Enduring Legacy of *Buffy the Vampire Slayer.*" Vulture, October 25, 2021. https://www.vulture.com/2021/10/buffy-the-vampire-slayer-twenty -years-greatest-legacy.html.

———. "The Grand Feminist Legacy of *Orphan Black.*" Vulture, August 15, 2017. https://www.vulture.com/2017/08/orphan-black-series-review.html.

Baugher, Lacy. "Twenty Years after *Alias,* TV Still Needs More Sydney Bristows." Den of Geek, September 29, 2021. https://www.denofgeek.com/tv/twenty-years-after -alias-tv-still-needs-more-sydney-bristows/.

Baumgardner, Jennifer, and Amy Richards. *Manifesta: Young Women, Feminism, and the Future.* New York: Farrar, Straus & Giroux, 2000.

Beaumont, Peter. "*Homeland* Is Brilliant Drama: But Does It Present a Crude Image of Muslims?" *The Guardian*, December 19, 2017. https://www.theguardian.com/tv-and-radio/2012/oct/13/homeland-drama-offensive-portrayal-islam-arabs.

Bennett, Alanna. "How 'Buffy' Changed Television for a New Generation." BuzzFeed, March 10, 2017. https://www.buzzfeed.com/alannabennett/what-it-means-to-honor-buffy.

Bergdahl, Esther. "The Kick-Ass Female Superhero We've Been Waiting for Is Finally Here." *Mic*, January 6, 2015. https://www.mic.com/articles/107766/marvel-s-agent-carter-promises-us-the-heroine-we-deserve.

"Bipolar Disorder." National Institute of Mental Health, 2022. https://www.nimh.nih.gov/health/statistics/bipolar-disorder.

Black, A. J. "*Alias* (Series Overview + Reviews)." We Made This, April 9, 2018. https://wemadethisnetwork.com/2018/04/09/alias-series-overview-reviews/.

Black, Audrey Jane. "Sisterhood, Science, and Surveillance in *Orphan Black*." In *Essays on Television Representations, 2013–2019*. Vol. 2 of *Fourth Wave Feminism in Science Fiction and Fantasy*, edited by Valerie Estelle Frankel. Jefferson, NC: McFarland, 2020.

Blake, Meredith. "President Obama Names His Favorite Show of 2015—and No, It's Not 'Homeland.'" *Los Angeles Times*, December 9, 2015. https://www.latimes.com/entertainment/la-et-st-president-obama-favorite-tv-show-the-knick-20151209-story.html#:~:text=Back%20in%202012%2C%20he%20was.

Blazina, Carrie, and Drew Desilver. "A Record Number of Women Are Serving in the 117th Congress." Pew Research Center, January 15, 2021. https://www.pewresearch.org/fact-tank/2021/01/15/a-record-number-of-women-are-serving-in-the-117th-congress/.

"Both Nature and Nurture Contribute to Signatures of Socioeconomic Status in the Brain." ScienceDaily, May 18, 2022. https://www.sciencedaily.com/releases/2022/05/220518140703.htm.

Boucher, Ashley. "Why 'Jessica Jones' Is the Superhero TV Show We Need in the #MeToo Era." *The Wrap* (blog), March 10, 2018. https://www.thewrap.com/jessica-jones-superhero-tv-show-we-need-in-metoo-era/.

Bowerman, Mary. "There's Even a Women's March in Antarctica." *USA Today*, January 21, 2017. https://www.usatoday.com/story/news/politics/onpolitics/2017/01/21/womens-march-on-washington-antarctica/96882184/.

Braude, Ann. *Radical Spirits: Spiritualism and Women's Rights in Nineteenth-Century America.* Bloomington: Indiana University Press, 2020.

Braxton, Greg. "TV Networks Pledged to Improve Diversity in 1999: Will This Time Be Any Different?" *Los Angeles Times*, July 27, 2020. https://www.latimes.com/entertainment-arts/tv/story/2020-07-27/tv-networks-diversity-pledge-naacp-boycott-1999.

Brayson, Johnny. "Why Nikita Is the Deadliest Woman in Pop Culture." CHARGE!, July 10, 2019. https://watchcharge.com/why-nikita-is-the-deadliest-woman-in-pop-culture/.

"Breaking Barriers." Pioneers of Television. https://www.pbs.org/wnet/pioneers-of
-television/pioneering-programs/breaking-barriers/#:~:text=Gradually%2C%20
people%20began%20to%20push.

Brennan, Matt. "Yes, 'Homeland' Is Still On: It's the Most Adaptable Show on Television."
Los Angeles Times, February 7, 2020. https://www.latimes.com/entertainment-arts
/tv/story/2020-02-07/homeland-showtime-claire-danes-mandy-patinkin-final-season.

Brost, Molly. "Spy Games: *Alias*, Sydney Bristow, and the Ever Complicated Gaze."
Americana: The Journal of American Popular Culture (1900–Present) 6, no. 1 (Spring
2007). https://www.americanpopularculture.com/journal/articles/spring_2007/brost
.htm.

Brown, Katie. "*Buffy the Vampire Slayer* and *Charmed*: The Re-feminization of Female
'Superheroes.'" *The Artifice*, February 4, 2015. https://the-artifice.com/buffy-the
-vampire-slayer-charmed-feminization/.

Bucksbaum, Sydney. "'Agent Carter' Bosses Discuss How 'Doctor Strange' Tie-In Impacts Peggy's Love Life." *Hollywood Reporter*, January 19, 2016. https://www.holly
woodreporter.com/tv/tv-news/agent-carter-how-doctor-strange-857229/.

Burt, Kayti. "*The Protege* Is a Reminder of Just How Good *Nikita* Was." Den of Geek,
August 26, 2021. https://www.denofgeek.com/movies/the-protege-review-nikita
-comparison/.

Butler, Bethonie. "Why the Success of 'The Equalizer' Is Bigger Than the Show Itself."
Washington Post, May 21, 2021. https://www.washingtonpost.com/arts-entertain
ment/2021/05/21/the-equalizer-queen-latifah/.

Caballero, David. "Peggy Carter, First Lady of the MCU." Digital Trends, May 6, 2022.
https://www.digitaltrends.com/movies/peggy-carter-hayley-atwell-first-lady-of-mcu/.

Calandrón, Sabrina. "Feminidad y uso de la fuerza: La fabricación de una heroína a
partir de la serie de televisión *Nikita*." Academia, September 21, 2016. https://www
.academia.edu/35765353/Feminidad_y_uso_de_la_fuerza_la_fabricaci%C3%B3n
_de_una_hero%C3%ADna_a_partir_de_la_serie_de_televisi%C3%B3n_Nikita.

Carilli, Theresa, and Jane Campbell, eds. *Women and the Media: Diverse Perspectives*.
Lanham, MD: University Press of America, 2005.

"Carl Clauberg." Auschwitz-Birkenau Memorial and Museum. https://www.auschwitz
.org/en/history/medical-experiments/carl-clauberg/.

Casey, Marcie, and Jay Clayton. "Queer Kinship: Privacy Concerns in *Orphan Black*."
Journal of Literature and Science 14, no. 1/2 (2021–2022): 125–39. https://www.liter
atureandscience.org/wp-content/uploads/2022/07/8.-CASEY-CLAYTON-Final.pdf.

Chang, Ailsa. "Joss Whedon Was Once Hailed as a Feminist: Then Came the Stories
about His Behavior." St. Louis NPR, January 18, 2022. https://www.npr.org/2022
/01/18/1073881791/joss-whedon-was-once-hailed-as-a-feminist-then-came-the
-stories-about-his-behavi.

Charmed Lover. "Shannen Doherty Talks about Her Clothes on *Charmed*." YouTube.
https://www.youtube.com/watch?v=t31rlqzeGIg.

Coffin, Lesley. "Women like Marvel Agent Carter Very Real Part of History." *Mary Sue*,
January 6, 2015. https://www.themarysue.com/real-women-history-marvel-peggy
-carter/.

Cole, Kai. "Joss Whedon Is a 'Hypocrite Preaching Feminist Ideals,' Ex-Wife Kai Cole Says (Guest Blog)." *The Wrap* (blog), August 20, 2017. https://www.thewrap.com /joss-whedon-feminist-hypocrite-infidelity-affairs-ex-wife-kai-cole-says/.

Collins, Hannah. "Ultimately, *Jessica Jones*' Feminism Fails Women of Color." CBR, March 25, 2018. https://www.cbr.com/jessica-jones-feminism-no-women-of-color/.

Combs, Holly Marie (@H_Combs). "Also we all chose our outfits . . ." Twitter, April 1, 2021. https://twitter.com/H_Combs/status/1377721365185273860.

Commerce, Jessie. "*Orphan Black*: How the Bechdel Test Helps Us Accurately Analyze Gender Equality." Media Production and Criticism. https://dmillef.wixsite.com /media-criticism/orphan-black.

"Commie Fighters of the '50s." For Your Eyes Only, https://www.for-your-eyes-only .com/Site/Commie_50s.html.

Cooley, Patrick. "Before 'Wonder Woman': How Female Superheroes Evolved." Cleveland.com, June 7, 2017. https://www.cleveland.com/entertainment/2017/06 /before_wonder_woman_how_female.html#:~:text=The%20character%20 started%20to%20evolve%20when%20then%20DC.

Crampton, Caroline. "Strong, Interesting Female Characters Are the Secret of *House of Cards*' Success." *New Statesman*, February 14, 2014. https://www.newstatesman.com /culture/2014/02/strong-interesting-female-characters-are-secret-house-cards-success.

Crislip, Anthony. "Why 'The Bionic Woman' Outshines 'The Six Million Dollar Man.'" Ultimate Classic Rock. https://ultimateclassicrock.com/bionic-woman/.

Crow, David. "*Homeland*, the Legacy of Carrie Mathison, and Why It's Time to Let Go." Den of Geek, April 27, 2020. https://www.denofgeek.com/tv/homeland-legacy -of-carrie-mathison/.

Crusie, Jenny. "*Totally Charmed*: Introduction." *Jenny's Blog*, 2005. https://jennycrusie .com/excerpts/totally-charmed-introduction/.

Daisley, Stephen. "How *Buffy the Vampire Slayer* Transformed Pop Culture." *The Spectator*, March 10, 2017. https://www.spectator.co.uk/article/how-buffy-the-vampire -slayer-transformed-pop-culture/.

D'Alessandro, Anthony. "Ray Fisher Demands WarnerMedia Reveal 'Justice League' Investigation Findings Following CEO Ann Sarnoff's Comments." Deadline, March 23, 2021. https://deadline.com/2021/03/ray-fisher-slames-warnermedia-ann-sarnoff -justice-league-joss-whedon-investigation-1234719795/.

DeBolt, Virginia. "Friends and Lovers on Marvel's *Jessica Jones*." Old Ain't Dead, December 3, 2015. https://oldaintdead.com/friends-and-lovers-on-marvels-jessica-jones/.

Deggans, Eric. "'Jessica Jones' Struggles in Life—but Triumphs on Screen." NPR, November 20, 2015. https://www.npr.org/2015/11/20/456812993/jessica-jones -struggles-in-life-but-triumphs-on-screen.

Desta, Yohana. "Kevin Spacey Is Seeking 'Evaluation and Treatment' after Allegations." *Vanity Fair*, November 2, 2017. https://www.vanityfair.com/hollywood/2017/11 /kevin-spacey-evaluation-treatment-allegations.

Dibdin, Emma. "'House of Cards' Says Time's up as Final Season Exposes Fears about Women in Power." *Hollywood Reporter*, November 4, 2018. https://www.hollywood reporter.com/tv/tv-news/house-cards-season-6s-all-female-cabinet-reveal-1157946/.

Dobbs, Michael. "Sexpionage: Why We Can't Resist Those KGB Sirens." *Washington Post*, April 12, 1987. https://www.washingtonpost.com/archive/opinions/1987/04/12/sexpionage-why-we-cant-reslst-those-kgb-sirens/900e1e59-1a7b-455f-93cf-22e67394512b/.

Dobbs, Sarah. "10 Ways *Buffy the Vampire Slayer* Changed the World." Den of Geek, March 10, 2017. https://www.denofgeek.com/tv/10-ways-buffy-the-vampire-slayer-changed-the-world/.

Dockterman, Eliana. "'Agent Carter' Creator on the Pressures of Creating Marvel's First Female Project." *Time*, January 15, 2015. https://time.com/3654883/agent-carter-creator-marvel-female/.

———. "*House of Cards* Creator Beau Willimon: Love Is 'Transactional.'" *Time*, February 16, 2015. https://time.com/3724484/house-of-cards-beau-willimon-season-3/.

Dowell, Meg. "We Need a New Agent Carter Series Now More Than Ever." Culturess, August 13, 2019. https://culturess.com/2019/08/13/need-new-agent-carter-series-now-ever/.

Dray, Kayleigh. "*Jessica Jones*: How a PTSD Survivor Came to Be the Greatest Feminist Superhero of Our Time." *Stylist*, February 19, 2019. https://www.stylist.co.uk/people/jessica-jones-ptsd-survivor-rape-feminist-superhero-comic-netflix/28808.

Durkay, Laura. "'Homeland' Is the Most Bigoted Show on Television." *Washington Post*, October 2, 2014. https://www.washingtonpost.com/posteverything/wp/2014/10/02/homeland-is-the-most-bigoted-show-on-television/.

Edwards, Brian T. "Moving Target: Is 'Homeland' Still Racist?" *Los Angeles Review of Books*, March 31, 2017. https://lareviewofbooks.org/article/moving-target-is-homeland-still-racist/.

Encyclopædia Britannica. "Coverture | Law." Last modified October 8, 2007. https://www.britannica.com/topic/coverture.

Esteban, Michelle. "Major FBI Milestone: This Year Marks 50 Years of Women Serving as Special Agents." KOMO, May 9, 2022. https://komonews.com/news/local/major-fbi-milestone-2022-marks-50-years-of-women-serving-as-special-agents.

Even, Rebecca. "Proud to Be a Woman: *Agent Carter*." *Cornell Daily Sun*, February 11, 2016. https://cornellsun.com/2016/02/10/proud-to-be-a-woman-agent-carter/.

"Faith Lehane." Buffyverse Wiki. https://buffy.fandom.com/wiki/Faith_Lehane.

Fambul, S. "17 Shows That Changed the Game for Black Women on TV." *Glamour*, August 6, 2020. https://www.glamour.com/gallery/tv-shows-that-changed-the-game-for-black-women.

Feasey, Rebecca. "The 'Charmed' Audience: Gender and the Politics of Contemporary Culture." In "A Screen of One's Own," edited by Heather Osborne-Thompson. Special issue, *Spectator* 25, no. 2 (Fall 2005): 39–48. https://cinema.usc.edu/assets/097/15720.pdf.

Feeney, Nolan. "*Homeland*: The Case against Calling Carrie a Bipolar 'Superhero.'" *The Atlantic*, October 7, 2013. https://www.theatlantic.com/entertainment/archive/2013/10/-em-homeland-em-the-case-against-calling-carrie-a-bipolar-superhero/280321/.

Feldman, Dana. "'Homeland' Ends on a High Note with Carrie and Saul in Cahoots." *Forbes*, April 27, 2020. https://www.forbes.com/sites/danafeldman/2020/04/27/homeland-ends-on-a-high-note-with-carrie-and-saul-in-cahoots/?sh=2e794cbd134b.

Fortin, Jacey. "That Time 'Murphy Brown' and Dan Quayle Topped the Front Page." *New York Times*, January 26, 2018. https://www.nytimes.com/2018/01/26/arts/television/murphy-brown-dan-quayle.html.

Foster, Tom. "The History and Evolution of Female Superheroes from 1940 to Present." TVovermind, October 6, 2017. https://tvovermind.com/history-evolution-female-superheroes-1940-present/.

Framke, Caroline. "*Orphan Black* Co-creator Graeme Manson on the Season Finale, a New Threat, and 'Shippers.'" *A.V. Club*, June 21, 2015. https://www.avclub.com/orphan-black-co-creator-graeme-manson-on-the-season-fin-1798280959.

———. "*Orphan Black* Flips the Sci-Fi Script by Putting Female Agency First." *A.V. Club*, July 18, 2013. https://www.avclub.com/orphan-black-flips-the-sci-fi-script-by-putting-female-1798239300.

———. "*Orphan Black*: 'History yet to Be Written.'" *A.V. Club*, June 21, 2015. https://www.avclub.com/orphan-black-history-yet-to-be-written-1798184133.

Frederick, Brittany. "10 Reasons 'Nikita' Doesn't Need Changing." TVovermind, October 14, 2010. https://tvovermind.com/10-reasons-nikita-changing/.

Frederick, Candice. "*The Equalizer* Season 2 Review: Queen Latifah Masterfully Flips the Script on Tired Procedural Dramas." *TV Guide*, October 8, 2021. https://www.tvguide.com/news/the-equalizer-season-2-review-queen-latifah-masterfully-flips-the-script-on-tired-procedural-dramas/.

Gallagher, Caitlin. "Why Jessica and Trish's Relationship on 'Jessica Jones' Is the Show's Real Love Story." *Bustle*, June 13, 2019. https://www.bustle.com/p/why-jessica-trishs-relationship-on-jessica-jones-is-the-shows-real-love-story-17992114.

Gardner, Kate. "Why Do Women Rarely Get Redemption Arcs?" *Mary Sue*, August 6, 2018. https://www.themarysue.com/female-characters-redemption-arcs/.

Gennis, Sadie. "TV's Most Important Political Debate Is Happening Right Now on *Orphan Black*." *TV Guide*, June 5, 2014. https://www.tvguide.com/news/orphan-black-feminist-reproductive-rights-1082607/.

Ghahremani, Tanya. "Why 'Orphan Black' Needs to Kill off Your Favorite Clone." Complex, May 19, 2014. https://www.complex.com/pop-culture/2014/05/orphan-black-kill-favorite-clone.

Gibson, Kelsie. "Actresses Who Have Played Catwoman through the Years." *People*, November 28, 2022. https://people.com/movies/actresses-who-have-played-catwoman/#:~:text=Julie%20Newmar%20played%20the%20very.

Gilbert, Sophie. "The Villainous Women of 'Jessica Jones.'" *The Atlantic*, March 15, 2018. https://www.theatlantic.com/entertainment/archive/2018/03/jessica-jones-season-2-review-netflix/555395/.

GLAAD Media Institute. "Where We Are on TV." GLAAD, 2021–2022. https://www.glaad.org/sites/default/files/GLAAD%20202122%20WWATV.pdf.

Goldstein, Jessica M. "The CIA Is Trying to Recruit Gen Z—and Doesn't Care If They're All over Social Media." *Washingtonian*, November 9, 2021. https://www

.washingtonian.com/2021/11/09/how-gen-z-and-the-tiktok-generation-are-becoming-spies/.

Griffiths, Kadeen. "Jessica and Trish's Relationship in 'Jessica Jones' Season 3 Will Be Complicated but Not Unfixable, according to Actor Rachael Taylor." *Bustle*, March 9, 2018. https://www.bustle.com/p/jessica-trishs-relationship-in-jessica-jones-season-3-will-be-complicated-but-not-unfixable-according-to-actor-rachael-taylor-8450629.

Gross, Ed. "*Charmed* Creator Spills Show Secrets in Our Decades-Old Interview." *In Touch Weekly*, February 16, 2018. https://www.intouchweekly.com/posts/charmed-cast-secrets-154161/.

Grossman, Pam. "Waking the Witch: The Feminist History of Spiritualism." *Ms.*, October 29, 2019. https://msmagazine.com/2019/10/29/waking-the-witch-the-feminist-history-of-spiritualism/.

Guerrasio, Jason. "The 'House of Cards' Star Who Plays Meechum Remembers the Show's Most Notorious Sex Scene." Insider, https://www.businessinsider.com/house-of-cards-meechum-sex-episode-2016-3.

Gurney, Karen. "Sex Lives of the Underwoods." Havelock Clinic, London, May 31, 2017. https://thehavelockclinic.com/bed-underwoods-sex-lives-frank-claire/.

Hale, Mike. "'The Equalizer' Review: Queen Latifah on the CBS Assembly Line." *New York Times*, February 4, 2021. https://www.nytimes.com/2021/02/04/arts/television/the-equalizer-queen-latifah-review.html.

Hammill, Geoff. "*The Mary Tyler Moore Show*." Museum of Broadcast Communications, archived from the original on February 1, 2015. https://interviews.television academy.com/shows/mary-tyler-moore-show-the.

Hanson, Dana. "The 20 Most Diverse Cities in the U.S. in 2022." Money Inc., September 26, 2022. https://moneyinc.com/most-diverse-cities-in-the-u-s-in-2022/.

Harold, Theresa. "Witchcraft Is More Popular Than Ever—but Why?" *Stylist*, March 1, 2017. https://www.stylist.co.uk/life/spells-in-the-city-why-an-increasing-number-of-women-are-practicing-witchcraft-digital-spiritual-modern/69261.

Harrington, Delia. "The Orphan Black Legacy: A Galaxy of Complex Women." Den of Greek, August 19, 2017. https://www.denofgeek.com/tv/the-orphan-black-legacy-a-galaxy-of-complex-women/.

Harris, Victoria. "Witches on Surfboards: How Witch Media Has Ridden the Waves of Feminism for the Classroom." *Cardinal Compositions* 4 (2020): 39–43. https://ir.library.louisville.edu/cgi/viewcontent.cgi?article=1007&context=cardcomp.

Harrison, Caitlin. "The Negative Effects of Purity Culture and How to Start to Heal." Kindman & Co., January 31, 2022. https://www.kindman.co/blog/the-negative-effects-of-purity-culture-and-how-to-heal.

Hartnett, Mary. "The Powerful Portrayal of *Homeland*'s Carrie Mathison." *TN2 Magazine*, March 31, 2017. https://www.tn2magazine.ie/the-powerful-portrayal-of-homelands-carrie-mathison/.

"Hayley Atwell's Machine Gun Fun." *Belfast Telegraph*, May 18, 2011. https://www.belfasttelegraph.co.uk/entertainment/film-tv/news/hayley-atwells-machine-gun-fun-28618734.html.

Heinecken, Dawn. *The Warrior Women of Television: A Feminist Cultural Analysis of the New Female Body in Popular Media*. Salzburg, Austria: Peter Lang, 2003.

Hibberd, James. "'Homeland' Showrunner Explains That Shocking Premiere Scene." *Entertainment Weekly*, October 5, 2014. https://ew.com/article/2014/10/05/home land-premiere-interview/.

Hill, Libby. "A Shocking, Horrifying Act on *Homeland* Aims to Build Empathy for the Indefensible." *Vox*, October 6, 2014. https://www.vox.com/2014/10/6/6900651 /homeland-carrie-drowns-baby.

Hipes, Patrick. "Streaming TV Series ahead of Broadcast in Featuring Women in Front of and behind Camera, Latest 'Boxed In' Study Finds." Deadline, October 18, 2022. https://deadline.com/2022/10/boxed-in-tv-study-2022-results-streaming-broadcast -series-1235147577/#:~:text=A%20new%20report%20from%20the.

"The History of the Female Superhero." YouTube. https://youtu.be/JG-AUqEsiNE.

"The History of Working Women, as Seen on TV." TV Professor, October 29, 2021. https://thetvprofessor.com/the-history-of-working-women-as-seen-on-tv/.

Hodge, Karl. "The Lazy Geek's Guide to *Alias*." Den of Geek, January 25, 2011. https:// www.denofgeek.com/tv/the-lazy-geeks-guide-to-alias/.

"Hollywood Diversity Report 2022." UCLA Entertainment and Media Research Initia- tive, October 27, 2022. https://socialsciences.ucla.edu/wp-content/uploads/2022/10 /UCLA-Hollywood-Diversity-Report-2022-Television-10-27-2022.pdf.

"*Homeland*." Television Academy. https://www.emmys.com/shows/homeland.

"*House of Cards*." Golden Globes, July 7, 2016. https://www.goldenglobes.com/tv-show /house-cards.

Housman, Patty. "*Roe v Wade* Overturned: What It Means, What's Next." American Uni- versity, June 29, 2022. https://www.american.edu/cas/news/roe-v-wade-overturned -what-it-means-whats-next.cfm.

Huddleston, Kathie. "Modern Day Hero." *SciFi Magazine*, February 2015, 34–36.

Idrees, Abdullah. "The Empowerment of Three: The Halliwell Sisters Charm Televisual Culture." *Studies in Visual Cultures—ENG 705* (blog), April 18, 2018. https://visual culture.blog.torontomu.ca/the-empowerment-of-three-the-halliwell-sisters-charm -televisual-culture/.

"International Women's Rights." Equal Means Equal. https://equalmeansequal.com /international-womens-rights/.

Isley, Sierra. "'Jessica Jones' Is the Feminist Show You Should Be Watching." @dolescent, July 5, 2018. https://www.adolescent.net/a/jessica-jones-is-the-feminist -show-you-should-be-watching.

Jasper, Marykate. "Jeri Hogarth: *Jessica Jones* and Female Capitalist Success." *Mary Sue*, March 13, 2018. https://www.themarysue.com/jeri-hogarth-jessica-jones-season-2/.

———. "*Jessica Jones* Is Great at Examining Trauma—unless It Happens to Women of Color." *Mary Sue*, March 14, 2018. https://www.themarysue.com/jessica-jones -women-of-color/.

Jenkins, Chris. "10 Surprising Ways 'Buffy the Vampire Slayer' Influenced Modern Culture." Listverse, May 16, 2015. https://listverse.com/2015/05/16/10-surprising -ways-buffy-the-vampire-slayer-influenced-modern-culture/.

Joho, Jess. "How 'House of Cards' Season 6 Fails Its Madam President." Mashable, November 7, 2018. https://mashable.com/article/house-of-cards-season-6-review -feminism-metoo.

Kang, Inkoo. "Maya vs. Carrie—Comparing the Feminism of 'Zero Dark Thirty' and 'Homeland.'" Yahoo, December 17, 2012. https://www.yahoo.com/entertainment /news/maya-vs-carrie-comparing-feminism-zero-dark-thirty-144513423.html.

Kantor, Jodi, and Megan Twohey. "Harvey Weinstein Paid off Sexual Harassment Accusers for Decades." *New York Times*, October 5, 2017. https://www.nytimes.com /2017/10/05/us/harvey-weinstein-harassment-allegations.html.

Keaney, Quinn. "What Exactly Did Trish 'Take' Away from Jessica Jones? The Answer Is Pretty Grim." Popsugar Entertainment, June 21, 2019. https://www.popsugar.com /entertainment/What-Did-Trish-Take-From-Jessica-Jessica-Jones-46258146.

Kennedy, Greg. "Female Super Empowerment: *Jessica Jones* Is Back." *The National*, March 5, 2018. https://www.thenationalnews.com/arts-culture/television/female -super-empowerment-jessica-jones-is-back-1.710419.

Kesby, F. R. "The Problematic Feminism of *Buffy the Vampire Slayer*." Women's Republic, October 15, 2018. https://www.womensrepublic.net/the-problematic-feminism -of-buffy-the-vampire-slayer/.

Khal. "'Jessica Jones' Is Marvel at Its Most Daring." Complex, November 17, 2015. https://www.complex.com/pop-culture/2015/11/jessica-jones-netflix-review.

"Kilgrave." Marvel Cinematic Universe Wiki. https://marvelcinematicuniverse.fandom .com/wiki/Kilgrave#cite_ref-JJ313_16-0.

Klett, Leah MarieAnn. "Purity Culture Harmed Thousands of Evangelical Teens; What Did the Church Get Wrong about Sex?" *Christian Post*, May 20, 2019. https://www .christianpost.com/news/purity-culture-harmed-thousands-of-evangelical-teens-what -did-the-church-get-wrong-about-sex.html.

Konopka, Blanka. "Horror Experience of Women Subjected to Bestial Experiments at WWII Concentration Camp Retold in Powerful New Exhibition." *FirstNews*, September 23, 2021. https://www.thefirstnews.com/article/horror-experience-of-women -subjected-to-bestial-experiments-at-wwii-concentration-camp-retold-in-powerful -new-exhibition-24909.

Krischer, Haley. "Why the Bathtub Scene on Last Night's 'Homeland' Was So Uniquely Disturbing." Salon, October 6, 2014. https://www.salon.com/2014/10/06/why_the _bathtub_scene_on_last_nights_homeland_was_so_uniquely_disturbing/.

L., Otto. "The *Black Widow* Effect, or Marvel and the Hidden Gem Called Peggy Carter." Medium, April 2, 2016. https://medium.com/@vivarium/the-black-widow -effect-or-marvel-and-the-hidden-gem-called-peggy-carter-bde6813bc140.

Lacob, Jace. "'Homeland' and 'Shameless': Television Tackles Bipolar Disorder with Realism." Daily Beast, April 10, 2012. https://www.thedailybeast.com/homeland-and -shameless-television-tackles-bipolar-disorder-with-realism.

Lang, Brent. "Number of Female Directors on Top Hollywood Films Declines in 2021." *Variety*, January 2, 2022. https://variety.com/2022/film/news/number-of-female -directors-on-top-hollywood-film-2021-1235145889/.

Latta, Corey. "Introduction: Part 2." In *Titans: How Superheroes Can Help Us Make Sense of a Polarized World*. Eugene, OR: Cascade Books, 2017.

Leon, Melissa. "Marvel's 'Agent Carter' Stomps on the Patriarchy." Daily Beast, January 7, 2015. https://www.thedailybeast.com/marvels-agent-carter-stomps-on-the -patriarchy.

Lepore, Jill. "The History Lurking behind 'Orphan Black.'" *New Yorker*, April 16, 2015. https://www.newyorker.com/culture/cultural-comment/the-history-lurking-behind -orphan-black.

"List of LEDA Clones." *Orphan Black* Wiki. https://orphanblack.fandom.com/wiki /List_of_LEDA_clones#:~:text=There%20are%20at%20least%20274.

Loofbourow, Lili. "The Many Faces of Tatiana Maslany." *New York Times*, April 2, 2015. https://www.nytimes.com/2015/04/05/magazine/the-many-faces-of-tatiana -maslany.html?ref=magazine&_r=2.

Los Angeles Times. "'Homeland's' Mandy Patinkin Describes the Dynamic between Saul and Carrie." YouTube, June 5, 2018. https://www.youtube.com/watch ?v=O_6AkiBsI_0.

Lutes, Alicia. "An Oral History of *Orphan Black* from the Women Who Brought It to Life." Nerdist, August 9, 2017. https://archive.nerdist.com/orphan-black-oral-history -women-bts/.

Lyons, Margaret. "*House of Cards* Has a Frank-and-Claire Problem." Vulture, March 3, 2015. https://www.vulture.com/2015/03/house-of-cards-frank-claire.html.

Makela, Mark. "Transcript: Donald Trump's Taped Comments about Women." *New York Times*, October 8, 2016. https://www.nytimes.com/2016/10/08/us/donald -trump-tape-transcript.html.

Maloney, Devon. "*Orphan Black* Science Consultant Cosima Herter Breaks down the Series Finale." *Vanity Fair*, August 13, 2017. https://www.vanityfair.com/hollywood /2017/08/orphan-black-series-finale-season-5-cosima-herter-interview.

Marcotte, Amanda. "Before Binge-Watching *Jessica Jones*, Read *Alias*, the Feminist Comic It's Based On." Salon, November 20, 2015. https://www.salon.com/2015/11/19 /before_binge_watching_jessica_jones_read_alias_the_feminist_comic_its_based _on/.

———. "*House of Cards* Goes Full Feminist in Its Second Season." *Slate*, February 18, 2014. https://slate.com/human-interest/2014/02/house-of-cards-season-2-goes-full -feminist-the-show-has-unflinching-honest-story-lines-about-rape-and-abortion.html.

Marlowe, Andrew, and Terri Miller. "Updating 'The Equalizer' for a New Era." Paramount, February 11, 2021. https://www.paramount.com/news/content-and-experi ences/updating-the-equalizer-for-a-new-era.

Martin, Michileen. "How *Buffy the Vampire Slayer* Changed TV and No One Noticed." Looper, June 18, 2019. https://www.looper.com/155959/how-buffy-the-vampire -slayer-changed-tv-and-no-one-noticed/?utm_campaign=clip.

Maurer, Elizabeth L. "Tuning in to Women in Television." National Women's History Museum, September 21, 2016. https://www.womenshistory.org/articles/tuning -women-television.

McDougall, Sophia. "I Hate Strong Female Characters." *New Statesman*, June 10, 2021. https://www.newstatesman.com/culture/2013/08/i-hate-strong-female-characters.

McFarland, Melanie. "'Jessica Jones' Tells Every Woman's Origin Story." Salon, March 17, 2018. https://www.salon.com/2018/03/17/jessica-jones-tells-every-womans -origin-story/.

———. "A Queen Becomes 'The Equalizer': What It Means When Black Women Take on Legacy Superhero Roles." Salon, February 7, 2021. https://www.salon.com/2021/02/07/the-equalizer-super-bowl-queen-latifah-cbs/.

Merrill, Laura. "Buffyversity: The Real Monster All Along." *Multiversity Comics*, April 6, 2021. http://www.multiversitycomics.com/news-columns/buffyversity-the-real-monster-all-along/.

Michael, Dennis. "*Charmed* Has That Spelling Magic." CNN, archived from the original on September 8, 2014. http://www.cnn.com/SHOWBIZ/TV/9810/23/charmed/index.html.

Milano, Alyssa (@Alyssa_Milano). "Well, this absolutely broke my heart." Twitter, April 1, 2021. https://twitter.com/Alyssa_Milano/status/1377699635838521346.

Milas, Lacy Baugher. "TV Rewind: How Spy Drama *Alias* Gave Us Television's All-Time Best Father/Daughter Duo." *Paste Magazine*, August 26, 2021. https://www.pastemagazine.com/tv/streaming/alias-tv-show-sydney-jack/.

Miller, Liz Shannon. "'House of Cards': What the Final Season Would've Looked like If Kevin Spacey Hadn't Been Fired." IndieWire, October 26, 2018. https://www.indiewire.com/2018/10/house-of-cards-season-6-if-kevin-spacey-hadnt-been-fired-1202015443/.

———. "What It's like to Be a 'Buffy' Fan in the Wake of These Joss Whedon Revelations." Collider, February 12, 2021. https://collider.com/joss-whedon-charisma-carpenter-allegations-buffy-fans-reaction/.

Miller, Ryan W. "Are You a Xennial? How to Tell If You're the Microgeneration between Gen X and Millennial." *USA Today*, December 20, 2018. https://www.usatoday.com/story/news/nation/2018/12/20/xennials-millennials-generation-x-microgeneration/2369230002/.

Mitchell, Jim. "How 'Homeland' Became a Pioneer in the Portrayal of Mental Illness." SBS, February 11, 2018. https://www.sbs.com.au/guide/article/2018/02/12/how-homeland-became-pioneer-portrayal-mental-illness.

Morrissey, Tracie Egan. "*House of Cards*' Claire Underwood Is a Feminist Warrior Antihero." Jezebel, February 17, 2014. https://jezebel.com/house-of-cards-claire-underwood-is-a-feminist-warrior-1524425272.

Mosher, Ella. "The Bechdel Test—Encouraging the Conversation about Women in Fiction." Communicator, December 19, 2014. https://chscommunicator.com/42578/opinion/2014/12/the-bechdel-test-encouraging-the-conversation-about-women-in-fiction/.

Mosley, Tonya. "'Me Too' Founder Tarana Burke Says Black Girls' Trauma Shouldn't Be Ignored." NPR, September 29, 2021. https://www.npr.org/2021/09/29/1041362145/me-too-founder-tarana-burke-says-black-girls-trauma-shouldnt-be-ignored.

Moss, Sophie. "Culture Throwback: Thinking Back on How *Charmed* Captured Contemporary Feminism." *Luna Luna*, November 23, 2015. http://www.lunaluna magazine.com/blog/culture-throwback-thinking-back-on-how-charmed-captured-contemporary-feminism.

Moylan, Brian. "*Orphan Black*: What I Learned Binge-Watching Seasons One and Two." *The Guardian*, April 18, 2015. https://www.theguardian.com/tv-and-radio/2015/apr/18/orphan-black-bbc-america-seasons-one-and-two.

Mudede, Charles. "The Karen Episode of Queen Latifah's *The Equalizer* Shows All That Is Wrong with the Current Anti-woke Movement." *The Stranger*, November 22, 2021. https://www.thestranger.com/slog/2021/11/22/63036726/the-karen-episode-of-queen-latifahs-the-equalizer-shows-all-that-is-wrong-with-the-current-anti-woke-movement.

"The New Normal: Actress Claire Danes, *Homeland* and Hollywood's New Take on Mental Illness." National Alliance on Mental Illness, March 6, 2012. https://www.nami.org/Blogs/NAMI-Blog/March-2012/The-New-Normal-Actress-Claire-Danes-Homeland-and-H#:~:text=Showtime%27s%20original%20series%20Homeland%20is.

Newburger, Emma. "Women Head the Top Three CIA Directorates for the First Time in History." CNBC, January 16, 2019. https://www.cnbc.com/2019/01/16/women-head-the-top-three-cia-directorates-for-the-first-time.html.

Nguyen, Nicole. "How *Orphan Black*'s Cosima Got Her Dreads." Popsugar Tech, July 26, 2014. https://www.popsugar.com/tech/Orphan-Black-Cosima-Hair-35337015.

Nilles, Billy. "Ranking TV's Top 20 Badass Female Characters." *E! Online*, April 26, 2020. https://www.eonline.com/news/1143325/ranking-tv-s-top-20-badass-female-characters.

Nowak, Kurt. "Coercive Sterilization in Nazi Germany." Museum of Tolerance. https://www.museumoftolerance.com/education/archives-and-reference-library/online-resources/simon-wiesenthal-center-annual-volume-4/annual-4-chapter-14.html.

Nussbaum, Emily. "Cheaper by the Dozen." *New Yorker*, April 21, 2014. https://www.newyorker.com/magazine/2014/04/28/cheaper-by-the-dozen.

———. "'Homeland': The Antidote for '24.'" *New Yorker*, November 29, 2011. https://www.newyorker.com/culture/culture-desk/homeland-the-antidote-for-24.

O'Connell, Mikey. "'Homeland' Declassified: Battles, Backlash, CIA Meetings and a Secret Call with Edward Snowden." *Hollywood Reporter*, January 16, 2020. https://www.hollywoodreporter.com/movies/movie-features/homeland-declassified-battles-backlash-cia-meetings-a-secret-call-edward-snowden-1269957/.

Oderberg, Isabelle. "*Charmed*: Sister Witches Juggle Life and Magic in This Oddly Relatable Late-90s Cult Hit Show." *The Guardian*, August 22, 2021. https://www.theguardian.com/culture/2021/aug/23/charmed-sister-witches-juggle-life-and-magic-in-this-oddly-relatable-late-90s-cult-hit-show.

Oliver, Amy. "The Real-Life Carrie from *Homeland*: CIA Drama Back on Screens Tonight." *Mail Online*, October 6, 2013. https://www.dailymail.co.uk/femail/article-2445871/Meet-real-life-Carrie-Homeland-CIA-drama--screens-tonight--reads-like-Valerie-Plames-amazing-life-story-But-does-think-plots-fact-fiction.html.

Oliver, James. "Women in Westerns." *Reader's Digest UK*, November 23, 2021. https://www.readersdigest.co.uk/culture/film-tv/women-in-westerns.

"*Orphan Black* (TV Series 2013–2017)." IMDb. https://www.imdb.com/title/tt2234222/faq/.

Parkinson, Hannah Jane. "Does *Homeland* Sensationalise Carrie Mathison's Bipolar Disorder?" *The Guardian*, December 1, 2014. https://www.theguardian.com/commentisfree/2014/dec/01/homeland-carrie-mathison-bipolar-disorder-claire-danes.

Paskin, Willa. "Nine Lives, at Least." *Slate*, April 18, 2014. https://slate.com/culture /2014/04/season-2-of-orphan-black-starring-tatiana-maslany-reviewed.html.

Patterson, Corey. *"Jessica Jones*: Freedom and Guilt." Pop Culture and Theology, March 9, 2018. https://popularcultureandtheology.com/2018/03/09/jessica-jones-freedom -and-guilt/.

Pence, Gregory E. "Sexuality, Gender Identity and *Orphan Black*." In *What We Talk about When We Talk about Clone Club: Bioethics and Philosophy in* Orphan Black. Dallas, TX: BenBella Books, 2016.

Pender, Patricia. "Buffy Summers: Third-Wave Feminist Icon." *The Atlantic*, July 31, 2016. https://www.theatlantic.com/entertainment/archive/2016/07/how-buffy -became-a-third-wave-feminist-icon/493154/.

Penny, Laurie. "Witch Kids of Instagram." *The Baffler*, December 13, 2017. https:// thebaffler.com/war-of-nerves/witch-kids-of-instagram.

Peterson, Todd. "Garner's Pregnancy Becomes Storyline." *People*, July 25, 2005. https:// people.com/celebrity/garners-pregnancy-becomes-storyline/.

Pilato, Herbie J. *"That Girl*: The One Who Changed Everything." Television Academy. https://www.emmys.com/news/online-originals/girl-one-who-changed-everything.

Piña, Christy. "Study: Diversity in TV Casting Increasing, More Lead Roles for Women." *Hollywood Reporter*, October 27, 2022. https://www.hollywoodreporter.com /tv/tv-news/ucla-hollywood-diversity-report-tv-2022-1235249634/.

Porter, Heather M. "In Search of the Complete Female Character in Marvel's Cinematic Universe." In *Marvel's* Black Widow *from Spy to Superhero: Essays on an Avenger with a Very Specific Skill Set*, 24–25. Jefferson, NC: McFarland, 2017.

Preece, Caroline. "Why *Charmed* Deserves to Be Celebrated." Den of Geek, January 13, 2017. https://www.denofgeek.com/tv/why-charmed-deserves-to-be-celebrated/.

———. "Why *Nikita* Will Be Missed." Den of Geek, January 15, 2014. https://www .denofgeek.com/tv/why-nikita-will-be-missed/.

"Prue Halliwell." In *Charmed*. *Charmed* Wiki. https://charmed.fandom.com/wiki /Prue_Halliwell.

Pyles, James. "Where Are the Families in Science Fiction?" Powered by Roots, March 25, 2021. https://poweredbyrobots.com/2021/03/24/where-are-the-families-in-science -fiction/.

Radish, Christina. "Marlo Thomas Talks Makers: Women Who Make America, *That Girl*, and More." Collider, February 26, 2013. https://collider.com/marlo-thomas -makers-women-who-make-america-interview/.

Raouf, Tariq. "'Orphan Black' and Trans Representation: Where They Went Wrong." Hypable, May 3, 2016. https://www.hypable.com/orphan-black-trans-representation/.

Reinstein, Mara. "Queen Latifah Explains How She Got Her Royal Name and Why Women Love Her as 'The Equalizer.'" *Parade*, September 30, 2022. https://parade .com/tv/queen-latifah-the-equalizer-season-3.

Renstrom, Joelle. "*Orphan Black* Was Never about Cloning." *Slate*, August 13, 2017. https://slate.com/technology/2017/08/orphan-black-was-never-about-cloning.html.

Richau, Amy. "Agent Carter Season 1 Episode 3 Review—'Time and Tide.'" Flicker- ing Myth, January 14, 2015. https://www.flickeringmyth.com/2015/01/agent-carter -season-1-episode-3-review-time-tide/.

Richenthal, Matt. "*Nikita* Spoilers: A Free Woman . . ." TV Fanatic, January 15, 2011. https://www.tvfanatic.com/2011/01/nikita-spoilers-a-free-woman/.

Roach, Araceli. "'Orphan Black' Season 3 Character Posters: I'm Not Just One, I'm a Few." ScreenRant, March 22, 2015. https://screenrant.com/orphan-black-season-3-character-posters/.

Robbins, Liz. "He Didn't like 'Homeland': Now He's Advising It." *New York Times*, March 12, 2017. https://www.nytimes.com/2017/03/12/nyregion/he-didnt-like-the-show-now-hes-advising-it.html.

Roffman, Marisa. "'Orphan Black's' Tatiana Maslany on Sarah's 'Selfless' and 'Painful' Decision." *Hollywood Reporter*, April 25, 2015. https://www.hollywoodreporter.com/tv/tv-news/orphan-black-spoilers-sarah-kira-791147/.

Rose, Lacey. "Krista Vernoff on Overcoming Her Past, Overhauling 'Grey's Anatomy' and (Finally) Emerging from Shonda's Shadow." *Hollywood Reporter*, April 1, 2021. https://www.hollywoodreporter.com/tv/tv-news/krista-vernoff-on-overcoming-her-past-overhauling-greys-anatomy-and-finally-emerging-from-shondas-shadow-4158013/?utm_medium=social&utm_source=twitter.

Roth, Rachel. "*Agent Carter*: Why ABC Canceled the Marvel TV Series." CBR, November 29, 2020. https://www.cbr.com/why-marvel-agent-carter-canceled/.

Salem, Rob. "Mandy Patinkin Says *Homeland* Is a Show about Choices and Family." *The Star*, March 6, 2013. https://www.thestar.com/entertainment/television/2013/03/06/mandy_patinkin_says_homeland_is_a_show_about_choices_and_family.html.

Sanders, Hannah E. "Living a Charmed Life: The Magic of Post-Feminist Sisterhood." In *Interrogating Postfeminism Gender and the Politics of Popular Culture*, edited by Diane Negra, Lynn Spigel, and Yvonne Tasker, 73–99. Durham, NC: Duke University Press, 2007.

"Sarah Manning." American Institute of Bisexuality. https://bi.org/en/bi-characters/sarah-manning.

Sarkeesian, Anita. "Some Thoughts on *Jessica Jones*." Feminist Frequency, December 1, 2015. https://feministfrequency.com/2015/12/01/some-thoughts-on-jessica-jones/.

Sarner, Lauren. "'Game of Thrones' and 'Jessica Jones' Owe Buffy's Success 15 Years Ago." Inverse, January 16, 2016. https://www.inverse.com/article/9852-game-of-thrones-and-jessica-jones-owe-buffy-s-success-15-years-ago.

Sava, Oliver. "*Agent Carter*'s Excellent Season Premiere Changes More Than Just the Scenery." *A.V. Club*, January 20, 2016. https://www.avclub.com/agent-carter-s-excellent-season-premiere-changes-more-t-1798186282.

Scherer, Jenna. "'Jessica Jones': We Finally Have a Superhero Icon for the #TimesUp Era." *Rolling Stone*, March 9, 2018. https://www.rollingstone.com/tv-movies/tv-movie-news/jessica-jones-we-finally-have-a-superhero-icon-for-the-timesup-era-127314/.

Schickler, Robyn, Michelle Whittum, Nicole Fanarjian, Rachel Rapkin, and Brian T. Nguyen. "The History of Female Surgical Sterilization: A Social and Ethics Perspective." *Journal of Gynecologic Surgery* 37, no. 6 (December 1, 2021): 465–69. https://doi.org/10.1089/gyn.2021.0102.

Schwab, Katharine. "Why Academics Love 'Buffy the Vampire Slayer.'" *The Atlantic*, October 1, 2015. https://www.theatlantic.com/entertainment/archive/2015/10/the-rise-of-buffy-studies/407020/.

Scream. Film. New York: Dimension Films, 1996.

Shapiro, Lila. "The Undoing of Joss Whedon." Vulture, January 17, 2022. https://www.vulture.com/article/joss-whedon-allegations.html.

"Shonda Rhimes Reveals How 'Buffy' Helped Her Rediscover TV." *Hollywood Reporter*, October 8, 2014. https://www.hollywoodreporter.com/news/general-news/shonda-rhimes-reveals-how-buffy-739109/.

Silverman, Stephen M. "Jennifer Garner's Baby Makes TV History." *People*, October 6, 2005. https://people.com/celebrity/jennifer-garners-baby-makes-tv-history/.

"Siobhan Sadler." *Orphan Black* Wiki. https://orphanblack.fandom.com/wiki/Siobhan_Sadler.

"The Slayage Conference." Association for the Study of Buffy+. https://www.whedonstudies.tv/conference.html.

Solomon, Dan. "How Netflix's 'Jessica Jones' Captures the Comic It's Based On—and How It Doesn't." Fast Company, November 24, 2015. https://www.fastcompany.com/3053946/how-netflixs-jessica-jones-captures-the-comic-its-based-on-and-how-it-doesnt.

Soloski, Alexis. "Kevins Can Score Improbably Attractive TV Wives." *New York Times*, June 9, 2021. https://www.nytimes.com/2021/06/09/arts/television/kevin-sitcom-attractive-wife.html.

Sontag, Deborah. "Anita Hill and Revitalizing Feminism." *New York Times*, April 26, 1992. https://www.nytimes.com/1992/04/26/nyregion/anita-hill-and-revitalizing-feminism.html.

Sophia, Gissane. "Character Deep Dive: Peggy Carter." Marvelous Geeks Media, December 18, 2020. https://marvelousgeeksmedia.com/2020/12/18/character-deep-dive-marvels-peggy-carter/.

Sperling, Nicole. "*Jessica Jones* Creator Melissa Rosenberg on Power and Pitfalls of Female Rage." *Vanity Fair*, March 21, 2018. https://www.vanityfair.com/hollywood/2018/03/jessica-jones-season-2-netflix-marvel-melissa-rosenberg-krysten-ritter.

St. Félix, Doreen. "Queen Latifah Obliterates Trumps N' Musks in 'The Equalizer.'" *New Yorker*, March 5, 2021. https://www.newyorker.com/magazine/2021/03/15/queen-latifah-obliterates-trumps-n-musks-in-the-equalizer.

St. James, Emily. "*Homeland*'s Carrie Mathison Is the Most Influential TV Character of the 2010s." *Vox*, November 11, 2015. https://www.vox.com/2015/11/11/9715382/homeland-season-5-claire-danes.

St. James, Emily, and Caroline Framke. "How *Buffy the Vampire Slayer* Transformed TV as We Know It." *Vox*, March 10, 2017. https://www.vox.com/culture/2017/3/10/14857542/buffy-the-vampire-slayer-explained-tv-influence.

Stacy, Shaun. "'Buffy' at 25: How the Show Changed Pop Culture Forever." GurlCulture, January 10, 2022. https://gurlculture.com/2022/01/09/buffy-at-25-how-the-show-changed-pop-culture-forever/.

Stahler, Kelsea. "Thank Hecate! Witches Are Here to Save the World." *Teen Vogue*, November 14, 2018. https://www.teenvogue.com/story/witches-pop-culture-sabrina-ahs-charmed-real-world.

Staszak, Elizabeth. "A Fantasy from a Fantasy: A Review of ABC's *Agent Carter*." CBE International, February 18, 2015. https://www.cbeinternational.org/resource/fantasy -fantasy/#_ednref1.

Steiner, Chelsea. "*Jessica Jones* and Its Legacy of Female Anger." *Mary Sue*, February 19, 2019. https://www.themarysue.com/rip-jessica-jones/.

———. "*Jessica Jones* Delivers Marvel's Best LGBTQ+ Representation." *Mary Sue*, June 25, 2019. https://www.themarysue.com/jessica-jones-lgbtq-representation-season -three/#:~:text=Jeri%20Hogarth%20(Carrie-Anne%20Moss).

Stelter, Brian. "Netflix Does Well in 2013 Primetime Emmy Nominations." *New York Times*, July 18, 2013. https://archive.nytimes.com/artsbeat.blogs.nytimes .com/2013/07/18/watching-for-the-2013-primetime-emmy-nominations/.

Still, Jennifer. "Why Delphine Cormier Is the Unsung Hero of 'Orphan Black.'" *Bustle*, July 28, 2017. https://www.bustle.com/p/why-delphine-cormier-is-the-unsung-hero -of-orphan-black-72939.

Stone, Sam. "*Jessica Jones*: Why You Should Have Sympathy for Trish Walker, Villain." CBR, June 22, 2019. https://www.cbr.com/jessica-jones-defense-trish-walker/.

Strause, Jackie. "'House of Cards': Robin Wright on Final Season's 'Vulnerability and Insecurities.'" *Hollywood Reporter*, November 2, 2018. https://www.hollywood reporter.com/tv/tv-news/house-cards-premiere-claire-underwood-speaking-camera -explained-1154454/.

———. "How 'House of Cards' Pulled off That Timely, Feminist Coup." *Hollywood Reporter*, November 8, 2018. https://www.hollywoodreporter.com/tv/tv-news/house -cards-final-season-claire-underwood-cabinet-twist-explained-1159290/.

Tait, Allison Anna. "The Return of Coverture." *Michigan Law Review*, January 28, 2016. https://michiganlawreview.org/the-return-of-coverture/.

Tallerico, Brian. "*Homeland*'s End Brings the Show's Defining Relationship Full-Circle." Vulture, April 26, 2020. https://www.vulture.com/2020/04/homeland-finale-carrie -saul-partnership-ending.html.

Tapp, Tom. "Gal Gadot Further Describes 'Justice League' Conflict with Joss Whedon." Deadline, October 18, 2021. https://deadline.com/2021/10/gal-gadot-joss-whedon -shocked-1234858052/.

Taylor, Charles. "'Alias' Grace." Salon, January 12, 2005. https://web.archive.org/web /20140821014601/http://www.salon.com/2005/01/12/alias_2/.

Taylor, Ericka. "'Hood Feminism' Is a Call for Solidarity in a Less-Than-Inclusive Movement." NPR, February 26, 2020. https://www.npr.org/2020/02/26/808943234 /hood-feminism-is-a-call-for-solidarity-in-a-less-than-inclusive-movement.

"10 Pioneering Female Superheroes We Saw on Classic TV." Heroes and Icons, August 13, 2021. https://www.handitv.com/lists/10-pioneering-female-superheroes-we-saw -on-classic-tv.

Theriault, Anne. "The Real Reason Women Love Witches." *The Establishment*, October 24, 2017. https://medium.com/the-establishment/the-real-reason-women-love -witches-647d48517f66.

"This Is What We Learned by Counting the Women's Marches." *Washington Post*, February 24, 2019.

Thomas, June. "Queen Latifah Makes the Impossible: A CBS Cop Show for the Black Lives Matter Era." *Slate*, February 7, 2021. https://slate.com/culture/2021/02/equal izer-queen-latifah-cbs-black-lives-matter-super-bowl.html.

———. "Secret Agent Woman." *Slate*, November 17, 2011. https://slate.com/culture/2011/11/covert-affairs-homeland-why-are-there-so-many-female-spies-on-television.html.

Thomas, Kaitlin. "Before 'WandaVision,' There Was 'Agent Carter,' and It Was Marvel's Best Show." Salon, January 31, 2021. https://www.salon.com/2021/01/31/agent-carter-wandavision-marvel-tv-shows-disney-plus/.

Thomas, Leah Marilla. "Jessica Jones' Mom Is in Marvel Comics, but Alisa Jones Is Drastically Different in the Series." *Bustle*, March 8, 2018. https://www.bustle.com/p/jessica-jones-mom-is-in-marvel-comics-but-alisa-jones-is-drastically-different-in-the-series-8445611.

Thorpe, Vanessa. "Claire Danes: Getting under the Skin of *Homeland*'s Troubled CIA Agent." *The Observer*, March 3, 2012. https://www.theguardian.com/tv-and-radio/2012/mar/03/homeland-claire-danes-carrie-mathison.

Timea. "Here's All of Tatiana Maslany's Clones in *Orphan Black*, Ranked." MovieWeb, January 18, 2022. https://movieweb.com/tatiana-maslany-clones-orphan-black/#:~:text=It%27s%20been%20years%20since%20Orphan.

Toby, Mekeisha Madden. "Queen Latifah: 'Black Women Have Been Equalizing for Years and Years, from Hatshepsut to Kamala Harris.'" TVLine, February 21, 2021. https://tvline.com/2021/02/21/the-equalizer-queen-latifah-black-women-interview-cbs-reboot/.

True Love Waits. "Three Million Teens Sign 'True Love Waits' Pledge." Oregon Faith Report, February 9, 2012. https://oregonfaithreport.com/2012/02/three-million-teens-sign-true-love-waits-pledge/.

Trzcinski, Matthew. "20 Things That Make No Sense about the Original *Charmed*." ScreenRant, January 10, 2019. https://screenrant.com/charmed-tv-series-original-biggest-plot-holes-no-sense/.

Tyree, J. M. "The Good Paranoia: Notes on *Jessica Jones*." *Michigan Quarterly Review*, July 31, 2019. https://sites.lsa.umich.edu/mqr/2019/07/the-good-paranoia-notes-on-jessica-jones%EF%BB%BF/.

VanDerWerff, Emily. "How *Buffy the Vampire Slayer* Transformed TV as We Know It." *Vox*, March 10, 2017. https://www.vox.com/culture/2017/3/10/14857542/buffy-the-vampire-slayer-explained-tv-influence.

Vaz, Mark Cotta. Alias *Declassified: The Official Companion*. New York: Bantam Books for Young Readers, 2002.

———. "Internal Memorandum." In Alias *Declassified: The Official Companion*. New York: Bantam Books for Young Readers, 2002.

"Very Special Episode." TV Tropes. https://tvtropes.org/pmwiki/pmwiki.php/Main/VerySpecialEpisode.

"'The Visionary'—Marlo Thomas as Ann Marie in *That Girl*." Comedy Hall of Fame. https://comedyhalloffame.com/celebrate/the-visionary-marlo-thomas-as-ann-marie-in-that-girl.

Wallace, Tim, and Alicia Parlapiano. "Crowd Scientists Say Women's March in Washington Had 3 Times as Many People as Trump's Inauguration." *New York Times*, January 22, 2017. https://www.nytimes.com/interactive/2017/01/22/us/politics /womens-march-trump-crowd-estimates.html.

Warn, Sarah. "'Buffy' to Show First Lesbian Sex Scene on Broadcast TV." AfterEllen, April 3, 2003. https://afterellen.com/buffy-to-show-first-lesbian-sex-scene-on-broad cast-tv/.

Watson, Stephanie. "Is Bipolar a Disability? Your FAQs." Healthline, March 4, 2021. https://www.healthline.com/health/bipolar-disorder/is-bipolar-a-disability#takeaway.

Weaver, Courtney, Joe Rennison, Lindsay Whipp, and Nicole Bullock. "Trump Reacts to Mass Protests with Conciliatory Tweet: More Than 2.5m People Gather around the World to Take Part in Women's March." *Financial Times*, January 22, 2017.

Weekes, Princess. "Alright, Let's Talk about Trish Walker." *Mary Sue*, March 21, 2018. https://www.themarysue.com/season-two-trish-walker/.

———. "'Jessica Jones' Has a Problem with How It Handles Race and Gender." *Mary Sue*, March 13, 2018. https://www.themarysue.com/jessica-jones-race-gender -superpowers/.

Wendig, Chuck. "On the Subject of the 'Strong Female Character.'" Terribleminds, March 8, 2013. http://terribleminds.com/ramble/2013/03/08/on-the-subject-of-the -strong-female-character/.

Whitney, Sarah E. "I Can Be Whoever I Want to Be: *Alias* and the Post-Feminist Rhetoric of Choice." Genders 1998–2013, March 1, 2013. https://www.colorado.edu /gendersarchive1998-2013/2013/03/01/i-can-be-whoever-i-want-be-alias-and-post -feminist-rhetoric-choice.

"Why Toronto Is the Most Multicultural City in the World." Study Abroad Foundation, November 8, 2022. https://www.studyabroadfoundation.org/blogs/why-toronto -most-multicultural-city-world#:~:text=Recognized%20by%20both%20the%20 United.

Wick, Julia. "Subverting Female Archetypes with the Clones of 'Orphan Black.'" Longreads, April 13, 2015. https://longreads.com/2015/04/13/subverting-female -archetypes-with-the-clones-of-orphan-black/.

Wilcox, Rhonda V. "About." Association for the Study of Buffy+, February 22, 2022. https://www.whedonstudies.tv/about.html.

———. "In Memoriam: David Lavery." Association for the Study of Buffy+. https://www.whedonstudies.tv/in-memoriam-david-lavery.html#:~:text=In%202008 %2C%20David%2C%20Tanya%20R.

Wilhelmi, Jack. "What Faith Did after *Buffy the Vampire Slayer* Ended." ScreenRant, April 4, 2020. https://screenrant.com/buffy-vampire-slayer-faith-after-finale-ending/.

Williams, Zoe. "*Jessica Jones*: The Timely Return of a Feminist Superhero." *The Guardian*, February 24, 2018. https://www.theguardian.com/culture/2018/feb/24/jessica -jones-mind-control-and-redemption-the-timely-return-of-a-feminist-superhero.

Windrem, Robert. "Hunting Osama bin Laden Was Women's Work." NBC News, November 14, 2013. https://www.nbcnews.com/news/world/hunting-osama-bin-laden -was-womens-work-flna2D11594091.

"Women Have Paid the Price for Trump's Regulatory Agenda." Center for American Progress, September 10, 2020. https://www.americanprogress.org/article/women-paid-price-trumps-regulatory-agenda/.

"The Women's March, 2017." National Museum of American History, March 2, 2020. https://americanhistory.si.edu/creating-icons/women%E2%80%99s-march-2017.

Wondemaghen, Meron. "*Homeland*, Carrie Mathison and Mental Illness on Television." The Conversation, October 24, 2014. https://theconversation.com/homeland-carrie-mathison-and-mental-illness-on-television-33458.

Wong, Claire L. "An Analysis: Female Villain Redemption Arcs That Paved the Way for Villanelle in 'Killing Eve.'" *Hollywood Insider*, January 14, 2021. https://www.hollywoodinsider.com/female-villain-redemption-arcs-tv/.

———. "Why 'Buffy the Vampire Slayer' Is Still One of the Best TV Shows Ever." *Hollywood Insider*, February 2, 2021. https://www.hollywoodinsider.com/buffy-the-vampire-slayer-success/.

Yasin, Sara. "Graffiti Artists Write '*Homeland* Is Racist' in Arabic on the Show's Set in Berlin." BuzzFeed News, October 14, 2015. https://www.buzzfeednews.com/article/sarayasin/graffiti-artists-homeland.

Yu, Su-Lin. "Reclaiming the Personal: Personal Narratives of Third-Wave Feminists." *Women's Studies* 40, no. 7 (October 2011): 873–89. https://doi.org/10.1080/00497878.2011.603606.

Zabinsky, Jamie. "Politics, Power and Queerness in 'House of Cards' Season 4." Feministing, May 31, 2016. https://feministing.com/2016/05/31/politics-power-and-queerness-in-house-of-cards-season-4/.

Zellars, Rachel. "Black Subjectivity and the Origins of American Gynecology." AAIHS, May 31, 2018. https://www.aaihs.org/black-subjectivity-and-the-origins-of-american-gynecology/.

Index

About the Author

Nicole Evelina is a huge fan of the shows in this book. She was in college when *Buffy the Vampire Slayer* first aired and watched it while discussing it with her friends throughout the country on AOL Instant Messenger, which was a new thing at the time. She also has the triquetra symbol from the *Charmed* Book of Shadows tattooed on her back.

Evelina is also a *USA Today* best-selling author and biographer who writes historical fiction, nonfiction, and women's fiction. Her other book in this series is Sex and the City: *A Cultural History.* Collectively, her books have won more than fifty awards, including four Book of the Year designations. Evelina is now a hybrid author but was named Missouri's "Top Independent Author" by *Library Journal* and Biblioboard as the winner of the Missouri Indie Author Project in 2018, and she has been awarded the North Street Book Prize and the Sarton Women's Book Award. One of her novels, *Madame Presidentess*, was previously optioned for film. She is represented by Amy Collins of Talcott Notch Literary.

www.ingramcontent.com/pod-product-compliance
Lightning Source LLC
Chambersburg PA
CBHW030302100426
42812CB00002B/538